No motorways or mobile phones. No video re
Sit back and enjoy the memories
memories of a time when cricket was still

It was born in me to play cricket. The days were never long enough.
Arthur Milton

Can you imagine going by train from Taunton? We spent about four hundred
hours each summer at Bristol Temple Meads, waiting for connections.
Ken Biddulph

We had to stay in two hotels. There wasn't anywhere big enough in the town.
Merv Winfield

Vic Munden was allocated the job of bringing some six inch nails
to make sure we'd got enough pegs.
Maurice Hallam

You came in on the first day. You took your tie off, you put it on the peg, and
there was this glorious uncertainty of not knowing what was going to happen.
Malcolm Heath

"Get padded up, you're in." "No, I've been in, skipper."
It was that kind of comedy.
Tom Cartwright

Les was the greatest. I could take a chair, sit down by the sight screen
and watch him bowl all day.
Bomber Wells

I didn't envisage having to bat again, but that's the game, isn't it?
That's what makes it so compelling.
Terry Spencer

There were three to win off four balls.
Why on earth did he keep trying to hit sixes?
Dickie Dodds

Cricket is a lifetime's job. You've got to eat, drink and play it.
Dennis Brookes

He used to phone Jim Laker at The Oval and say, 'I've lost my mechanics, Jim,
I can't bowl,' and Jim would say, 'What do you expect me to do, Roly?
I can't see what you're doing wrong from a hundred miles away.'
Martin Horton

You didn't always think so then, but it was the most wonderful time.
Bryan Stott

Stephen Chalke was born in Salisbury in 1948 and now lives in Bath. Prior to writing this book, he worked full-time in adult and further education, but he now combines cricket writing and publishing with part-time university lecturing.

Runs in the Memory (1997) was his first venture into writing, and he has subsequently added three books:
Caught in the Memory (1999), its sequel about the 1960s,
One More Run (2000), with the old Gloucestershire spinner Bomber Wells, and
At the Heart of English Cricket (2001), based on the life and memories of Geoffrey Howard, the 92-year-old retired cricket administrator.

He now writes a regular column in Wisden Cricket Monthly and has published *Fragments of Idolatry* (2001) by David Foot.

Still a keen cricketer with the wandering side The Journeymen, he describes in the introduction to this paperback edition how his quest to revive his own game led by chance to the writing of this book.

Ken Taylor was born in Huddersfield in 1935 and now lives in North Norfolk. He trained as an artist at the Slade and has been a teacher of Art for thirty years. For several years he has been building up a substantial collection of portraits of sportsmen.

A batsman, occasional bowler and brilliant fielder, he played cricket for Yorkshire from 1953 to 1968 and three times for England. He also played football for Bill Shankly's Huddersfield Town in the old First Division. An old-fashioned centre half, he played in the same side as the young Denis Law.

His illustrations also appear in *Caught in the Memory* and *One More Run* and in Ian Botham's new book, *Botham's Century*.

RUNS IN THE MEMORY

County Cricket in the 1950s

Stephen Chalke

with illustrations by Ken Taylor
(of Yorkshire and England)

FAIRFIELD BOOKS

Fairfield Books
17 George's Road, Fairfield Park, Bath BA1 6EY
Tel 01225-335813

First published 1997
Reprinted with minor revisions 1998
Second reprint with further minor revisions 1999

First published in paperback 2002

ISBN 0 9531196 5 3

Printed and bound in Great Britain by
Bookcraft Ltd, Midsomer Norton, Bath

For

Ken Biddulph

Time past and time future
What might have been and what has been
Point to one end, which is always present.

T.S.Eliot, 'Burnt Norton'

CONTENTS

FOREWORD 9

INTRODUCTION TO THIS PAPERBACK EDITION 11

INTRODUCTION TO THE ORIGINAL EDITION 19

CARRYING THE BAGS
Middlesex v Glamorgan *Don Shepherd* 21

HIT HARD AND ENJOY IT
Essex v Lancashire *Dickie Dodds* 33

A LEARNING ENVIRONMENT
Surrey v Warwickshire *Tom Cartwright* 46

A GOALKEEPER'S TRIP TO OLD TRAFFORD
Lancashire v Northamptonshire *Dennis Brookes* 61

WHAT MIGHT HAVE BEEN AND WHAT HAS BEEN
Yorkshire v Leicestershire *Terry Spencer & Maurice Hallam* 75

MEMORIES ARE MADE OF THIS
Gloucestershire v Nottinghamshire *Bomber Wells & Merv Winfield* 88

ROSES IN DECEMBER
Worcestershire v Yorkshire *Martin Horton* 101

HERE COMES THE SUN
Kent v Surrey *John Pretlove* 112

THE GLORIOUS UNCERTAINTY
Derbyshire v Hampshire *Malcolm Heath, Harold Rhodes & David Green* 125

WE'LL HAVE A RESULT
Essex v Gloucestershire *Arthur Milton & Richard Bernard* 139

THEY COULD NOT BE BEATEN
Somerset v Yorkshire *Ken Biddulph* 151

THE END OF AN ERA
Sussex v Yorkshire *Jim Parks, Bryan Stott & Ken Taylor* 163

THE STUMPS ARE DRAWN 178

COUNTY CHAMPIONSHIP TABLES 1952-1959 182

ACKNOWLEDGEMENTS 184

INDEX 187

ILLUSTRATIONS

Denis Compton   20
Brian Statham   32
Jim Laker   45
Frank Tyson   60
Len Hutton   74
Arthur Milton   87
Roly Jenkins   100
Tony Lock   111
Colin Ingleby-Mackenzie   124
Trevor Bailey   138
Bill Alley   150
Fred Trueman   162

The illustrations in this book are all of cricketers from the 1950s, but Ken Taylor has many more drawings of sporting personalities. He has already printed and distributed portraits of Fred Trueman, Brian Close, Ray Illingworth and Dickie Bird, but he can supply prints from a much wider list and in several formats: postcard size, a picture for framing or an even larger scale portrait for a cricket club wall. His subjects include players both from his own playing days and from the modern game.

Full details are available from Ken Taylor at The Red House, Stody, Melton Constable, Norfolk, NR24 2EB.

The illustrations are interpretations of old photographs. The ones of Roly Jenkins and Tony Lock are by Ken Kelly, and Ken Taylor and the publishers would like to thank him for granting permission for his photographs to be used in this way. The one of Fred Trueman is with the kind permission of the Yorkshire Post. Most of the other photographs appeared originally in the now defunct Playfair Cricket Monthly magazine. The publishers have tried to find out the copyright owners of these photographs, and if any photographic source believes that they are theirs they should contact the publisher to rectify the matter.

FOREWORD

by Tom Cartwright

Any decade in cricket history will have special significance to players who played at that time. I'm equally sure that cricket lovers who follow the game have special periods in their memories that they revisit for pleasures that only cricket can give.

Stephen Chalke has chosen a most fascinating decade, a period of reconstruction when many Test and County cricketers were picking up the pieces of their careers blighted by a long war. Young people like me were just starting careers, hoping that we might emulate them after being excited and inspired by their wonderful spirit and application in getting the show back on the road in the late forties.

There was also much activity in the re-construction of our cities and industries. My own home town, Coventry, had reverted from producing munitions to building a wide range of motor cars again. So successful was this that throughout the country Coventry was known as "Boom Town". Life was good, plenty of jobs, housing was becoming more available and county cricket was attracting thousands of spectators every match.

It must be very difficult for the modern county cricketer to grasp just how much glamour there was being a player in those days. Saturday mornings - the first day of a Championship match - at Edgbaston you would see huge queues at every entrance. It was not unusual to see the gates closed before lunch.

It was a huge privilege as a sixteen-year-old to be part of this scene. My first class debut at Trent Bridge in 1952 will always remain one of the very special days in my life, and I'm sure other contributors to this book will have similar memories. Walking out to bat and seeing many of my cigarette cards coming to life was both thrilling and daunting. They were all there - Simpson, Butler, Jepson, Stocks, Poole and, above all, Joe Hardstaff. It was thanks to "Mr Hardstaff" that I managed to bat for a few hours. It was his advice, coaching, encouragement and sometimes mild rebuke that kept me at the crease. Imagine that happening today where abuse - sledging - seems necessary to support the lack of skills.

In the early fifties the MCC set about establishing a Coach Education scheme. Early meetings and seminars were held at Lilleshall. County coaches and top players with years of experience were invited to help devise syllabus and method. The resulting structure has changed little over the years and has been the basis of both National Cricket Association and England and Wales Cricket Board schemes.

It never seemed quite right to me that the national cricket future should be shaped in theory and practice in a multi-sport complex. Sadly the multi-sport syndrome still prevails. Many of the new cricket Centres of Excellence are based in multi-sport halls, not cricket-specific centres.

It was inevitable that towards the end of this decade social changes would as always be reflected in how we enjoyed our recreation. Numbers of spectators at county matches started to fall. The administrators and decision makers started to talk about the need for "brighter" cricket, whatever that meant. Much of the fun and style of the fifties were soon to be lost.

There have been many changes since - some good and some not so good. It's interesting to reflect that in the fifties most counties carried between 22 and 28 players on their staffs with probably four full-time people on administration, including the county secretary. Recent years have seen playing staff numbers fall while administration increased, hugely in some cases. I'm grateful that my early years were spent in this era. There were so many people to learn from and enjoy - both home and overseas players.

There were many overseas players at that time but no "hired guns". They came with a love of cricket and a desire to be part of something unique. The two years qualification they had to serve speaks volumes for their desire to be part of the fun.

The publication of 'Runs In The Memory' will give insight and pleasure to those who didn't experience the fifties. To those who did, it will be a welcome reminder of a magic time.

T.W. Cartwright

July 1997

INTRODUCTION
TO THIS PAPERBACK EDITION

"How did you come to write this book?" I am often asked, and my reply always starts in the autumn of 1993. I was 45 years old, suffering from back problems for the first time, and the statistics of my cricketing summer made depressing reading, even by my own modest standards. I had just 23 wickets to show for 22 games.

My wandering side, The Journeymen, had a last weekend in Essex in late September, and my season ended on Great and Little Warley's sloping ground. The leaves of the chestnut trees had turned brown and were starting to fall, the pitch was soft, and the raised wooden pavilion with its verandah had seen better days. It was the perfect setting for a bout of melancholy.

I bowled seven innocuous overs, and I went out to bat at number nine with 39 runs wanted from the last five overs. It was a wonderful opportunity to end my summer in glory. But, as the bowler ran in, the low sun flashed through the half-bare branches, and the ball was almost upon me before I realised that it was short and would sit up nicely for a pull shot. I hurried into the stroke, and I watched in despair as my effort sent the ball looping gently into the hands of short mid-wicket.

Back in the pavilion the thoughts started to run through my head. "It's time to call it a day. Don't go on and on like Dad did. Retire now before it gets worse."

Over the following weeks another voice started to answer back. "Don't be silly. Dad was 62. You're just 45. You're not ready to walk away from it all – the friendships, the fun. Why don't you work on your game, get some coaching? You're never too old to learn. You teach adults; that's what you're always telling them."

I made enquiries, and I found myself on the telephone to Ken Biddulph, the old Somerset bowler.

"What did you have in mind?" he asked me.

"Well, I thought maybe we could meet for half an hour each week."

"Half an hour? You can't do anything in half an hour."

"Well, an hour, then."

He rang a few days later to say that he had booked the net at the Stratford Park Leisure Centre in Stroud. Just him and me. Friday afternoons, from 4 to 5.30.

I got away early from work in Bristol, and I drove up the A46 to find him in the entrance hall. A slim, upright man with immaculate grey hair and a Somerset blazer.

"Stephen? Good news. There's nobody in after us till six o'clock."

He told me that I had a good bowling action, but he was soon reconstructing it. My hips swivelled as never before, my feet landed awkwardly in chalked footmarks, and the ball flew into the roof or the side of the net with alarming frequency.

"That's much more like it, Stephen. Now we're getting somewhere."

I had my doubts, but I soon realised that he knew his business. One week he brought in a batsman, then gradually we grew into a group session that lasted for three happy winters.

I took 39 wickets in 1994, 50 in 1995, an astonishing 82 in 1996. Well, I did play a lot of matches that summer – but that was because I was enjoying my cricket more than I had ever done.

That first evening with Ken was the fifth of November, and I had promised that I would be home for the local fireworks display. It was a 30-mile drive back to Bath, and I had expected to be setting off at 5.30.

At six o'clock Ken and I made our way up to the balcony. The cricket net was pulled away, the five-a-side football took over the main hall, and Ken started to reminisce about his days at Somerset. How he lay awake the night before he had to bowl at Roy Marshall, how he shed a tear when they made him twelfth man for the West Indies match, how he edged Frank Tyson for four at Bath when the ball was so fast that he had not even started his back-lift. "I knew you were slow, Kenny," Tyson had laughed. "I didn't realise you were that slow."

"You'll have to go up to the fireworks without me," I rang home to say.

Some evenings I was still there after 7.30, but I seldom heard a story twice.

I was enchanted. Ken was bringing back to life a distant past, reminding me how different was the world I knew as a child in the 1950s. He was giving me such an insight into the life of the professional cricketer: the routine and the emotions. And he talked of my 45-year-old aspirations with just the same respect and enthusiasm as he told me of his own encounters with Peter May and Fred Trueman.

Some weeks I could feel my back stiffening up as I stood on the balcony in my damp shirt, but it never seemed to matter.

In the autumn of 1996 I signed up for an extra-mural class at the University of Bath. It was called 'An Introduction to Feature Writing'. I had a Masters Degree in English Literature and a drawer full of short stories, but I thought a course like this might give me more realistic goals for my writing. The tutor, Hazel Shaw, was hostile to anything that sounded at all academic – "You can throw that paragraph away. That's how they teach you to write in universities." – and that was fine by me. She certainly sharpened us all up.

"Now you have to start thinking about your special interests," she said one evening and, as she continued, my mind drifted away to Ken and his wonderful stories. Was there a feature-length article there? And who would be interested?

Ken Biddulph. He played 91 times for Somerset between 1955 and 1961. An interview with Ken would hardly have the sports editors sitting up.

Then I thought, "I could ask him about the best game of cricket he ever played. I could write it as a story."

So we sat with a pint of beer each, in a pub just outside Stroud, and he talked me through the Somerset–Yorkshire match at Bath in 1959.

"Yorkshire were always a bit different. They had this self-belief. ... I always thought Closey was a genius and a bit thick at the same time. If you listened to him, he was never wrong. You tended to get into the habit of believing everything he said."

The next day I was in the library, looking up the Times report of the match. *'Yorkshire had got their teeth into Somerset and were not letting go.'* And inevitably my eyes drifted across to the rest of the paper: the M1 under construction, the Queen expecting her third child, the advert for Phosdrin, an insecticide with dramatic killing powers. The elements started to mix together in my head, and a cocktail emerged.

"My goodness," Ken said after he read it. "You seem to have remembered more of this match than I have." I could tell that he was delighted, and my mind was now running ahead.

"I wondered about doing this with the other counties. Is there anybody you would recommend?"

I wanted sixteen more people like Ken, with good memories, a telling turn of phrase and a sense of humour, but I had no idea who they might be.

"You could try Martin Horton in Worcester," he said immediately. "I think he'd be your sort of person."

I sent Martin my account of the Bath match, and he was soon on the telephone. "I'd love to help you. The only problem is that I'd also like to choose a match against Yorkshire."

This was my first interview with a stranger, and in the days before our meeting I read up all that I could about Worcestershire. Half of the names were unfamiliar to me, and I was anxious not to appear a complete ignoramus.

I need not have worried. I arrived at Martin's house at eleven in the morning, and I did not leave till half past three. Margaret cooked us a lunch, we drank a bottle of wine, and the stories flowed, the best of them about Roly Jenkins, their ever-enthusiastic but highly-strung leg-spinner.

"It didn't feel like you were interviewing me," Martin told me recently. "It was just a pleasant conversation."

A friend, who read my first efforts, offered an image that stuck in my mind. "It's like I'm watching the match as I read it," he said. "Only the match is forty years ago, and the person chatting away next to me is playing in it."

Arthur Milton was next. He is the last man to have played both football and cricket for England, and it always caught my fancy that, when he retired from sport, he became a postman, spending twenty years delivering the mail in North

Bristol. He was retired now. "Don't come too early," he told me. "Only I've got three paper rounds to get done."

We met one afternoon, and he too was starting to choose a Yorkshire match. For a moment it occurred to me that that could be the organising principle of the book – 'The Day We Beat Yorkshire' – but I stopped him. "No, let's pick another match. I've done Yorkshire twice already."

It was only at this point that I decided to make it a book about county cricket in the 1950s. Don Shepherd was my next contact, and he wanted to relive Glamorgan's victory over the Australians in 1968. "No," I said. "I want a county match, and I want it to be in the 1950s."

By happy coincidence Harold Rhodes in Derby and Malcolm Heath in the Cotswolds selected the same 1958 match, and I tracked down David Green, the young Derbyshire amateur whose father was the ill-fated Ind Coope groundsman on that occasion.

Harold put me onto Ken Taylor, and I drove all the way to North Norfolk to see him. Ken had been teaching Art for 25 years, and he seemed more distant from his life as a cricketer than the others I had met. The memories were harder to tease out of him, and he had a disconcerting habit of strolling across to the fire, away from my tape recorder. Back home I spent hours trying to decipher his barely audible voice.

When I rang Ken's friend Bryan Stott at his company in Leeds, it was a different experience. The memories flooded down the telephone line as he resisted his secretary's attempts to attract his attention. "When we got to Scarborough ... Just a minute, I'm busy on the phone. ... I shall never forget the crowds. ... Put it in on the desk for now, will you? ... Stephen, there are tears in my eyes as I tell you this."

I had spoken on the telephone to Doug Insole about Arthur Milton's match, and I asked him to recommend an Essex player of that time. I could have asked Doug himself or Trevor Bailey, but I had become intrigued by those whose voices were less often heard.

"If you like your humour bucolic, try Tonker Taylor. If you'd like it religious, you might prefer Dickie Dodds."

I have no idea why, but I opted for the religion.

When I arrived at Dickie's house in St Neots, he presented me with several pages of typed manuscript. "I've written it all down for you," he said. "I thought it would save time." That was exactly what I did not want. I was trying to catch the personal idioms of each cricketer's voice, and I insisted on talking it through with him.

He wrote back with alarm after I sent him the chapter. "Did I really say all these things? ... You'll have to take them out. ... Only I've never been interviewed like this before."

Dickie played 14 summers for Essex. He came close to selection for the tour of the West Indies in 1947/8. Yet he had never been the subject of a feature-length

14

interview. He had begun his career in the days of print rationing, and he had finished before the cult of celebrity started to dominate the sports pages.

After several letters we had produced a chapter that satisfied us both, and undoubtedly it was a better piece of writing for his involvement. He failed to convert me to Moral Re-Armament, but his words did echo around my head long afterwards.

I went to see his opening partner Sonny Avery in Monmouth. Sonny was close to death, and his wife cancelled my visit twice.

"Shall we leave it?" I asked her, feeling that I was becoming a pest.

"No," she said. "He does want to see you, but you'll have to come on the right day."

We sat in the two armchairs of his living room, and I could feel the immense effort he was making, trying to pull memories out of a deep mental fog. He talked about his debut in 1935. "I was helping on the ground at Chelmsford, and this girl came across. 'You're playing at The Oval tomorrow,' she said. I thought she was pulling my leg."

Essex promised him that he would play every game the following summer.

"In actual fact, I played none."

Foolishly I interrupted him. "Did anybody ever speak to you about it?" And he sat in silence for almost a minute.

"It's a long time ago, you know, to remember a detail like that."

"We always told him he should write a book," his wife said to me. "He had so many lovely stories that he used to tell."

The memories had already faded, and within weeks Sonny was dead.

Some weeks later I met Bernie Constable, the Surrey batsman, in a pub near Sandown Park, and he too died soon afterwards. He told me the story of his championship debut at the end of 1939. With war imminent, the match was rerouted from The Oval to Old Trafford. They arrived at 4 a.m., slept in the pavilion, and on the third morning play was abandoned and they caught the train back to Euston. "Kids being evacuated were all over the station when we arrived."

This is our history, and with each death it slips further away from us.

By this stage I was sending sample chapters to publishers, and the replies all found ways of saying the same thing: 'It fully deserves publication, but it would represent a risk for us. ... I am somewhat doubtful about being able to make it financially viable. We would need to sell at least two thousand. ... Wonderful but a little too specialised. ... Ideally I am looking for biographies fronted by well-known and established names.'

Only John Gaustad, the owner of Sportspages Bookshop in London, struck an optimistic note. "Oral history is where American sports writing has been going. I'm sure you're on the right track."

Dennis Brookes was the oldest cricketer to choose a match for me. He made his debut for Northamptonshire in 1934, and he lives still in Wantage Road, a few doors down from the main entrance to the County Ground. We sat in his front room with a pot of tea and, when he selected a match at Old Trafford in 1953, I pulled a face. Half of the Northants first team were absent, and I had been hoping he would pick a game against Kent. At that point I had covered all the counties except Kent and Leicestershire.

I should have known better than to try to deflect him from his story – because it was as good a story as there is in this book. It had so many ingredients, and the best was the last-minute call-up of a local footballer, who was working at the time for British Timken, the company of the club's chief benefactor. His name was Peter Pickering. The reference books told me that it was his only first-class appearance and that he was still alive. It took weeks of searching to discover that he was in South Africa, then weeks of waiting before his letter arrived.

"At about 9.15 a.m.," he wrote, "an announcement over the public address system summoned me to the chairman's office. I arrived there at the double to find his personal secretary waiting for me at the door. 'Get in there quick – it's urgent,' she said."

On the telephone I used to say that my interview would last about two hours, and some were happy to leave it at that. "That's enough of me," Arthur Milton announced. "What about you, Stephen?" He then started to interview me.

I set off each time with a small tape recorder and two 90-minute cassette tapes. Sometimes, when I sensed somebody might be a real talker, I would throw in a third cassette. Even three tapes – 4½ hours of conversation – was inadequate, though, for Bomber Wells. "Do you want stories?" he asked and, before I had even settled down, he was off. We had a sandwich lunch, his wife took the old dog for three walks, and I tried several times to say that I had to go. But nothing stopped him. I arrived at ten, and I left after half past four. He made liberal use of exaggeration, but everything he said fitted with what all the others had told me.

That was what was so striking. Bomber Wells was a comedian, Dickie Dodds an evangelist, Tom Cartwright a craftsman. John Pretlove was a Southern amateur who left cricket for a career in the construction industry, Ken Taylor a Northern professional who became an Art teacher. Terry Spencer ran his own window-fitting business in Leicester, Malcolm Heath was cricket coach at St Paul's School, and Arthur Milton cycled across the Bristol Downs with the morning papers. They lived their different lives, but certain themes recurred in all their contributions.

They grew up in a world without television sets and home computers, with only a handful of motor cars and most workers in manual jobs with just two weeks of paid holiday a year. They had known war, and their values were permeated with ideals of public service, hard work and fair play, ideals that have long been eroded by affluence.

My journey had started on the balcony of the Stratford Park Leisure Centre with Ken's delightful tales of his Somerset team mates: "Peter Wight had this high-pitched, West Indian voice and, when the bowling was quick, he used to back away. 'Oh, flippin' 'eck,' he'd say. But he still managed to flick the ball away for four."

I had driven to Worcester and North Norfolk, to Derby and South Wales, and at the end of it all I had collected so many lovely cricket stories. But it was not just the stories that captivated me. It was the way they brought alive for me the England in which I had grown up, an England I had almost forgotten.

I still had no publisher, and I could not put it all away in the drawer with my short stories. "It's wonderful," Bryan Stott said about his chapter. "I've read it three times already this morning, and I'm still finding new things in it." Tom Cartwright was just as enthusiastic: "Apart from John Arlott," he said. "I've never read anything like it." I had no choice. It had to be published, and I would have to do it.

I remembered the pictures Ken Taylor had shown me in his studio, scores of portraits that had never seen the light of day, and I asked him if he would agree to my putting some of them in the book. Then I spent several fraught weeks learning about scanning, post-scripting files and all the technicalities of computer age printing. People in the know told me that the book would sell 800 to 1000 copies, but I was quietly determined to do better and I printed 1500.

My first review was by Frank Keating in The Guardian. He rang me one Saturday night while I was watching 'Casualty' and told me that in his opinion it was the Sports Book of the Year and he would be saying so in his column.

A few weeks later I took my daughter for her Saturday afternoon cricket session with Peter Wight, and the mother of another girl told me casually, "I saw your book mentioned in The Week. Some writer named it as one of his six best cricket books of all time."

"Really? Can you remember his name?"

"Um .. Swinson. Something like that."

"Swinson? Not E.W. Swanton?"

"Yes, that's right. Swanton."

Dickie Dodds went to the Christmas festivities of his local Conservative Association. His M.P. John Major was present, and Dickie reported back to me the conversation. "'Ah, Dickie,' he said to me, 'I've just been reading a book you're in.' He said it was the best book about cricket he'd ever read."

"The best?" I repeated incredulously.

"Well, one of the best, something like that."

Such was the way the compliments trickled back.

Then the Daily Telegraph rang to say that Michael Parkinson had submitted a column based on my book, and the orders came in thick and fast. By Spring 1998 I was asking the printer for another 1000 copies, then a year later a further 800. A total of 3300 books, and now they are all gone.

I have written a sequel on the 1960s and books with Bomber Wells and Geoffrey Howard. I have a regular column in Wisden Cricket Monthly, and I have published a book for David Foot. The house is full of boxes of books, and I wrestle with self-employed tax returns and files of invoices.

I have had so many lovely letters, but none of all this would have been possible without the co-operation of the old cricketers. They shared their memories freely, and it is the wonderful mix of their voices that gives this book whatever charm it has. "As an evocation of sporting memory," a professor in sports studies wrote to me, "your work says far more than most of the jargon-laden texts that I'm obliged to read." How Hazel Shaw would approve of that!

This is not a book that offers answers; you must think what you like. I am just the chap standing in a damp shirt on the balcony of the Stratford Park Leisure Centre, drinking a bottle of wine with the Hortons, sitting beside the dying Sonny Avery. Listening. Receiving from an older generation their deep love of cricket and passing it on.

Too specialised? Lacking a big enough name on the front cover?

I am not convinced.

The voices will not be there much longer. Bomber Wells has had to fight back from a debilitating stroke, and in the autumn of 2001 Dickie Dodds died.

Soon enough there will be nobody left who knew cricket before the war. Then there will be nobody who knew the 1950s. There will only be books and tapes to tell us of the world that is gone. Good riddance to some of it – the long hours of low-paid work, the diseases that had no cure, the widespread colour prejudice – but I doubt if you will read this book and feel that all the changes have been for the better.

*

Last summer my wicket tally was down to just 29. In our last match we were on Kew Green, playing the journalists of The Observer newspaper. The captain put me at silly mid-on, and the batsman chipped the ball past me before I had even started to move for it.

Time to call it a day? The thought did cross my mind again, I am 54 next summer, but the friendships are so important. And I am sure that I have got a few more wickets left to take. If all else fails, perhaps I can get Ken to convert me into an off-spinner.

"Now then, Stephen, did I ever tell you about the winter Malcolm Heath and I spent felling trees?"

I did decide that I would not reprint this book again, but it has given me such great pleasure. I am not sure that a paperback edition makes sense as a commercial venture but then, as all the big publishers told me, the book never did make commercial sense.

It was a labour of love. As cricket should always be.

Stephen Chalke

Bath, January 2002

INTRODUCTION

The aim of this book is to recreate the county cricket of the 1950s by telling the story of twelve games played during these years. I have set them in chronological order, starting at Lord's in May 1952 and ending at Hove in September 1959. So we begin in the Spring of Queen Elizabeth's accession, with food rationing and uncleared bomb sites, and we end in the Autumn of Harold Macmillan's 'You've never had it so good' election, with Independent Television and the Mini car. They are years of change, but we only realise the full impact of these changes in the years that follow.

The twelve games feature all seventeen counties and have been chosen by men who played in them. They are games that have stayed in their memory for forty years. Some recall triumphs, some disasters, some thrilling finishes. There are games in which individuals achieve brief greatness and games in which unfashionable counties beat their richer counterparts. They have all stayed alive in the memory.

The format of the county championship is unchanged during these years. Each county plays 28 three-day games, with points only for winning and for first innings lead. The wickets are left uncovered during the games, though there is some covering of bowlers' run-ups. Players are divided into amateurs and professionals, and most counties still have amateur captains.

I have constructed these stories from interviews with players and from contemporary reports. I have tried to set each game in the context of its time, and I have incorporated the players' thoughts on the game then and now. I have also tried to bring alive some of the characters in each team, the differing temperaments and the humorous incidents. I want it to read as if you are at the game and you are sitting next to one of the players, though the game is forty years ago and the player is sitting in 1997.

I hope that I have recreated these games as they really happened, but the memory can play tricks. My own first memory of cricket is at Hastings in 1956, A.E.R. Gilligan's XI against the Australians, and I can still see Arthur Milton hitting the tourists all round the pretty ground, the tourists whose faces I have collected on sweet cigarette cards. What a lovely day it is as I look at it in my memory! How strange to read in Wisden that 'rain spoiled the opening match of the Festival' and 'a biting wind blew across the ground'.

At the end of the book, I have drawn the stumps and reflected on what I have learnt during its writing. It has been a pleasure to meet so many old players, their love of the game undimmed by the years, and I hope that this book communicates that pleasure. You may mourn the loss of a golden age, or you may be glad that we live in more affluent, sophisticated times. Whichever way, I hope that you will enjoy the stories of these games.

Denis Compton

CARRYING THE BAGS

Middlesex v Glamorgan
May 1952
with Don Shepherd

Don Shepherd played for Glamorgan from 1950 to 1972. Originally a fast-medium bowler, he switched to off-spin in 1956. He took 2218 first-class wickets, and he was a member of the Glamorgan side that won the championship in 1969. He remembers a match at Lord's in the early days of his career.

Lord's Cricket Ground, the game's headquarters, always has that special atmosphere. Walking out to bat through the Long Room, with its portrait of Thomas Lord and its bust of W.G. Grace. Looking up from the square and seeing the weather vane of Old Father Time on top of the Grand Stand. Running in to bowl with the great crowd all round, the M.C.C. members in front of the pavilion, the beer-drinkers in the Mound Stand. It is another world from the sandy bays and winding country lanes of the Gower Peninsula.

It is May 1952. Memories of the war are receding slowly, just like the ration books. But Denis Compton and Bill Edrich, Middlesex's leading batsmen, have brought dash and colour to those hard years after the war, and there is still expectation whenever they walk to the wicket. Denis, the Brylcreem Boy, his cavalier grin is on all the advertising hoardings. Bill, the wartime bomber pilot, no bowler is ever too fast for him to hook. What runs will 1952 bring for them?

Gentle sunshine and a soft breeze make a pleasant Saturday for cricket at Lord's. "Lord's on a warm day," A.A. Milne writes, "with a bottle, a mixed bag of sandwiches and a couple of spare pipes in a despatch case, and I don't care who is playing whom." It is May 1952. Middlesex are entertaining Glamorgan. Middlesex have begun their summer with victory over Derbyshire, but for Glamorgan this trip to Lord's is their first fixture. "You just want to get started," Don explains. "You want to get into the routine of cricket every day."

According to the Times, *'a large and responsive crowd'*[*] gathers. "The crowds were enormous in those days, and Glamorgan always had a very special following. There were so many exiled Welsh people who religiously followed you when you were in their area." Three Welsh lords sit on the balcony of the Lord's pavilion. The football season is over, with 55,000 cheering Cardiff City to a last victory promotion to Division One. Now they turn their attention to cricket.

Denis Compton. Is there any truth in the story that he strolls in on the morning of the first game, borrows a bat and steps out to play as if he has never been away? Against Derbyshire he is stumped for 85, Bill Edrich is caught out for 60, and they both look forward to this Glamorgan game to continue their early

---

[*] Quotations from contemporary newspaper reports are in italics throughout.

season form. They bat at three and four, behind Jack Robertson and Sid Brown. Robertson, Brown, Edrich, Compton are Middlesex's first four in July 1938, two months before Neville Chamberlain proclaims 'Peace in our Time', and they are Middlesex's first four in August 1955, a year after the last of the wartime rations is lifted. In that glorious summer of 1947, they score over twelve thousand runs. Has ever a county boasted a better top four? There is many a disappointed groan around the ground when the news comes through that Glamorgan are to bat.

It is May 1952. Identity cards have finally been abolished, and the last London tram is about to run.

Wilf Wooller is the Glamorgan captain. He is county secretary, too. They call him Skipper, and at times he is like a Roman emperor as he rules them with a discipline that is extraordinary, even in 1952. They have their positions on the field, and they have their duties off it. "When you came in as a young player," Don recalls, "you just played. You more or less did what you were told." Don is the youngster; it is his job to carry the bags.

"Wilf once said to me," Warwickshire's Tom Cartwright recalls, "that he wanted his players to be more afraid of him than of the opposition." Tom smiles. "He probably achieved that."

The Glamorgan team travels on Friday evening, Cardiff to Paddington by train. "I had to make sure the bags were on a trailer with a porter, I had to count them onto the guard's van and count them out the other end, I had to make sure the taxis were over, and that I had a half-crown tip for the porter and the guard. It wasn't just cricket kit, either." It is the start of eleven days away, and all the players have cases full of clothes. "The old leather bags were heavy, too." They stay at the Portland Arms in Maida Vale, and on Saturday morning it is Don's job to get the bags to Lord's. Then Wilf walks the players there – a short journey compared to the three or four miles they have to walk to some county grounds. Wilf is a big man, a Welsh rugby international in the '30s. He is over six foot tall, but he has been down to eight stone in the war, force-marched twenty miles in a day by the Japanese, and by comparison these early morning walks are a light stroll.

Wilf wins the toss, and he elects to bat. It is not a difficult decision. Not like the day at Derby when he asks Allan Watkins and Haydn Davies what they think. "Put them in," they suggest, and Wilf comes on first change and his five for 64 takes 52 overs. "His knee was like a balloon. You couldn't get the ball off him." "I'll never listen to you buggers again," he curses.

Emrys Davies and Phil Clift open for Glamorgan. Emrys Davies, what goes on beneath that calm exterior? He looks more like a chapel minister than a professional sportsman. "Emrys was the rock of Glamorgan's batting," Don explains. "He would bat for ever and ever. Phil was more inclined to get on with it." 'On a quiet, unresponsive wicket,' the Times reports, 'the Middlesex bowlers were treated firmly, at times even unceremoniously, by Davies and Clift. Indeed, at luncheon, these two had already gathered 135 runs to deserve an appetite.'

Emrys is forty-seven now, and he has played for Glamorgan since 1924. He carries the memory of those early championship years. The season of six captains and five wicket-keepers. The portly gentlemen at first slip, the ball bomp onto the chest and down to ground, a weary "Well stopped, sir" from the bowler. The difficulty of raising a team for Trent Bridge when Larwood was in his prime. And he himself averaging just 13.96 after eight summers of batting. Did he ever dream that he would score 2000 runs and take 100 wickets in the same season? Or that he would be picked for an M.C.C. tour of India? Or that, after the war that deprived him of that tour, Glamorgan would win the county championship? "Emrys was the senior pro," Don explains. "I was just starting my career. He wouldn't have talked to me about any of that."

Emrys is the second Welsh professional taken on by Glamorgan. The first, Dai Davies, is an umpire now. How fitting that on that historic day at Bournemouth when the county clinches the championship it should be Dai at the bowler's end for the vital lbw shout. Some tell how he led the appeal, others how his finger went up with the words, 'That's out, and we've won.' There are better batting sides in 1948, better bowling sides, too, but "in fielding," Wilf Wooller writes, "we give first to no side".

Emrys has five when he edges Moss to slip, 'a straightforward catch' that Denis Compton spills. 'It left the fieldsman owing his side a lot of runs,' the Times adds. Phil Clift gives a sharp chance to Jim Sims at short mid-wicket, but that too goes down. Jim is forty-eight years old and, when he almost fires his top-spinner through Emrys's defence, 'the patriarchs grinned, recognising the experienced skill in each other'. They have lost six years to the war, and they are determined to enjoy these years in their late forties. It will be another two summers before Emrys is bowled Tyson 0, declines a second innings and calls it a day. And who should open in his place but the forty-one-year-old Wilf Wooller? "Bugger off, Tyson," he growls when hit under the heart. "You're not fast enough to hurt me." "You'd never get the better of Wilf," Don remembers.

Luncheon at Lord's is formal. "However sweaty you were, you had to put a blazer on. There was no chasing round, bringing down trays." Don knows Lord's better than most. In 1948, while Glamorgan are deposing Middlesex as county champions, he is on the bowling staff. "I never saw anyone. I was in digs in St John's Wood Road, thinking 'What's it all about?'". He practises his bowling in the morning and, for the rest of the day, he is available for members who want a net. "It was hard work. We put up with things they wouldn't do now." He bowls to the Australian Bill Brown, "you could have two or three thousand people watching", to the Duke of Buccleuch, to the opera singer Dennis Noble and to Gubby Allen, just back from captaining the MCC in the West Indies. "Two bowlers, please," Gubby Allen calls, and he puts a half crown on the stumps. "He had a big pair of pads, and of course you could never get him out lbw." Don does not know it, but he is preparing his body for 20,000 first-class overs. "It was a process of getting fit by doing what you've got to do, which I'm afraid doesn't happen now."

Before this summer of '48, he has played so little cricket. On a mat for the parson's team in Porteynon, three or four wartime games for his school and a little for his R.N.A.F. station near Worcester. "The bowling action was just there, I never had any coaching. I didn't even know a batsman could play forward or back." He watches Bradman as he hits 150 in his last innings at Lord's, and it is his job to open the dressing-room door for him.

'If the batsmen had gained free rein in the morning, the afternoon was to perform something of a somersault.' Jack Young, the master of 'smile and guile', removes both openers, and Denis Compton, with his chinamen, gets the better of Parkhouse, Watkins and Jones. 152 for no wicket becomes 208 for five.

Little Willie Jones, like Wilf, is a Welsh rugby international. A fly half. A small man with an amazing burst of speed and a supreme ability to kick a ball. On the cricket field his speed in the covers is legendary. But he is the most nervous of batsmen and Wilf is not always the best of captains for him. Seven times he scores 1000 runs in a season, yet he is often in a crisis of self-doubt. "I can't get a bloody run, man. I don't know where the next one's coming from." He is so anxious that he gets his wife to ring Wilf to check if he is playing. "In the evening, when he'd had a couple of drinks," Don says, "he became a much better player".

Wilf towers over him, and Willie is afraid of making mistakes. "We were no strangers to a row in the dressing room if Wilf didn't agree with what was going on." There are even days when Wilf threatens to send him home. "Many's the time I wish I'd gone," Willie confides to Dennis Brookes at Northampton. But back he comes, and sometimes his wife comes with him 'to sort Wilf out'. "Willie's great shot was the late cut," Don recalls. "It looked glorious if he hit it well. But, if he got out, it'd be 'If I ever see you playing that bloody dob shot again, …'" Today, he is caught Edrich, bowled Compton, 10. In the words of the Times, Compton's three wickets were *'a contribution on the part of this compelling cricketer which served as part payment towards the earlier and important catch he had dropped'*. There are still runs owing, it seems.

It is May 1952. The United States has tested its first H-bomb, and Allied planes drop napalm over Korea.

'The Glamorgan batting dwindled quickly so that by five o'clock the pitch was being rolled in preparation for the Middlesex reply.' The last wicket falls when Don is bowled by Alan Moss. "Making hay, I expect. I don't suppose I ever had a practice with the pads on in all the years I played." Don has played two half-seasons for Glamorgan, and this is his seventeenth duck. He pushes open the dressing-room door, the door he once opened for Sir Donald Bradman, and do his team-mates laugh? "I think they'd gone past that by then. Anyway, the crowd like to see the stumps flying. Specialists were specialists in those days. It was only when bonus points came in that we started to bat a bit properly."

Glamorgan, 266 all out. "Quite a good score for Glamorgan, a decent total to bowl against." It is ten past five, and Don is taking the new ball. This summer presents a fresh opportunity for him to establish himself as the spearhead of the attack. He spends the winters in the family shop on the Gower Peninsula, and he does two paper rounds a day. He walks back towards the pavilion, and he measures his fourteen pace run. "I think you'll find that my run-up was from the start of one of the white lines on the middle of the road to the far end of the second one." All winter, up and down hill on his paper round, he strives for that extra yard of pace, and against the low wall in front of the shop he strives for consistent length with his tennis ball. "I had to bowl a half-volley to get it back. If I didn't, it would go through the hedge." And pre-season at Cardiff there is just a dirty corridor in the old North Stand. It is a different world from a well-filled Lord's on a sunny Saturday afternoon.

'The fourth ball of Shepherd's first over moved late from leg to find the inside edge of Brown's bat, so that the unfortunate batsman played on.' Middlesex, 1 for one, and Bill Edrich joins Jack Robertson. "Jack was a beautifully fluent player." He has scored 2000 runs each season since the war, but "I remember dropping him, a caught-and-bowled. It was an absolute dolly." The score moves on to 53 for one, and the Middlesex supporters are enjoying their batsmen at last. But Don is young and supple, and his day is not over. With the first ball of a new over he sends downs a well-pitched delivery that bowls Bill Edrich, and it is time to renew acquaintance with Denis Compton. That year on the bowling staff, Denis is a regular visitor to their young pro's room, king of the shoveha'penny board. "You wouldn't take him on at that even." The Times correspondent is still reflecting on the 85 runs Emrys Davies has scored after that fateful drop when, with the last ball of the same over, 'Shepherd persuaded the great Compton to play on to a ball short and wide of the off stump.'

Brown 0, Edrich 24, Compton 1. Don stares with disbelief at Wisden's printed page. "I could have sworn those three boys all had nought." For forty-five years he has looked back with pride at the evening he bagged them all for ducks. "I hadn't looked at Wisden. God knows who bought them. My mother, I expect. There wasn't a thing then about cricketers looking up papers and taking note of what went on. You just played." His brother will deliver the newspapers that spread the news of his wickets to the Gower Peninsula, and Gowerton Grammar School's magazine will publish the card in its old boys' notes. Harry Sharp is bowled by Allan Watkins, and Middlesex end the day on 76 for four.

It is May 1952. The B.B.C. begins an experiment in television for schools, and a new board game Scrabble is marketed.

Glamorgan may have won the championship in 1948, but they have never won in Yorkshire and never won here at Lord's. For the pre-war players these are mountains still to climb. At Harrogate in 1955, Don will clout a 'vigorous' 48 to save the follow on and Glamorgan will beat Yorkshire in a thrilling run chase. "I never thought I'd live to see this day," Haydn Davies will say through forming tears, and their newly-acquired physiotherapist will openly weep. Did Don remember any such talk at Lord's? "I was just starting out. I'm not sure I would have been too involved with their chatter."

He is part of the team, though, when they visit the London Welsh club in the evening. No drinks here, this is a dry house, so they stop first at The Green Man in the Gray's Inn Road. Wilf may be a hard captain on the field, but he is always there for their Saturday evening get-togethers. And for the singing that develops. 'Calon Lan' and Willie Jones' favourite, 'Bugeilio'r Gwenith Gwyn'. 'Bringing In The White Wheat.'

> *'Myfi sy'n dachgen leuance ffôl*
>
> *Yn byw' yn ôl fy ffansi.'*

"Everybody knew the words, even if they couldn't speak the language." Even Len Muncer, the North Londoner, and Jimmy McConnon, the Geordie. 'I am a foolish young man, living on my fantasies,' they sing, though they do not know it.

Then Willie tells them of the three great kickers in Welsh rugby: Rees, Sullivan and Jones. Another drink, and there are only two: Sullivan and Jones. A third drink, and, well, even Sullivan is forgotten.

At the London Welsh club, they are taken up onto the stage to receive the plaudits. There are student doctors, office workers, milkmen. "I think every milkman in London was Welsh, wasn't he?" Many of them have been at the game and, each time Don has knocked down the stumps, their cheers have filled the Middlesex silence. Does Don dream of such an evening as he runs up along the white lines of his village road?

Back at the Portland Arms, Don shares a room with Bernard Hedges, and somebody shares with Willie Jones. "Run up!" Willie mutters in his sleep. "There's three runs here."

Rain on Sunday leaves the wicket on Monday *'unpleasant before luncheon'*, and the first hour sees just 25 runs added for the loss of Routledge. *'As soon as Muncer came on, however, his run-up marked out by sawdust like so many paving stones against the green background, things began to happen.'* Len Muncer has spent his war on the Burma-Siam railway, reflecting on a cricket career here at Lord's that has seen him achieve few of his ambitions. A leg-break bowler at a county rich in such bowlers, he moves to Glamorgan in 1947 and he turns to off-spin, taking 159 wickets in championship year. He has a flatter trajectory than Jim McConnon, but he makes the batsman play at every ball.

It is 1952. Law 39, L.B.W., stipulates that the point of impact shall be between wicket and wicket. There is no additional law for not playing a stroke outside the off stump. "Somebody like Washbrook would come in with those big old floppy pads bending over. If it hit him on the knee roll an inch outside the off stump, it's not out. So the whole line of our game was different. We used to bowl straight with short legs." And what short legs! Allan Watkins, Phil Clift and Wilf himself. "Three great catchers there." *'Muncer carried all before him. He pitched to a length and turned awkwardly from the off. He was helped on the way by a really brilliant catch close in by Watkins.'*

Glamorgan bustle through their overs. There is no clapping of hands to attract attention. It is the fielder's job to look at Wilf between each ball, and field changes are made with quiet gestures. It is a Glamorgan tradition developed by Maurice Turnbull before the war. Maurice was Glamorgan's first Test player, and he was a martinet. Not for him drinks with the team, the professionals had to write for appointments to see him. George Lavis, now the county coach, tells how he would make signals behind his back. "If he gestured for you to move ten yards and you didn't see it, you wouldn't play the next game." He dies in the Normandy invasion, but some of his spirit lives on in Wilf's determination to make Glamorgan successful. "Even if you lost, you could always say you'd been in a game. Wilf would never be dominated."

"We have attempted to make each fielder an integral part of a machine," Wilf writes. It is not always easy. Emrys is at mid-on, and Len Muncer is down on the boundary. At Westcliff in July, Essex are 82 for nine, wanting four for victory when the batsman edges Don to fine leg. Len lumbers round and sticks out a boot. "The ball hopped over," Don recalls, "and that was the game." They go down to Bournemouth on the train, and Don is distraught. "It'll happen again," Emrys says comfortingly. And it does. 45 years on, Don can laugh.

'But for a gallant little innings by Titmus - 11 runs well made at a time of crisis - Glamorgan would have been in a position to require the follow-on.' There is a shower before lunch, a heavier one after. Time perhaps for a game of cards in the Glamorgan dressing-room. "Just poker, sixpenny limit. It never got a bad school." *'Muncer finally trapped Moss at three o'clock to end a great spell of bowling. Five wickets for seven runs speaks for itself.'* Sims, Young, Moss, four runs between them, did they make hay like Don? "No, they were very straight, coming from Lord's." Middlesex, 123 all out, trail on first innings by 143 runs.

Batting is hard now on the wet pitch, and Emrys Davies looks down the wicket as his congregation comes and goes. Phil Clift is acrobatically caught by Les Compton, and Gilbert Parkhouse is lbw. Then Willie Jones calls 'Ie', Emrys calls 'Na', and Emrys watches *'Compton (L) falling full length as he broke the wicket with Jones also prostrate in the middle of the pitch'*. Poor Willie, do the runs he calls in his sleep ever end this way? *'It was a scene of sheer destruction.'* The score is 28 for three.

Emrys makes a *'serene'* 29, Allan Watkins hits *'some powerful hooks and cuts'* in his 65, and Wilf himself sweeps two sixes into the grandstand. Allan and Wilf add 60 in half an hour, and, though they are both out by close of play, the score reaches 169 for six, a lead of 312. 'Glamorgan Well Placed' is the Times headline. *'Their greatest danger would now seem to lie in the uncertain weather.'*

Jim Sims is forty-nine tomorrow, and the hours of fielding are growing longer. Alan Moss is twenty-one, racing in off his long run and giving his all to the game, an exciting career ahead of him. Alan tells of the day he is driven to long-on and turns in his follow-through to see Jim edging from mid-on to square leg, saying from the corner of his mouth, "I'm sorry, Al old boy, but you'll have to go." It could not happen at Wilf's Glamorgan. In 1955 at Lord's, John Dewes, "he was the big white hope, wasn't he?", is edging the ball everywhere, and Wilf is starting to boil. He puts every fielder behind the bat." "Whatever you do," he says to Don, "don't pitch the ball up." And he stands at short gully. "Well, of course, the next ball goes straight down the ground to the corner of the Middlesex stand, and he suddenly realises that he's got to go for it. As he passes me, he says, 'You must be the dullest bugger who's ever played first-class cricket", and off he goes into the distance."

Fielding theories, Wilf is full of them. "Wooller may be a Welshman," Somerset's Colin McCool writes, "but like everybody else in English cricket he is theory-crazy." Colin McCool, he is the quiet Australian, smoking his pipe in the dressing room corner, but his team mates see another Colin when they play Glamorgan. He is hit on the pad, and he protests at Wilf's absurd appeal from short leg. "You squealing Aussie bastard," Wilf retorts. "Get back to Wagga-Wagga." By the time they finish Colin's bat is cocked like a hammer. "I called him every name known to man, and yet, truth was I loved the bloke."

"Among his own team," Colin adds, "his word carried the weight of a High Court Judge." But Wilf is one of the lads in the bar at the end of the day, and, when he buys an Austin Sheerline with a number plate of 111, Don recalls, "we bitched him so much he had to sell it". "He was a tough nut all right," Colin writes, "but there was more gold in his heart than there is in Fort Knox. He would have trampled roughshod over a baby for the good of Glamorgan cricket, but it was all forgotten once he had climbed out of his flannels."

Wilf is a hard man in his own public school, Oxbridge way, and Freddie Brown of Northants is another. Later this summer they will grind out the most tedious of draws, and in front of the pavilion they will exchange their end-of-match pleasantries. "Thanks for fuck all, Wilf." "Bugger off, Freddie." Behind them, Len Muncer turns to Dennis Brookes. "I'm glad I sent my children to elementary school," he says.

It is May 1952. BOAC runs its first jet passenger service, and the city of Manchester introduces a smokeless zone.

Glamorgan, 194 for six, 194 all out. Is this the game when Wilf plays hell with Denis for trying to claim that Jimmy McConnon is too late out to bat? "I used to sit and laugh sometimes when I got home," Colin McCool writes, "wondering what those innocent spectators would have said had they known what was cooking in the middle." Don Shepherd once more passes the bust of W.G. Grace in the Long Room. And once more the stumps go back as he is bowled for nought. "Heave-ho, I should think." His eighteenth duck. He may be 'a foolish young man living on his fantasies', but in time there will come days when he will connect, when the bars will empty as he bludgeons fifties in 15 and 16 minutes. '*Middlesex, shortly after midday, were left with the task of getting 338 for victory at the rate of some 65 runs an hour.*' "You could base a declaration on 60 runs an hour. 65 was on, especially with those great players."

28 runs in the first hour, '*a panting jog trot instead of a smart gallop*'. Jack Robertson falls, trying to hook Don, and Sid Brown struggles. Eight runs in three innings this season, this is no time to play himself into form. '*His bat was all*

edge and, unhappily, he was all too conscious of it.' "Sid was a better player when the others around him were going well." *'Edrich did his best to keep things moving, sending the 50 up just before luncheon.'* Bill Edrich piloted Blenheim twin-engine bombers in the war, and one in three did not return some nights. Wilf Wooller played cricket on Christmas Day at Changi prisoner camp, eight stone of skin and bone. Hooking the bouncer, standing at short leg, these do not rank as acts of courage.

'For half an hour after luncheon Brown continued the struggle, which was as much with himself as with the Glamorgan bowlers. At last, dancing hopefully out to McConnon, he lost his middle stump to a shorter ball cleverly held back.' It is 85 for two, and *'with Edrich and Compton (D.) together this now was the heart of the matter'*. Wilf delights in giving Test batsmen a hard time, and none more than Denis Compton. In his first ever innings against Glamorgan he walks down the 84 steps at St Helens to be bowled for one, and he walks back up again. Hardly long enough at the crease for Wilf at short leg to make his presence felt. As he walks out to bat on this Tuesday afternoon, he has scored 211 runs, average 23.44, against Glamorgan, and, though he does not know it, this will be his last chance to improve these figures. "Wilf and Denis had many a tussle, but, when I see Denis now, he always asks after Wilf."

'McConnon left Compton stranded and looking suspiciously leg-before-wicket to his very first ball', but 'not out' is the verdict, and 13 runs are added without incident. On Saturday, Don has bowled Edrich and Compton with the first and last balls of an over. Today it is Allan Watkins's turn, Compton and Edrich, first and last balls. *'The left-handed Watkins, who bowled finely at medium pace, first made Compton play outside a ball that moved down the hill, and then had Edrich beautifully taken at first slip by Parkhouse. The score was 99 for 4 and the heart of the Middlesex innings had been cut out.'*

Compton, bowled Watkins, 2. Denis Compton walks away with a smile, perhaps a toss of the head as he pulls off his gloves. Not for him a long dressing-room mope. "Tomorrow is another day," he says. And tomorrow he will be back here at Lord's for his 98th first-class century. And in four weeks, he will be here again, waving his bat at a midweek crowd of several thousand as they cheer his hundredth hundred. Great bundles of letters arrive, and he leaves them to his agent to answer. But these failures against Glamorgan are not the only ones of the summer, and another type of letter starts to arrive. Parents travel miles so that their children can see the great Denis Compton, and today he walks off with three runs to show for his two innings in the match. "What *has* happened to you?" they ask. He drops out of the Test side and, according to Wisden, 'his temporary eclipse became regarded as the main cause of the Middlesex slide'. It is his worst season, yet in its course he gathers 1880 runs, 77 wickets and 26 catches.

Jimmy McConnon bowls Routledge, and Middlesex are 100 for five. *'Father Time on the roof of the grandstand pointed clearly to the west, and that was where the victory seemed sure to go.'* Muncer and McConnon wheel away, and the Middlesex lower order does rather better. Leslie Compton hits *'some powerful blows'*, and Jim Sims and Jack Young take the game into its final session.

There are bags to be packed and carried down to the taxis. Cases full of clothes, too. "Cricket kit wasn't very clever. I'd have had quite a few pairs of socks. Welsh wool, bought on Swansea market and knitted at home. We had pretty heavyweight boots, too, with big studs." They will all have to be counted onto the porter's trolley at Euston, counted onto the guard's van, too. The days of the team van are still a long way away. "Mind you, that broke down once on the way to Middlesborough. They got a lorry driver to tow them, he wasn't very happy. The rope broke, and off he went. They arrived in the morning on a double decker bus." As Young and Sims play confident shots against the off-spinners, does Don start to fear the last ball finish, the mad dash for the taxis, the changing on the train? "The trains were packed. We didn't know when we'd be finishing so we couldn't book a compartment. We often had to stand in the corridors."

'All through Shepherd played his youthful part with some distinction,' the Times records, *'and he ended the gay abandon of it all with a new ball.'* Middlesex are all out for 206, and Glamorgan have won by 131 runs. In two years' time, Wilf will bowl them to a second victory at Lord's, but a third is still to come. Are there tears among the senior pros? Emrys Davies with his minister's smile, Haydn Davies who has swapped his science degree for a pair of keeper's gloves, Len Muncer who is tasting success he never knew at Lord's, and Wilf himself, one up on his old foe Denis Compton. Don is too busy heaving the bags to the taxis to share whatever moments there are.

It is May 1952. By the end of the year, 'The Mousetrap' will open in the West End, and the New Musical Express will print its first Top Ten.

A glorious summer is ahead for Don. The thud of the ball against Gubby Allen's pads, the white lines beneath his paper round run-up, the half-volleys against the low shop wall, they bring him 120 wickets and a county cap. He will never again taste such success as a fast bowler. Wilf will rest him for just one game all summer, and he will spend it on the sands near home, bowling his heart out. At least it will be three days away from the bags.

2218 first-class wickets. No bowler has taken more without a Test cap. "I never picked up a Sunday paper expecting to see my name there. You just played. I don't think I knew anything about myself until these last few years." Just scattered memories, like the evening he bowled Compton, Edrich and Brown at Lord's. Not for noughts, alas, but for few enough that he can still hear the cheers that night in the London Welsh club.

MIDDLESEX v GLAMORGAN

Lord's. 10, 12 & 13 May 1952

GLAMORGAN WON BY 131 RUNS

GLAMORGAN

E. Davies	c Edrich b Young	90	c L.Compton b Young		29
P.B. Clift	c L.Compton b Young	72	c L.Compton b Moss		0
W.G.A. Parkhouse	b D.Compton	13	lbw b Moss		8
W.E. Jones	c Edrich b D.Compton	10	run out		1
A.J. Watkins	b D Compton	6	b Moss		65
*W. Wooller	b Young	15	lbw b D.Compton		37
B. Hedges	b Moss	19	b Moss		26
B.L. Muncer	c Sharp b Young	27	c Sims b Young		18
J. McConnon	not out	9	c Titmus b Young		0
+H.G. Davies	b Moss	0	not out		0
D. Shepherd	b Moss	0	b Young		0
Extras	b 1, lb 4	5	b 7, lb 2, nb 1		10
		266			**194**

1-152, 2-167, 3-179, 4-185, 5-208, 6-214, 7-251, 8-265, 9-266, 10-266
1-1, 2-21, 3-28, 4-90, 5-130, 6-158, 7-194, 8-194, 9-194, 10-194

Moss	21.1	1	65	3	28	10	44	4
Edrich	10	2	28	0	3	0	15	0
Young	32	12	61	4	26	9	63	4
Sims	8	1	29	0				
Routledge	4	0	8	0				
Titmus	3	0	8	0	10	3	28	0
D.Compton	22	4	62	3	9	1	34	1

MIDDLESEX

J.D. Robertson	c H.Davies b Muncer	52	b Shepherd		12
S.M. Brown	b Shepherd	0	b McConnon		40
*W.J. Edrich	b Shepherd	24	c Parkhouse b Watkins		34
D.C.S. Compton	b Shepherd	1	b Watkins		2
H.P. Sharp	b Watkins	5	c & b Muncer		21
R. Routledge	b Watkins	3	b McConnon		0
+L.H. Compton	c Watkins b Muncer	15	c Shepherd b McConnon		20
F.J. Titmus	not out	11	b Muncer		0
J.M .Sims	c Watkins b Muncer	0	c H.Davies b Shepherd		27
J.A. Young	lbw b Muncer	4	not out		22
A.E. Moss	lbw b Muncer	0	b Shepherd		12
Extras	b 1, lb 6, nb 1	8	b 13, lb 3		16
		123			**206**

1-1, 2-53, 3-55, 4-69, 5-79, 6-102, 7-105, 8-109, 9-115, 10-123
1-18, 2-85, 3-98, 4-99, 5-100, 6-124, 7-124, 8-153, 9-189, 10-206

Shepherd	18	4	38	3	10.2	3	29	3
Wooller	12	3	33	0	4	0	15	0
Watkins	17	7	37	2	20	5	30	2
Muncer	7.5	3	7	5	16	4	34	2
McConnon					24	1	82	3

Umpires: G.S. Mobey and H.G. Baldwin

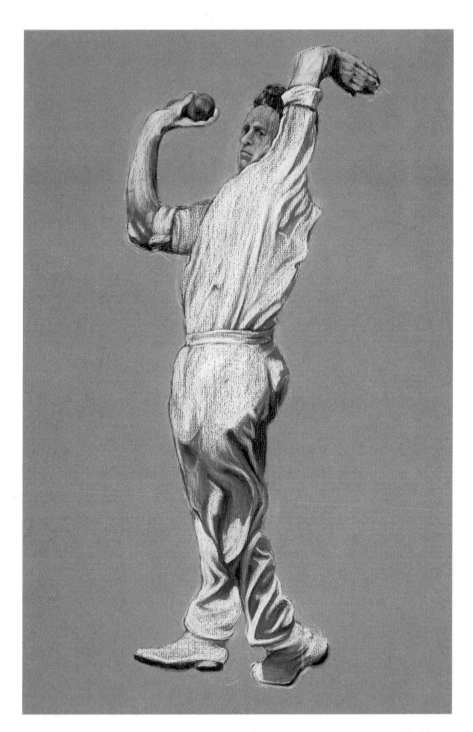

Brian Statham

HIT HARD AND ENJOY IT

Essex v Lancashire
June 1952
with Dickie Dodds

Dickie Dodds played for Essex from 1946 to 1959. A hard-hitting opening bat, he scored 1000 runs in a season eleven times. The son of a country vicar, he decided at the end of the Second World War to devote his life to the cause of Moral Re-Armament, to which he gave all the proceeds of his 1957 benefit match. He remembers an Essex run chase at Brentwood.

Trevor Bailey. It is June 1952, and his two-year Test place is lost to Glamorgan's Allan Watkins. He is not yet a hero of English cricket nor yet is he the central figure of this wandering Essex side. In twelve months his determined batting will be at the heart of England's Coronation Year Ashes victory. In ten years he will be both captain and secretary here at Essex. But these are just future possibilities in 1952. His typewriter keys have not yet tapped out the first words of his first cricket book. The radio waves have not yet transmitted the first judgements of his expert analysis. It is the summer of 1952. For now his cricketing career must develop in the cavalier world of Doug Insole's Essex side.

"Bailey to me was an enigma," Dickie recalls. "I expect I was to him."

Back in 1946 Trevor and Dickie have both arrived as amateurs at Essex. Dickie has spent his war years in Signals in India and Burma, but Trevor is five years his junior and his Royal Marine battalion embarks for Europe just as Germany is surrendering. Dickie has grown up in a country vicarage, and he has a summer-long struggle with his God before he resolves to become a professional cricketer. Trevor, meanwhile, goes up to Cambridge University and retains his amateur status as Essex's Assistant Secretary.

It is June 1952, and at Brentwood against Lancashire each finds his own way of rising to the challenge of a thrilling run chase.

Brentwood is the loveliest of Essex's many venues. There are trees on three sides of the ground, and by late June there are splashes of red among the various greens of the oaks, elms and planes. The ground belongs to Merrymeade, the adjoining stately home, and in a semi-circular enclosure an old lady sits under a parasol, watching the play. She is Mrs Hall Payne, widow of the tea trader who built this house and who raised money around Brentwood for the Canadian Pacific Railway. The old wooden pavilion is painted white, and it is so tiny that it contains just one hand basin for washing down after the game.

It is June 1952, and the visitors at this year's Brentwood week are Leicestershire and Lancashire. The Leicestershire game has come to a thrilling climax on Friday evening. Essex chase 195 in 100 minutes and make them with one ball and two wickets to spare. This is how Essex like to play, and at the end of the summer they will win the newly inaugurated News Chronicle Trophy for Brighter Cricket. They will win it again in 1953, and the cups still stand on Dickie's mantelpiece. Dick Horsfall, Ray Smith, Doug Insole, Dickie himself, they hit the ball hard and score their runs fast. 'Hit Hard And Enjoy It', that is the spirit in which Dickie expresses God in his cricket, and that is the name of the book he will write twenty years later to explain this philosophy.

Now it is the turn of the formidable Lancashire team, unbeaten after twelve fixtures and lying third in the championship table. Their openers, Cyril Washbrook and Jack Ikin, are unfit, but the side possesses great depth of talent, with three young Test players in their bowling attack: off-spinner Roy Tattersall, slow left-armer Malcolm Hilton and the young quick bowler Brian Statham. It is an attractive fixture for the inhabitants of this small town, nestled on the edge of London's Green Belt.

It is June 1952. Hotels line the nearby High Street, a reminder of the days when the town was a staging post for mail coaches. There is still a market day on Wednesdays.

Lancashire bat first on Saturday and, according to the Manchester Guardian, *'for long periods of the day their batsmen played as though they suspected both bowlers and the wicket of being possessed of some hidden venom'*. Wharton and Lomax are the makeshift openers, Trevor Bailey bowls his first five overs for one run, and after 45 minutes the score is just 20. Then Lomax edges Ken Preston to Paul Gibb behind the stumps.

"Paul Gibb, what a wonderful character," Dickie remembers. "When he was small, he wanted to be heavyweight boxing champion of the world. Then he got glandular fever or rheumatic fever, one of those, and he never grew much after that. His doctor said he had a bad heart, he mustn't do anything energetic. So Paul took up squash, tennis and cricket. And his appetite was the same as if he had been a heavyweight boxer. He was the most enormous trencherman."

Lancashire are 96 for one at lunch, Wharton 52 not out. "People used to love coming to Essex. There were so many different grounds, the cricket was enjoyable, and the food was always good." And nobody likes his food more than Paul Gibb. In Australia he challenges Joe Hardstaff to an ice-cream eating competition, and he wins easily. Extra vegetables, second helpings, left-overs, they all go down, and there is always the bottle of liquid paraffin handy to help them on their way.

It is June 1952. The young Queen Elizabeth has been four months on the throne, and it will be another year before the news of the conquest of Everest brings extra glory to her Coronation day.

Dickie will spend Coronation night in Paul's small Ford van, working their way from Ilford to Llanelli on winding roads. "He started off with the most exaggerated sports car you've ever seen. It was fibreglass, with a great big bonnet. Then he bought this van." Paul has piloted Sunderland flying boats in the war and, before they set out, he carries out a general inspection of the vehicle. Tyres, oil and water; back door locked, windscreen wiped. "He used to settle into the driving seat as if he was wiggling into a cockpit." A check of the dashboard instruments, a waggle of the pedals, and away they trundle, a 30 mile an hour limit for commercial vehicles. While Edmund Hillary and Sherpa Tensing stand on top of Everest with their British flag, Paul and Dickie meander lost around the Welsh mountains. Sheep bleat by the roadside, Coronation bonfires blaze from distant peaks, and they reach their hotel just before dawn. They spend all day in the field and lose by an innings.

It is June 1952. A plan is announced to light zebra crossings with blinking beacons.

After lunch, Geoff Edrich and Alan Wharton continue steadily until *'at 111 Edrich lofted a drive off Smith and was well caught by Insole running swiftly from long on to long off.'* Is this the short straight boundary that Trevor Bailey analyses in his autobiography? "'I was always fascinated," he writes, "by the number of batsmen unable to resist the very short boundary at one end and holing out." *'As if to avenge Edrich, Wharton then pulled a long hop from Smith into the crowd and in a subsequent over from Smith made one grand cover drive for four followed by a crisp square cut also to the boundary.'* It is 150 for two.

Brentwood's square is tended by Bill Hansell. Gone are the days when he uses his horse to pull the roller, but he still sprinkles wet cow dung over the wicket and rolls it till it dries like concrete under the hot sun. It is known for many years as a batting paradise. In 1934, when county cricket returns to Brentwood after a break, Kent score 803 for four, with Bill Ashdown making 332. "What do you remember of that day, Bill?" they ask him when he is an old man, and once more he recalls the hot sun beating on the freshly rolled wicket. "The smell," he says. It is not a ground for a bowler to lick his fingers.

On that day in 1934, a nineteen-year-old Ray Smith makes his first home appearance for the county. One for 115 in 22 overs as Ashdown, Woolley and Ames despatch the ball to all corners of the pretty ground. Now he is thirty-seven, and he bowls 39 overs in the day, 1417 in the season. Seam and swing at a lively pace, then off-spin with his cap on. A thousand runs with the bat, too, and some magnificent fielding. "He came off the farm in April. He went to bowl in the nets, didn't like bowling much in the nets either. He never did any press-ups or laps. He smoked like a chimney. And I never remember him once on the physio's table. He probably thought a ham string was something to do with his mother's ham curing." At Leicester one year he bowls 56 overs in a day. "Nowadays you train up every flipping muscle in the body. Ray only trained the muscles he used." His back is ramrod straight, and he is dark and handsome. "He was a wonderful human being, loved cricket. It was a calling for him. He didn't do it for the money." Essex are on two pounds bonus for a win, one pound for a draw. "To me, it was an insult. Would Ray Smith bowl any harder because there was two pounds for a win? Of course he wouldn't." At 153, he traps Wharton lbw for 85. And how does he appeal? "He was the only bowler I have encountered," Trevor Bailey writes, "who whispered his appeals to the umpire." "I don't remember that," Dickie says. "Ray's appeals weren't like today's dramatics, but they were normal for the time as I recall."

It is June 1952. 64% of the workforce have manual jobs. The average working week is 46 hours.

'Place and Grieves now settled down to grim defiance in murky light and, in the fifty minutes before tea, they added 32 runs.' Place, one day he will come to be known as 'the saintly Winston Place', the hero of author Peter Tinniswood, and Ken Grieves, the slashing Australian stroke maker. What heavy weather they make of batting at Brentwood! For those hoping for more of the fireworks of Essex's run chase the previous evening, it is a dull day's cricket and *'save for a spell by Preston the Essex bowling never really looked hostile. True, the keenness of the fielding saved many runs, as did the slowness and undulating surface of the outfield, but the wicket looked easy.'*

Trevor Bailey is a fine swinger of the ball, and Ray Smith will bowl all day. Ken Preston has fought his way back from a badly broken leg, and Bill Greensmith is a promising leg-spinner. But this Essex side is not known for the strength of its bowling, and they prefer to bat second and chase runs on the last afternoon.

247 for three. Ken Preston has Place caught off *'a sharply rising ball'*, then *'the batting wilted pathetically'*. 266 all out. Five wickets each for Ken and Ray, but it is not they who are lying on the physio's table at the end of the day, but Trevor Bailey. Harold Dalton is the masseur, and he doubles up as electrician, tailor and boot-mender when he is not putting Trevor's body back into service. This summer there are more Bailey aches than usual, and he sets to work as Essex's opening batsmen negotiate twenty minutes in the dying light. There is *'an expectant array of behind-the-wicket fieldsmen, but Dodds and Avery seemed in no way perturbed'*. 8 for no wicket.

Sunday is the Sabbath for Dickie, a day away from cricket. But cricket is never time away from God. "The highest form of prayer I knew," he explains, "was to try to play beautiful shots for a creator who loved beautiful things. You almost look and say, 'Look what I've done.' Cricket can be so deadly dull. Today they play like automata. If you bowl a ball, there are about four shots you can play to it. For one thing, you can play it on the up. Do they do that?"

He takes from his jacket pocket the diary where he has written the words that Ian Botham has used on television to describe one of his great 1981 innings. "You've got to enjoy it, let it go, let it speak for itself, let it take you over. You've got to set it free, not get in its way." He travels to Ian's house, and he asks him, "Did you really say these words?" "Yes, I did." "You know, Dickie," a priest says later, "that is a perfect expression of the Holy Spirit."

Rain on Sunday does not affect the easy pace of the pitch, and Monday morning sees Brian Statham and Geoff Lomax in action with the new ball. Brian Statham, has ever a genuinely quick bowler been as accurate? If he hits you on the pads, they say, you might as well walk. *'Dodds made good use of his favourite stroke, the drive, at the expense of Statham.'* "You were playing cricket with Brian," Dickie remembers. "You weren't trying to stop him knocking your teeth out. He bowled you bouncers, but he wasn't trying to hit you. It was a technical thing."

At the other end, Sonny Avery plays with a quiet grace. Dickie is the vicar's son, the public schoolboy from Warwick; he has learned to bat in a cricket net on the back lawn of a country vicarage, and he hits the ball with stylish force. Sonny is the barber's son, the elementary schoolboy from East Ham; he has learned to bat in the streets beside the Royal Albert Dock, and he strokes well-timed shots off his legs.

Sonny starts at Essex as a young office boy, with a desk looking down the wicket of the county's Leyton ground. "When I should be working, I was watching," he recalls sixty-five years later. "I remember Patsy Hendren getting 200, and he never once lifted the ball off the ground." And at Brentwood when Bill Ashdown is scoring 332, Sonny is frantically pulling the rollers of the scoreboard. This is his cricketing education. As a boy, batting in front of the lamp posts, he has never imagined that he will keep such company. "I never had any ambitions really," he reflects, "but if I had had some coaching, I could have improved my off-side play."

Dickie's first ambition is to play for Middlesex, and it takes him some time to grow to love Essex's flat lands. For Sonny, this journey into county cricket in rural Essex is all pleasure and surprise. So unlike in background, they enjoy nine happy years together at the top of the Essex order. "Sonny was such an unselfish man to bat with," says Dickie. "Dickie was a lovely stroke player," says Sonny. "They were a great partnership," their team mate Colin Griffiths reflects, "as people as well as cricketers."

Soon it is 86 for no wicket. Brian Statham glides in off his silky smooth run, a world-class quick bowler, and at the other end Geoff Lomax lopes in, an average county medium pacer. "The contrast could disorientate you," Dickie recalls. Lomax starts a spell at the pavilion end. *'His first and third balls all but bowled Dodds, and the last one Dodds pulled into the hands of Howard at mid-wicket.'* Sonny falls to the same bowler and, when Dick Horsfall is caught at short extra cover off Hilton, Essex take lunch at 92 for three.

It is June 1952. The Census reveals one in three households without a bath, one in twenty without piped water. The new Conservative Government pledges itself to build 300,000 houses a year.

By the 1980s, Brentwood pavilion will be replaced by a modern brick building, complete with hot showers. Dutch Elm disease will thin out the trees, and the 1987 hurricane will sweep down one whole side of the ground. In 1994 the square will be relaid as layer upon layer of Bill Hansell's work will be excavated. Malcolm Webb of Brentwood Cricket Club laughs. "There were all sorts of things we found down there," he says. But Mrs Hall Payne's legacy will ensure that the ground is there for cricket, and it is still possible to erect a parasol in the semi-circular enclosure and to watch Brentwood cricketers at recreation.

"My job was to give recreation to those who came to watch," Dickie explains. "Re-creation. Lift their spirits. I believe that we can all find re-creation when we glimpse creativity. If what we see is materialism, it will be dull."

'So well did the Lancashire bowlers and fieldsmen perform during the afternoon that just before five o'clock Essex had lost eight wickets for 187 and Lancashire seemed assured of the lead.' Gibb, Horsfall and Bailey, all fall to Malcolm Hilton, still known to many as 'the boy who bowled Bradman'. At the age of nineteen, in only his third first-class match, he twice captures Bradman's wicket cheaply; now at the age of twenty-three he struggles to fulfil the expectation of those early headlines. Here at Brentwood Ray Smith runs an overthrow, only to find his wicket thrown down from fine leg, and Colin Griffiths provides Edrich with his third catch.

Colin Griffiths is one of the amateurs that Essex pluck out of club cricket to supplement their small playing staff. "It was a good policy," Dickie thinks. "They brought a different dimension to the game, and it fed back into the clubs where they played." Colin has been a pupil at the next door Brentwood School, and he is just twenty-one, fitting in a summer of county cricket between National Service and a job in his father's demolition company. "My career was charted out for me," he reflects. "In those days, you didn't rebel against your family." It is his eleventh game for the county, and he leaves the wicket with a batting average of just 12. "I was being picked as a batsman and being asked to go in at nine. Then I'd have to go in at three or four in the run chase and throw my wicket away. I never had my eye in." What is the extra dimension that he is bringing? His team mates will discover later in the week at Tunbridge Wells when he will share an eighth wicket partnership of 183 with Trevor Bailey. But that is another day, and it is another Trevor Bailey, not the batsman whose steady 34 has taken much of this Monday afternoon.

'Greensmith batted with determination and Vigar with such stubbornness that hope gradually began to revive for Essex.' Frank Vigar is another specialist batsman in the tail. 1700 runs in 1947, but he too gets few chances of a long innings. "Our batting had to be that way," Colin admits. "We had no bowling." Bill Greensmith at ten hits 56, and next year at Blackheath he will find himself at three, scoring a magnificent leg-side century. Frank and Bill, their ninth wicket stand at Brentwood adds 72, and Essex close the second day on 260 for nine, six runs behind Lancashire. The game is effectively set for a one innings contest on the third day.

"Hit the ball hard and enjoy it," Dickie advocates, and Essex win the News Chronicle Brighter Cricket Trophy. Are they not a one-day side before their time? Would Dickie not have loved the limited over game? "All the excitement is that they've got to get a result. During the game the spectators have all got these bits of paper saying it's 3.2 an over, 4.6 an over. It's an accountant's day out. Look at these games at Brentwood. They are of the spirit in which we played our cricket.

38

Because that spirit went, they tried to legislate to make people play the game the way it should be played."

Or, as Neville Cardus writes, "It is the individual art and presence that have made cricket the great national summer game; it will not survive if it tries to compete strictly as a competition."

It is June 1952. Plastic flowers are advertised, fireproof and washable.

On Tuesday morning, Essex are all out for 261, and first innings points go to Lancashire, who set about building a total for the declaration. Ray Smith comes on early, and he bowls unchanged for 33 overs for another six wickets; eleven in the match, 136 in the season. Is he the best all-rounder never to play for England? "I remember him bowling his swingers at Charlie Harris of Notts. It was like Charlie was playing an invisible ball." Then Charlie takes out his false teeth and bares his gums at Ray, who cannot continue for laughing. "His bowling never quite recovered that day."

At 138 for five, Essex fancy their chances of chasing less than 200, but *'brave batting by Edrich and Hilton'* adds quick runs. Paul Gibb injures a finger, and Doug Insole takes the keeper's gloves. He never quite stands up to Ray's off-spin, but he is near enough, it seems, to stump Edrich for 69. The declaration comes at half past three. 232 to win, 140 minutes to score them in.

"Our characters are reflected in the way we play," Dickie explains. "You'll never hit the first ball for six if you've never thought of it. So you do play the way you think, and you choose the way you think."

Essex's batting order bears no resemblance to that of the first innings. This is now an order for fast scoring, and Doug Insole pads up with Dickie Dodds to lead the way. "We didn't have very serious sessions in the dressing room. You couldn't have a serious session with Insole around." Trevor Bailey and Sonny Avery are down at eight and nine, when all the hitters have had their go, and poor Frank Vigar is at eleven. It worked against Leicestershire on Friday evening. Will it work now against Statham and Tattersall? Doug Insole is no slouch when it comes to fast scoring, but against Leicestershire in the previous run chase Dickie's whirlwind 25 is over before he gets off the mark. He looks down the wicket with anticipation as Dickie prepares to take strike from Brian Statham.

Statham glides in with his long silky smooth run up and releases the ball. "It left his hand like a stone from a catapult. So accurate. What must he think when he sees the English bowlers today spraying it all over the place?" *'There was no doubt about Essex's intentions for Dodds pulled Statham's first ball for four and hooked the next over the tented licensed bar."* Brian stops in mid-pitch, bewildered. "Hey, Dick, what's going on?" he asks. The crowd are on their feet, and they stay there as *'Insole set about Lomax and then in Statham's next over Dodds hooked another six to a similar vicinity as his last.'*

They say of Dickie that he is fearless, but a whole chapter of his autobiography tells how hard he works to cope with his fear of the bouncer. Late in his career he starts to take refuge at the non-striker's end, and for a while the dressing room is a tense and bitchy place. Finally he admits his fault, and in the next game at Clacton he blazes 97 and 81 against Kent's Fred Ridgway. "You've got to stop fear, ambition, jealousy blocking you." There are no blocks today as he follows up his hook *'with an off-drive for three and a cover drive which was only saved from a boundary by Wharton's alacrity.'* 33 for no wicket, and just eleven minutes gone. "Dodds is almost an anachronism," the Playfair Annual writes. "He should be knighted for his spirit of adventure." Doug Insole is less certain: "his appearance is sufficiently dignified to qualify him for a bishopric, the Cabinet, or a television panel game," he writes in 1960, "while his batting is fit for a World Eleven or the madhouse."

'This was too good to last and Dodds, having disdainfully driven Lomax for four, lofted the next ball to Tattersall at long off.' Is this the short straight boundary that Trevor Bailey writes about? Dick Horsfall waits nervously to bat, a cigarette in his hand, and, when he replaces Dickie, he cuts a four, sees a wild throw give him a five, then feels a ball from Statham hit him on the pads. If Brian hits you on the pad, they say, you might as well walk, and he is back with his cigarette in the pavilion. 50 for two. 25 minutes gone.

Doug Insole is bowled by Statham, then Colin Griffiths brings the extra dimension of his amateur approach. The Brentwood schoolboys are all there to cheer on their ex-captain. "I've got a recollection," he says, "of top-edging Brian Statham over the keeper's head for six." He hits a four and a six off successive balls, then he is caught behind off Roy Tattersall. 89 for four, and he settles back to watch Ray Smith and Paul Gibb take up the chase. *'Smith smote Hilton for six into the tea bar'*, and the 100 comes up in fifty minutes. Ninety minutes left, another 132 to win.

Amateurs and professionals. On the scorecard, the amateur has his initials before his name, the professional after. So it is Gibb, P.A., keeping wicket for Essex since 1951, and he is the same man as P.A. Gibb, who opened the Yorkshire batting in 1946. His M.C.C. membership is suspended now that he has turned professional. "I first came across Paul at Harrogate," Dickie recalls. "Norman Yardley was away, and he was the only amateur available to captain Yorkshire. I noticed how he spent his time at third man and deep fine leg while the game was conducted by a sort of shop steward's committee of senior pros." His 120 in the timeless Test at Durban remains for some years the slowest Test century by an Englishman. He is a hard man to get out, but this is Doug Insole's Essex, and in a run chase he can be counted on to play his golfing chips in the direction of long on. *'Gibb departed from his usual sedateness to keep the pace of run-scoring well in front of the clock.'* In half an hour, the score moves from 100 to 150 and no more wickets are lost. 82 to win, an hour to get them in. *'An electric excitement hung over the ground,'* "Mac" writes in the Brentwood Gazette. *'Even the sedate occupiers of the members' enclosure were on their feet when Essex were racing towards the 232 they had been set.'*

Roy Tattersall bowls a long spell of off-spin from the school end. "He was a tall man, loose jointed," Dickie remembers. "He had a long curving run up." In the first four summers of the fifties, he takes more wickets than any other bowler. Alas, he is born in the same year as Jim Laker, "my recollection is that Jim spun the ball more", and he plays in just sixteen Tests. He tosses the ball up to Ray Smith, who is out to *a well-judged catch in the deep by Wharton.'* 150 for six. He tosses the ball up to Paul Gibb, and Paul, still playing his golf chip, is *'equally well caught at long on'.* 156 for seven. 76 to win, and the hitters all gone.

Sonny Avery and Trevor Bailey take up the challenge. "I wasn't a fast scorer," Sonny admits, and he is *'lured from his crease by Hilton and stumped by yards'.* 183 for eight. 49 to win, less than half an hour left, but *'Bailey refused to be flurried'.* No painted circles for any of the fielders to stay inside. The crowd stay on their feet as Trevor and Ken Preston add 23 for the ninth wicket before Ken, too, falls to a catch in the deep. There is only Frank Vigar now between Lancashire and victory. A tall, swarthy-complexioned man from the West Country, he has twelve first-class centuries to his name, but in a run chase he goes in at number eleven. *'Still Essex pursued their run-seeking way and thus it came to pass that in the last over only nine runs were needed for victory with Bailey and Vigar a defiant last wicket pair.'* Malcolm Hilton, 'the boy who bowled Bradman', will bowl his slow left arm from the pavilion end.

It is June 1952. Gene Kelly stars in 'Singin' In The Rain' and Gary Cooper in 'High Noon'.

Nine runs to win, six balls to get them. Trevor Bailey, on strike, surveys the field and calculates his options. "He was a walking computer," Colin recalls. "He always knew every detail of the game." He tugs his batting gloves tight with his teeth while Ray Smith and Dick Horsfall chain-smoke in the pavilion. Trevor is the Barnacle, England's great stonewaller. He will enter the record books with the slowest first-class fifty ever, his 68 at Brisbane taking over seven and a half hours. It is scored at a rate of nine runs an hour, and here at Brentwood he has to score nine runs in one over.

The first ball arrives, and Trevor meets it with an immaculate forward defensive. A groan is heard all round the ground. Nine runs to win, just five balls to get them. "You play the way you think," Dickie says, "and you choose the way you think."

Is it going to be a repeat of the run chase at Romford two weeks ago? 183 to win, a rapid 76 from Dickie, then a funereal 11 not out from Trevor. "He would never throw his wicket away," Sonny recalls. "A big storm was coming up, black as thunder, and Trevor still couldn't make an effort to get on with it." 'Essex began splendidly,' Wisden records. 'Then the batsmen, despite threatening skies, slowed their pace.' The match is washed away. "I didn't know it was going to rain," Trevor protests to general amazement.

Trevor, the Barnacle. In twelve months' time, he will become the hero of the nation as he bats almost all day at Lord's to defy an Australian victory. "His batting was far from attractive to the eye," Wisden will write, but "the mood so infected spectators that often cheers broke out for purely defensive strokes." At

Romford on that same day, the Essex game finishes early, and the team huddles round a flickering television, cigarette smoke everywhere as the tension mounts. Then suddenly Trevor "shook off his self-imposed shackles and essayed a cover drive which resulted in a fairly easy catch." Doug Insole describes the picture. "For what seemed an eternity he stood there, swayed slightly to and fro, and then drew his gloved hand across his forehead in a gesture of despair." His Essex team-mates explode with laughter as Trevor departs from the flickering screen.

Trevor again tugs with his teeth at his batting gloves, and he waits for the second ball of the final over. Is it any different in length or flight from the first? Can the watching Essex players fathom what is in his mind as once more he lifts his bat? There is a gasp of astonishment as *'Bailey off-drove the second ball from Hilton for six.'*

It is now three runs to win off four balls, Trevor has a competent partner, and the game is back in manageable Bailey territory. Great cheers greet his six, and the chattering is still dying down as Hilton once more approaches the wicket. Even Mrs Hall Payne beneath her parasol is caught up in the excitement. "The one thing that the batsman must avoid," it says in Trevor Bailey's 'Cricket', "is to lose his head." But what is this? A second time the Bailey blade flashes and the ball rises high into the air. Has he really let the spirit take him over? Has he really set it free? "He must avoid having a death or glory swing," his book declares in italics. Whatever is going through his mind, the shot is timed less sweetly, and the ball starts to fall to earth within the boundary. *'Wharton, running hard round the pavilion rails'*, Alan Wharton the Colne schoolmaster whose one Test selection owed much to his brilliant fielding, *'took the ball waist high but could not hold it'*. The batsmen scamper two, the crowd are beside themselves, and Ray Smith and Dick Horsfall draw deeply on their cigarettes.

Three balls left, one run to score. The work is all done now, and Trevor has only to survey the gaps and push the ball into one of them. And who is there better than Trevor to play the forward prod? On Friday a two wicket victory with one ball to spare. Today a one wicket victory with two balls to spare. What a splendid Brentwood week! "Now they try to legislate to bring back that spirit."

But wait! What is happening? Malcolm Hilton tosses up the ball, and there is no sign of the forward prod. Trevor opens his shoulders and tries for a third time to blast the ball out of the ground. He catches it low on the bat and, according to "Mac" in the Brentwood Gazette, *'over 2000 sun-drenched cricket lovers let loose a yell that was thrown skywards and must have reverberated throughout the county. They were all of one opinion that Trevor Bailey had made the winning hit.'* It is not even the tempting short boundary that he is aiming to clear. He has won the game in the most glorious fashion. Hasn't he? *'He hadn't. Nigel Howard, the Lancashire captain, scooped the ball from nowhere, and the game was tied.'*

"I don't know why he did it," Dickie says. "I'd never seen him hit a straight six before. There were three to win off four balls. Why on earth did he keep trying to hit sixes?"

"No, that's not quite right," Colin says. "You see, this is 1952. He could be quite impetuous in those days. All that Barnacle Bill stuff came later. Mind you, even impetuosity couldn't explain his rush of blood in that last over. He was a difficult man to understand, very difficult to put in any box."

This is June 1952, and this is Doug Insole's Essex. The post-mortem is a jocular affair, but for once in his life Trevor is momentarily speechless. Ten years later he will write in another book that he lost count of the score. "I remember," Colin says, "how Trevor always knew every detail of his figures while he was bowling." "Bailey forgotten what the score was," Dickie laughs with great merriment. "Bailey who always knew everything about everything."

Dickie turns the pages of Wisden to find what happens to this new Trevor in Essex's next fixture. Paul Gibb trundles his small Ford van to Tunbridge Wells. Is this the occasion when they stop in heavy traffic in the middle of the Blackwall Tunnel to change a tyre? The Kent ground's rhododendrons are in full bloom and, after a typically breezy fifty by Dickie, they watch Trevor hit 155 not out in four hours. "With two sixes and sixteen fours," Dickie reads. "And this is Bailey." Colin Griffiths, highest score 31, batting average 12, drives and pulls with such abandon that his only first-class hundred is the fastest century of 1952. "It was a lovely, hard, fast wicket," Colin recalls. "A strokemaker couldn't go wrong." He will celebrate with a weekend in Paris, then score a vigorous 89 against Middlesex, again in partnership with Trevor. "Whenever he was at the wicket with me, he made me feel very confident." Then Colin will tear a back muscle hitting a six, and he will fade from this county scene. Eventually he will rebel against his family and will finish up as head of a residential unit for disturbed adolescents. "They paid me to pursue all my interests." Mountaineering, water-skiing, canoeing; but never again cricket. "After Essex, I lost interest in the game."

Trevor will play for another fifteen years. Then there will be a lifetime of expert analysis. "Bailey to me was an enigma," Dickie reflects. "I expect I was to him."

Dickie will play for seven more years. Then he will give his summers as well as his winters to Moral Re-Armament. But he will always find time to have his spirits lifted by the beauty of cricket played creatively. "When Brian Lara started, he loved to hit the ball. He had no fear, only love." And Ian Botham, the words in the back of Dickie's diary, "You've got to enjoy it, let it go, let it speak for itself, let it take you over. You've got to set it free and not get in its way."

ESSEX v LANCASHIRE

Brentwood. 21, 23 & 24 June 1952

MATCH TIED

LANCASHIRE

A. Wharton	lbw b Smith	85	c Avery b Smith		16
J.G. Lomax	c Gibb b Smith	10	c Bailey b Greensmith		47
G.A. Edrich	c Insole b Smith	35	st Insole b Smith		69
W. Place	c Avery b Preston	63			
K. Grieves	b Preston	34	c & b Smith		0
*N.D. Howard	c Avery b Preston	0	b Smith		5
P. Greenwood	b Smith	14	b Smith		8
M.J. Hilton	b Preston	8	not out		48
R. Tattersall	b Smith	1	not out		7
J.B. Statham	b Preston	1	c Greensmith b Smith		15
+A. Wilson	not out	0			
Extras	b 10, lb 3, nb 2	15	b9, w 1, nb 1		11
		266		(7 wkts, dec)	**226**

1-20, 2-111, 3-153, 4-237, 5-237, 6-240, 7-255, 8-265, 9-266, 10-266
1-32, 2-103, 3-104, 4-114, 5-138, 6-175, 7-208

Bailey	21	6	44	0	14	3	34	0
Preston	20.3	2	49	5	11	2	26	0
Smith	39	5	105	5	33	4	122	6
Greensmith	24	12	30	0	12	5	33	1
Insole	4	0	23	0				

ESSEX

T.C. Dodds	c Howard b Lomax	46	c Tattersall b Lomax		26
A.V. Avery	c Wilson b Lomax	41	st Wilson b Hilton		4
+P.A. Gibb	c Edrich b Hilton	13	c Grieves b Tattersall		33
R. Horsfall	c Edrich b Hilton	3	lbw b Statham		10
*D.J. Insole	b Lomax	2	b Statham		18
T.E. Bailey	c Wharton b Hilton	34	c Howard b Hilton		52
R .Smith	run out	27	c Wharton b Tattersall		48
F.H. Vigar	not out	25	not out		1
C. Griffiths	c Edrich b Tattersall	6	c Wilson b Tattersall		19
W.T. Greensmith	b Statham	56	b Statham		5
K.C. Preston	b Statham	1	c Grieves b Tattersall		10
Extras	b 4, lb 2, nb 1	7	b 3, lb 2		5
		261			**231**

1-86, 2-89, 3-92, 4-104, 5-111, 6-164, 7-181, 8-187, 9-259, 10-261
1-33, 2-50, 3-61, 4-89, 5-150, 6-156, 7-167, 8-183, 9-206, 10-231

Statham	24.4	3	50	2	12	1	59	3
Lomax	21	4	37	3	3	0	14	1
Tattersall	25	5	46	1	18	3	61	4
Hilton	37	15	47	3	10.4	0	69	2
Grieves	22	7	44	0				
Wharton	3	0	11	0				
Greenwood	12	4	19	0	3	0	23	0

Umpires: T. Spencer and C.H. Welch

Jim Laker

A LEARNING ENVIRONMENT

Surrey v Warwickshire
May 1953
with Tom Cartwright

Tom Cartwright played for Warwickshire from 1952 to 1969, for Somerset from 1970 to 1976 and for Glamorgan in 1977. Originally a right-hand batsman, he became also a medium-pace bowler, doing the double of 1000 runs and 100 wickets in 1962. He was a member of the Warwickshire side that finished second in the championship in 1964 and won the Gillette Cup in 1966. He played in five Test matches for England and is now National Coach for Wales. He remembers a game early in his career at The Oval.

"Most modern players would have the technique if they had the environment to learn it," Tom believes and, when he thinks of his own cricketing education, he recalls his first encounter with Stuart Surridge's great Surrey team. "I was just seventeen, a little lad walking out to bat at The Oval, trying to grasp what was going on, trying to learn from the experience. I think I learnt more in my time at the wicket in that game than I've learnt in any period of any other game."

Surrey versus Warwickshire. The reigning county champions versus their predecessors. It is May 1953, and London is buzzing with excitement. The Australians have arrived to defend the Ashes, and preparations are under way for the Coronation of the young Queen Elizabeth. "It was all a little bit overpowering. You're taking in an awful lot. It's not just coping with the action on the field of play. Even staying in hotels at that stage was exciting."

Surrey, the reigning county champions, many believe that they are the finest county side of all time, and Warwickshire, their predecessors, "an extraordinary team of ordinary cricketers," their captain calls them. They are an ageing team when they win the championship in 1951, and Tom Cartwright is in the first wave of a new generation of young professionals.

The Warwickshire coach travels down from Trent Bridge to Maida Vale where they stay at the Portland Arms. Two, three, even four to a room. It is cramped, but it is pleasanter than some. 'Harkness specials', they call the worst ones - after the assistant secretary whose job it is to book them. "There was one at a seaside town," Eric Hollies writes. "It was built as near to a railway line as any place could be without getting in the way of the trains. We slept by the timetable." At breakfast another guest laughs at their complaints. "You don't know the half of it," he says. "If you leave the door and the window open, the trains go right through." Eric loves to collect these stories and tell them.

They eat together as a team, Tom remembers, "then it was straight into the lounge for a couple of halves of beer, and they just talked cricket all evening." Tom is seventeen, and most of the team are over thirty. Eric Hollies plays for

Warwickshire in 1932, in the month before Hitler comes to power, and he is in the England team before Tom is born. Tom Dollery, the captain, spends the war on Artillery observation posts, directing fire from as little as fifty yards from the enemy, while young Tom, a small boy in Coventry, survives the air raids in a night shelter. Charlie Grove, the senior pro, is a promising fast bowler of twenty-six when war is declared and he is thirty-four when he next plays for the county. He is forty now, more medium than medium-fast, but his cricketing brain will bring him success for this one last season. "I would sit in the corner," Tom recalls. "At about twenty past ten, Charlie would look across at me, and he'd tap his watch. I'd plead for ten minutes, but I knew not to push it. I loved sitting there, listening to them talking, but I never said anything."

Charlie and Eric are forty, Tom just seventeen. The wisdom passes down a generation as Tom listens to their talk. "A bowler is at his best when he is near finishing," Eric says. "That's when he's accumulated the vital experience. He's like an old fisherman with the patience to sit and wait for the inevitable nibble."

It is May 1953. John Christie awaits trial for the murder of four women at 10, Rillington Place, London. Timothy Evans has been hung for the murder of his wife and child at this address, and now their bodies are to be exhumed. Evans, a lorry driver of low intelligence, has he been wrongly hung?

Torrential rain falls in the night. "It really did come down," Tom remembers. The Australians are due to play the M.C.C. at Lord's, and a queue long enough to fill the ground is disappointed when the 'No Play Today' signs go up. The sun shines brightly on the waterlogged square. *'On these occasions,'* E.W. Swanton writes, *'the advocates of covered wickets play insidiously on the feelings of the multitude, like the hanging abolitionists at an execution. If the wicket had been covered, they say, we should have seen a day's cricket.'* Meanwhile at the Oval, "it was a blue sky, absolutely clear, very strong sun. It was evident that we were going to play."

What a transformation there has been at the Oval! Hit by three bombs in 1940, it is requisitioned as a prisoner of war camp with a great cage erected on the square and outfield. Then it is an anti-aircraft site, a barrage balloon and searchlight base, finally an assault course. By 1945 there is little left of the beautiful turf where Len Hutton compiled his record 364 against Australia. In October Bert Lock, the old Surrey player, is demobbed from the R.A.F. and given the job of rehabilitating the ground. He walks for miles across the Gravesend marshes, looking for weed-free turf. He sits for days in freezing winds, stitching up the rat-gnawed nets. 'SOS The Oval. Come and help your local ground,' read the handbills distributed around the neighbouring flats, and Bert supervises shilling-an-hour volunteers as they lay the 80,000 turves. He is a countryman, his choice of fast-knitting grass is inspired, and he pulls the hand-drawn roller up and down all Spring. By early May the crowds are back, the volunteer turf-layers among them, and they watch Sarwate and Banerjee of India add 249 for the tenth wicket, the only time in cricket history that numbers ten and eleven have both scored centuries. Alec Bedser is leading the Surrey attack, returning "physically hardened and mentally far more mature", and Bert Lock, for all his loyalty to Surrey, watches the ease of the Indian stroke-play with relief and pride.

The Oval pitch. It seems that nobody discusses Surrey's success in the fifties without referring to it. Surrey have the finest bowling attack in the country, perhaps the finest county attack of all time - Laker and Lock, the Bedser twins and Peter Loader - and at the Oval they play on wickets that help the bowler. What is it that changes a good county side in 1951 to the great, all-dominating side of subsequent years? Peter May writes of three main factors: the appointment of Stuart Surridge as captain, the transformation of Tony Lock's bowling action and the change in the character of the Oval square. "The ball began to move about," he writes, "to turn by the second innings and to have a sort of rounded bounce, not especially quick but useful to good bowlers. The outfield, once rough and brown, was now lush and green, and the ball retained its shine longer." It is not true of all their glory years, but in 1953 Surrey will play thirteen county games at the Oval and win ten of them. Elsewhere they will win three out of fifteen.

There is not just second innings turn and a longer-shining ball for Warwickshire to contend with. Twelve months ago they arrived as reigning champions and, by the end of the first day, twenty-one wickets had fallen, with the turf, according to Wisden, 'so loose and dusty that the ball continually turned quickly and hurried through at awkwardly varying heights'. Then on the second morning, with Surrey facing a nightmare session of batting, the worst holes have all been filled. As the Oval's historian reports, "considerable repairs had been effected, involving substantial time, materials and a tool of some kind". Nobody ever does get to the bottom of the mystery, and Tom Dollery is too much of a sportsman to make a fuss. Eric Hollies is never one to miss the chance of a joke, though - "he was so full of devil," Tom says - and at this, his next visit to the Oval, he presents Bert Lock with a trowel and a small bag of cement.

Tom Dollery and Eric Hollies inspect the wicket, and they take the young Tom with them. "I just walked up and down as they were talking about the pitch, and at seventeen that was brilliant. It was like I was in Santa's Grotto." Tom Dollery wins the toss, a good one to win, and he elects to bat. 'The speed at which the turf dried out,' E.W. Swanton writes, 'was remarkable evidence of the success of the aeration and drainage work that has been done there these last few years.' By twelve o'clock, the young Tom Cartwright is walking to the wicket with Freddie Gardner. He has no county cap, not even a second eleven one, and he wears a little blue cap that his mother has insisted on buying him in Nuneaton. Meanwhile Alec Bedser marks out his run and watches the pair approaching the wicket, the seasoned professional and the apprentice. Alec will be an England selector in time, and Tom will be in some of his Test sides, but he will always think of him as the lad in the blue schoolboy cap. Freddie Gardner clips a three off the sixth ball, then the rain returns, a sharp downpour that drives them off the field.

Tom Cartwright the young opening batsman. He has scored 82 on his debut at Trent Bridge last year, and two days ago he scored 83 on his return there. "Do you think we'll make the grade?" the young players ask each other. "That was not a nice agenda at all," Tom reflects. It will be another two summers before his contemporary Clive Leach makes his championship debut, bagging a pair against Essex. Then, when Clive gets his first bowl, Dick Spooner the keeper stands up to his slow left-arm. Dick is a hard man from the North-East, "not the greatest encourager", and he puffs out his cheeks as he receives the ball. "He's not spinning the thing, skipper," he keeps saying, and Clive is soon back in the second eleven. Some seasons with Durham, a job selling paint, a cover version of 'The Yellow Rose of Texas', sports commentaries on Tyne Tees television. "Clive was like a little bumblebee, buzzing about. He was always going to be chasing something." In time, he will become a director of Yorkshire Television, making the grade with a large house and a Rolls Royce. Tom is happy with the achievement of less materialistic targets. "I've never had a sponsored car in my life. A young pro moving from college to a county playing staff, he'll talk to you about a flat and a car straightaway. Okay, they're living in a pretty tough world. Nevertheless it detracts from their pursuit of playing cricket in the way we did."

'With only a fortnight to go before Coronation Day,' the Times writes, *'the seconds are being measured out in hammer beats as the vast stage is set for pageantry. A lot remains to be done, but London's face already beams through its bone-deep grime.'*

The rain passes, and Tom prepares to take strike for the first time. "I hadn't played against that Surrey team. I hadn't even seen some of them until I walked out onto the field. I was seeing figures I'd only ever seen on cigarette cards. It was an awful lot to take in." Alec approaches the wicket, past the umpire Lawrie Gray who is standing to the legside of the stumps. "He had a bit of a gammy leg; he used to give the bowler a bit of room." Tom's education continues as the ball strikes his pad and the umpire's finger goes up. A golden duck. By the end of the over, New Zealander Don Taylor is back in the dressing room with him. 3 for two.

Warwickshire regroup in 1946 with just five professionals on their staff, and Tom Dollery and Eric Hollies carry a struggling side. The improvement in their fortunes comes as they start to recruit far and wide. Alan Townsend and Dick Spooner from the North-East. Tom Pritchard, Ray Hitchcock and Don Taylor from New Zealand. Keith Dollery from Australia. The Pakistani Hafeez Kardar, the Jamaican Derief Taylor, then later Billy Ibadulla and Swaranjit Singh. "There are critics of a policy which has turned the Warwickshire staff into a cricket League of Nations," the 1950 Wisden declares, "but the Birmingham public will not worry where their cricket favourites come from so long as they play attractively and win matches." Don Taylor is a wartime friend of Jim Laker, but Surrey offer him just six pounds a week for twelve weeks to travel from New Zealand. Warwickshire are less wealthy, but their need for new players is greater. "They weren't hired guns," Tom explains. "They came and did their two-year residence. It was the hired guns, the Australians especially, that brought all this sledging into the game."

Stuart Surridge has revolutionised the Surrey fielding. He has put his best fielders close to the bat, even though they are the bowlers, and it has allowed him to move the leg trap much closer to the batsman. ""Stuart was a noisy, demonstrative man, very much a physical presence close to the wicket. Just handling the attack, moving the field, you were aware of him." There is no limit on how close they can stand, and some say that their backchat is just the same as the modern sledging. Tom disagrees. "It was very daunting, but it wasn't sledging. It was a positive assertion that they were going to get you out, and this was how they were going to do it." Don Taylor is caught in the leg trap off Alec Bedser, and Freddie Gardner follows soon after in the same way. 8 for three. *'There followed a more or less lucid interval for Warwickshire,'* the Observer reports, *'during which Spooner and his captain Tom Dollery promised to return the innings to something like normal.'*

Stuart Surridge the captain. 'Surrey will win the championship for the next five years,' he writes in his diary at the start of his first season in charge, and his great self-belief is a key component of its achievement. Monty Garland-Wells, Surrey captain before the war, sets up an accumulator bet on their success, and long before the end of their reign the bookmakers have taken fright and agreed a handsome settlement. What a wonderful party he lays on at the Oval when he collects his winnings!

It is May 1953. Colonel John Hunt and his team of mountaineers are at Camp Six, 24,000 feet up Everest. They are in Abominable Snowman Country, waiting for high winds to drop, before they move up to Camp Seven and prepare for the final assault.

Alec Bedser bowls unchanged till lunch. 'Big Al', they call him, he has a massive frame and it makes his run-up look quite laboured. But he has a classical action that swings the ball in to the bat, he generates pace off the pitch and, with his enormous hands, he can bowl as good a leg-cutter as the game has ever seen. In 1953 he is at his peak. "On a rain-affected wicket," Freddie Trueman writes, "he could be virtually unplayable. No batsman in the world really has an answer to the delivery which starts outside off stump, pitches leg stump and hits the top of the off." Tom traces the skill back. "Alec learnt his leg-cutter from George Pope, and he learnt it from Sydney Barnes." To devotees of the Edwardian Golden Age, Barnes is the greatest bowler of all time, and his magic has passed in a chain to this damp morning at the Oval, some fifty years on. But where is it in the modern game? "It's gone. Like all things, they're not passed on anymore." *'Spooner was meeting Bedser on equal terms until he mistimed a drive and gave a catch to mid-off. That was the beginning of the end.'*

Stuart Surridge himself bowls with the new ball, then he gives way to Tony Lock. The Oval pitch, Surridge's captaincy and Lock's new bowling action, these are Peter May's three explanations for Surrey's great leap forward in 1952. Gloucestershire's Tom Graveney recalls Lock in the late forties. "I played against this soft, gentle little floater. It was a case of 'down the wicket and help yourself'. I never thought he would amount to much." Then in the winter of 1951 Lock becomes the coach at Croydon's indoor cricket school, and the roof is supported by a low-slung beam. "It curbed the trajectory of my flight," he writes, "and I started to bowl a little quicker." He perfects a fast ball that turns viciously and, though he is called for throwing by one umpire in 1952, he wins his first Test caps and he bowls unchallenged through Surrey's glory years. They mutter about this quicker ball all round the circuit and, when Essex's Doug Insole is bowled by it, he asks the umpire, "Was I bowled or run out?" Here at the Oval in May 1953 he has Ray Hitchcock caught in the leg trap, then gives Alec Bedser his fifth wicket by catching Tom Dollery *'with quite a gymnastic roll'*.

Tony Lock is the great exhibitionist when it comes to taking catches, and it is part of Stuart Surridge's strength that he keeps on top of all the characters in this Surrey side. Gloucester's Bomber Wells remembers his different approach for each bowler. For Tony Lock, the abuse is endless: "That's the bloody biggest load of rubbish under the sun. I could get ten kids in the local park who could bowl better than you." It enflames Lock, and he bowls with fire and purpose. For Jim Laker, it is all encouragement: "Come on, Jim, you're the best bowler in the world. Let's be having you." "I swore at Jim only once," Stuart Surridge writes, "and he couldn't bowl for an hour." It is 38 for six at lunch, and Jim has not even bowled. "Bedser bowled brilliantly," Tom remembers. "It was very wet when we started, and it was a good toss to win. To be honest, we batted badly."

It is no better after lunch. "You could see the ground steaming as you looked across it. It was that kind of day, and it did crust." Alan Townsend falls to Lock, caught behind by McIntyre. Little Arthur Mac is one of the few small men in this Surrey side, and even on pitches like this he stands up to the bowlers. "If the ball seems to take a long time to get to the gloves," Tom explains, "you try to bowl quicker and you destroy your shape. You don't achieve the skill levels because of that. If the keeper's stood up, it's pitch, boom and it's into the gloves." Tom's coach at Warwickshire is Tiger Smith, and Surrey's scorer for this match is Herbert Strudwick, England's finest two keepers in the prime of Sydney Barnes. Tiger is sixty-seven and, when the new coaching centre opens at Lilleshall, he is the one who stands on a table and demonstrates the art of keeping. So impressive is his display that nobody wants to follow it. Alec Bedser bowls his leg-cutter like Sydney Barnes, and little Arthur Mac takes it like Tiger and Struddy.

"Day in, day out," Peter May writes, "Arthur Mac was the most reliable wicket keeper of the 1950s. He should have played many more times for England. He was never acrobatic. There was no need, as he was always in the correct position on his two feet." And who is the best keeper that Tom bowls to in his career? "Derek Taylor," he says. Derek is Somerset's gloveman when Tom moves there in the seventies. "I wouldn't have swapped him for anybody at that time." And where has Derek learned his skills? "He'd been at the Oval with Arthur Mac as coach." And now? "The environment isn't there to hone the skills."

Alec Bedser starts his fourteenth over, and he claims the last three wickets. Charlie Grove, Keith Dollery and Eric Hollies. In the history of non-batsmen, there are not many to rival poor Eric. He has been to the wicket almost 500 times now, and his highest score still stands at just 24. The first sight of Eric through the pavilion gate is usually enough for the groundsman to start up the engine of his roller. It is half past two, and the scoreboard shows a total of just 45.

It is May 1953. 'Yes sir,' the advertisement says. 'Brylcreem gives your hair that clean, smart look that goes with success.'

Tom Dollery prepares to lead the Warwickshire team onto the field. He has a little brylcreem on his hair, but he is not one to fuss over his appearance. "If he saw players in front of the mirror," Tom recalls, "he'd give them terrible stick." He has directed fire from Artillery observation posts, and he has no time for such preening. "How would you cope with cold steel?" he asks. Charlie Grove is a different sort of man. "He was very meticulous. He was a sergeant major in the war. Didn't smoke, didn't drink. You jumped to attention when he looked at you." Charlie tends his kit with immense care while Tom breezes through, grabs any bat, puts on anybody's clothes as he goes out. "There were these trousers in the early fifties called duck-egg blues. They were seven pounds a pair, ludicrously expensive. Charlie got some, and Tom put them on one day to bat. He got 150-odd, and Charlie found them all concertina-ed on the floor. He couldn't believe that somebody had destroyed his new trousers." In later years Tom will run a pub in Hatton, and he will refuse to serve men with long hair. "He couldn't come to terms with that. What he'd be like now with ear-rings and things, I don't know."

Tom Dollery has a book for sale. 'Professional Captain' is its title. 'Player, spectator, student and the man who watches over a hedge will each find enjoyment and wise counsel in this book by one of England's foremost cricket strategists.' "The blokes would have gone anywhere with him," Tom recalls. "To speak to him in the field, I never felt he was there at that moment. He'd already planned that. He always seemed to think two weeks ahead." In two weeks Edmund Hillary and Sherpa Tensing will stand on top of Everest. With 45 runs for a first innings score, Tom Dollery has an Everest to climb here at the Oval.

Young Tom Cartwright takes his position in the gully, and he already knows to chase the ball to the boundary, regardless whether he can catch up with it or not. The day he gives up the chase, he turns to see Dick Spooner advancing towards him. "Never, ever ... ," Dick starts. "But .. but ... ," Tom interrupts. "No 'but'. You chase it all the way." "That was the schooling," Tom says. "It was very hard, and you had to know your place." His team-mate Alan Townsend remembers the young Tom. "We nurtured him," he says. "In life today there isn't the discipline. If you made a mistake, you didn't want to do it again." Alan, like Tom, will take up coaching when he is older, but he will not find the young players so keen to listen. "Nowadays they think they know it all at eighteen. They want to be professional cricketers, but they aren't prepared to work hard enough." "There are so many more distractions now, aren't there?" Tom adds. "The professional game has become so much more conscious of money."

Eric Bedser is soon out. 5 for one. Then Fletcher and Constable set about grafting out a score. *The Oval pigeons were left undisturbed on the outfield while the score crept to 27.'* Perhaps it is the moment for the gruff-voiced Surrey secretary to make one of his booming loudspeaker announcements: "Go away, you pigeons, go to Lord's." Eric Hollies and Ray Weeks come on to bowl, leg spin and orthodox left-arm slow, and *'it was seen that the ball was turning and occasionally sharply'*. Tom is a specialist opening batsman in 1953, and it will be another five years before he is bowling regularly for the county, a further five years before he is bowling for England. He is a medium-pacer, and Eric is a leg-spinner. "It was strange in a way, but I learnt more about bowling from Eric than from anyone. I used to sit and listen, and he'd talk to me." And what is the advice he passes down? "You've got to conquer yourself ... You must be in control of your end before you worry about controlling the other end .... Be honest with yourself ... If you bowl a bad ball, don't look for any reasons other than yourself."

"I was always determined to bowl," Tom reflects. At school he bowls out-swing, but in the adult game he can only master in-swing till that wonderful day at Dudley in May 1958. He is bowling to Martin Horton and Dick Richardson, and the ball suddenly swings away. Is it a fluke? Or can he repeat it? "It was the training of Eric Hollies. Know yourself. I knew the shape of my hand when I let it go. I was able to do the quick analysis." He bowls a whole over of out-swing, then starts to mix the two. Martin and Dick are both caught in the slips, and he completes a career-best five for 36 in 23 overs. "And I never lost it from that moment." For Eric and for Tom, bowling is a craft skill, and it is there to be analysed. That is the Warwickshire tradition. "Tiger Smith taught me, you never tell anybody anything unless you can break down the mechanics in detail."

It is May 1953. In the journal 'Nature', two Cambridge scientists describe how DNA, the material of genes, has a double helix structure.

Fletcher edges Ray Weeks into Alan Townsend's safe hands in the slips, Clark skies Eric Hollies to cover, but Bernie Constable grafts away. He is one of the unsung heroes of this Surrey side, and his 37 on this treacherous Oval wicket is worth more than many a fancy century. "People used to go on that Ted Dexter was a good player," Bernie reflects, "but you couldn't have asked him to play out an hour and a half on a dodgy wicket." What can it be like to be a Surrey batsman? "We never got our full quota of innings. And when we did bat, we had to get on with it and get out. So our records were nothing. We didn't mind while we were winning but, when people look at averages, they're very false, aren't they? Only the greedy people want to get averages." There are no greedy people in this Surrey side, least of all Stuart Surridge who strides to the crease at 81 for seven, the lead just 36. *'There was no substance in the middle of the Surrey batting,'* the Sunday Times reports, *'but when the need was for quick runs to give their bowlers a second chance, the tail played their part manfully.'*

Eric Hollies is a remarkable bowler, a leg-spinner who concedes just 2.2 runs an over throughout his long career. Tom Dollery calls him 'the toothache bowler'. In that first summer after the war, he bowls over 80% of the overs at one end. "He hardly ever went to nets. He had this innate ability to bowl accurately. He could bowl close to the wicket, wide of the crease, from 24 yards; he could bowl it from anywhere and still drop it on a spot. Then when the wicket wore, he would impart more spin." Some batsmen never learn to play him. Jack Parker of Surrey is one. "Come on, Jack, let's see if you can spot this one," he teases. "How were you out today, Jack?" his wife asks. "Bowled Hollies or lbw Hollies?" Then, when Jack appears on a cereal advert, Eric draws a cricket ball in front of his pad and sends it to him. "l.b.w. Guess who?" "He had this Indian sign on a lot of people. He made people understand that. He didn't let them rest." This is the first summer of Jack's retirement, and he sits among the Oval members, waving at Eric: "You won't get me today." Everybody likes Eric and his sense of humour. "He was very sharp, but he could have fun and not disturb his concentration at all."

The pitch is taking spin, Eric is looking for the wickets that will wrap up this Surrey innings, and Stuart Surridge is looking for the quick runs that will allow him to get Warwickshire back in this evening. This is his style of captaincy, always pressing for the result, and in August 1954 he takes this to an impossible extreme. Worcestershire, all out 25. Surrey, 92 for three, then out of the blue he calls his batsmen in. Worcestershire are bowled out for 40, and no sooner have they left the field than the rain sets in. In such moments legends are born.

Eric Hollies has his legend, also here at the Oval. Don Bradman's last Test innings. Four wanted for his 7000 runs and an average of 100. The crowd stands, the players give him three cheers, and Eric bowls to him. It is Eric's first Test of the summer, and in the county game he has noticed that Bradman is not reading him from the hand. "I'll bowl the googly second ball," he tells Tom Dollery before he leaves for the Oval, "just in case he's expecting it first one." Tom Cartwright is a boy of just thirteen, listening to the wireless as John Arlott describes that second delivery. "Hollies pitches the ball up slowly, and he's bowled. Bradman, bowled Hollies, 0." It is only as the batsman walks away that Eric realises the wicket is down. "Bradman went forward," John Arlott explains. "It was Hollies' googly. It clean bowled him groping right down the pitch, and he was just beaten all the way." "John Arlott was one of the key people that inspired me to play cricket," Tom reflects. "He painted pictures that made it inevitable that I wanted to play cricket." And Test Match Special now? "I haven't been able to listen to that for a long time. It's almost self-promotion. It's not about what it was at all."

Eric has played for England at the Oval in 1948 and 1949. The next Warwickshire player to play there will be Dick Spooner in 1955. His county colleagues will be on the coach from Dover to Nottingham when he goes out to bat in the second innings. He is on a pair, facing South Africa's Hugh Tayfield, and this time Tom has no chance to savour John Arlott's word pictures. "The roar went up in the coach," Tom explains. "'He's bagged them'. I can remember that ever so clearly. Poor old Dick. It was the only time they played him at home."

Eric Hollies bowls to Stuart Surridge. The patient fisherman, waiting for the nibble, to the belligerent leader, striving for the immediate victory. "I can remember him slogging and just getting away with it." Three times in four balls he clears the boundary, and *his third six sent up the hundred, a figure one had forgotten existed*. Then Jim Laker joins in the fun, depositing the ball into the pub on the other side of the road. "I never hit one better," he writes, "and I hit it with a Harrow bat." It is 119 for nine by the time they are both out, then Tony Lock weighs in with a quickfire 27. *'Lock was batting gaily,'* the Observer reports, *'until, trying to hook a ball, he was struck so violently on the head that he had to be carried off the field.'* "Locky had a sweep at Charlie Grove," Tom remembers. "I was very close in the gully, and I saw him go down. He went down in stages. He rolled over, almost by my feet. Just before the blood came, I could see the vein glinting in the sun." He will spend the rest of the match in hospital, and Warwickshire's batsmen will have one less problem to face. The wicket is at its worst now. "It would have been horrendous trying to bat against Locky."

It is May 1953. Colonel Hunt's Everest expedition is at Camp Six still. He has studied scientifically the weather patterns. They are wearing new high-altitude nylon clothing and carrying lightweight oxygen equipment. From below, the summit has seemed a harsh, rocky ridge, but, when Edmund Hillary and Sherpa Tensing reach it, it is a symmetrical and beautiful cone of snow.

What peaks can Tom reach if he studies this game of cricket? At half past five he puts on his blue schoolboy cap and he steps out once more with Freddie Gardner to face the Surrey attack, the great bowlers and the ring of close fielders, the cigarette cards come to life. "It was an amazing experience for me." The deficit is 101, the pitch is at its worst, and there is an hour's play to survive. Over forty years later Tom will still remember the innings.

It is May 1953. The Coronation, the Conquest of Everest, the Ashes victory, athletics records for Roger Bannister and Chris Chataway. This is a summer of joy and celebration. A fortnight ago, in front of the Queen and Prince Philip, Stanley Matthews has led Blackpool to the most dramatic of FA Cup victories at Wembley. 3-1 down, they beat Bolton Wanderers 4-3, and for many it is still the greatest final of them all. Wherever there is sport, there are spectators. "On a Saturday morning," Tom remembers, "you had to fight your way through the hordes to get into the ground. The gates were shut often, certainly by lunchtime." People have less money, and there is not the diversity of leisure-time attractions. "It's all become so materialistic now," Tom reflects. "It's very sad, really. People had small targets: getting out into the country, doing the garden, going to cricket. You could achieve these targets and be quite satisfied with them. Now people seem to be pursuing things that are beyond their reach."

An hour to survive on a pitch that has been changing in character as it dries out and is now at its worst, the ball flying off a length and turning square. Freddie Gardner has a simple batting strategy. If he is not playing a shot, he lets his body take the ball. "He was the most uncompromising batter of pace that I've ever seen." No chest protector, no arm guard, not even a thigh pad. Just a small hand towel tucked inside his trousers. "That little ball can't hurt you," he always says, and his body is forever covered with bruises and weals. "Tom Dollery's thigh pad was a roll of fivers in one pocket and a handkerchief in the other," Tom remembers. "Always keep a roll of fivers," he tells his team. "You never know when you're going to come across a down-and-out old player."

Alec Bedser and Jim Laker are the bowlers. "It was very difficult to put a bat on Bedser. He was bowling on a length, and I remember Arthur Mac was standing up, leaping and taking the ball high in the air. And Laker at the other end, that again was something unique for me." Stuart Surridge's Surrey want instant results, and it is not long before Eric Bedser at first slip is berating his brother. "I can remember Eric screaming at Alec." "Rubbish ... Bowl straighter ... Make him play." Tom is on a pair, and he struggles for a seeming age before he decides to take a chance. He sweeps at Jim Laker, and the ball flies off his top edge, over Arthur Mac's head and away for three runs. Time passes, the score creeps along and the humiliation of the first innings, it seems, is not to be repeated.

Back in the pavilion, Alan Townsend starts to relax. He is down to bat at number seven, and there is little more than half an hour left to play. It has been a hot afternoon in the field, and he retires to run a bath.

Batting on a sticky dog wicket. What is the art? "You could never let the ball hit the bat. You always had to have the bat playing the ball. There is a difference. You learnt that very quickly. People say we're not competitive enough in our game now. On uncovered pitches you had to compete almost all the time. And if you survived, you learnt." Tom is learning fast here at the Oval, and Warwickshire proceed to 20 without loss when, alas, *'disaster, swift and sudden, overtook them'*. Tom is lbw Laker, 9, the most memorable innings of his life, and Freddie is caught Laker bowled Bedser, 7. Surrey have bowlers for every sort of wicket, and *'certainly Laker was spinning the ball. The one, which stood upright, was a horror to avoid.'*

Tom has scored 0 and 9, and he drops back to the second eleven. It has been a tough experience for the seventeen-year-old, but he is true to the Warwickshire philosophy, "Be honest with yourself", and he is keen to learn. "Tom had all the qualities but he lacked confidence," Tiger Smith writes. "My job was to be gentle with him and keep hoping his enthusiasm remained high. I'm delighted to say it did, and his success gave me great pleasure." Tiger Smith has kept wicket to WG Grace and Sydney Barnes, and Tom is still putting his wisdom into practice in the 1970s. But by then cricket is becoming a different game. "My philosophy in one-day cricket was not to swing the ball too much because I didn't want the edges."

Warwickshire are 26 for two at the start of another Laker over, and Alan Townsend's bath is filling up. Three balls later it is 26 for five, and Alan is walking to the wicket, his bath still running. Spooner, Dollery, Hitchcock, *'a pretty formidable trio for any bowler to bag'*, are the victims of Jim Laker's hat-trick, and the dressing room is in pandemonium. Don Taylor is still at the crease but *'Townsend, possibly to get away from Laker, was run out,'* he can have his bath now, *'and there was no one to stay with Taylor.'* Ray Weeks is the fourth to return with a duck, and the scoreboard reads 32 for seven. Back in the dressing room, Tom Dollery is issuing instructions: "Get padded up. You're in." "No, I've been in, skipper." "It was that kind of comedy," Tom remembers.

The Birmingham Post carries an editorial on the day's play. *'With wickets all the time a-tumble, the game can scarcely yield its full riches. Cricket is a game of majesty, and its majesty does not consist in processions to and from the wicket.'*

20 for no wicket has become 32 for seven, and Jim Laker has a hat-trick. Yet how mild are the celebrations compared with the modern game! "I think it's terrible," Bernie Constable says. "All this business when somebody gets caught on the boundary and they've all got to run out to kiss the fielder. Just because he's caught a ball. That's what he's there for. Think of the wickets Laker and Lock got. If we'd kissed them every time they got a wicket, we'd all have had sore lips."

Charlie Grove hits *'two hearty blows'* to lift the score beyond the first innings 45, but the extra half hour is taken and by twenty to seven Eric Hollies, the eternal number eleven, is making his way to the wicket. There is hardly even time for him to cook up one of his little jokes. Like the day at Derby when Cliff Gladwin runs through them with a magnificent mixture of deliveries. He gets one of his team mates to write them down on a piece of paper, and he presents it to Cliff. "There you are," he says. "Bowl them in that order, and I'll see what I can do." Or the day against Worcestershire when all the fielders are clustered close for his arrival. He gives his bat to the square leg umpire, and unobtrusively he crouches down in their leg trap. This evening at the Oval he is on a pair, and he passes Alec Bedser on his way to the crease. Alec already has match figures of eleven for 35 off 27 overs. As the Birmingham Post says, *'it is not often that the man and the occasion are so happily wedded as they were in this fantastic match.'* "Give me one to get off the mark," Eric pleads. "I won't hit it far." Alec smiles. "All right. I'll bowl one down the leg side for you." He is as good as his word, and Eric hits it straight at short leg. Alec has twelve for 35, Warwickshire are 52 all out, and the 1951 champions have been beaten in the day with forty-five minutes lost to rain and twenty minutes of the extra half hour unclaimed.

"Once they'd got to 146," Tom reflects, "we'd got no chance. It really was down to our poor batting in the first innings." It is a traumatic defeat, but it does not break the Warwickshire spirit. Back at the Portland Arms the lessons of the day are learnt, there is admiration for their Surrey opponents, and the victories soon come again, none sweeter than in the return game at Edgbaston.

The story of the game is the story of the pitch. *'Deadly it certainly was, and at the end it stood out as a black strip contrasting with the surrounding green.'* At Edgbaston it is Surrey's turn to inspect the wicket with suspicion. "The suggestion was that there was grit in the top dressing," Tom recalls. "Surridge walked around on the second morning, and he came off with a matchbox full of bits of grit and a piece of cup handle that he reckoned he'd dug out of the pitch."

Here at the Oval *'Surrey members rose as one in tribute to their team,'* the Observer tells. *'And well they might, for one has to go back nearly a century to discover when the Oval was last the scene of a one-day triumph for Surrey.'* In three weeks' time, Lancashire will beat Somerset in one day on the newly-laid Bath square. Then in 1960 Kent will do the same to Worcester at Tunbridge Wells. But pitches will be covered, and these will remain the last entries on the page. "The game was something that I shall never ever forget," Tom says. "It taught me an awful lot about playing under difficult conditions."

"We were thinking we'd be going home," Alan Townsend recalls. "Then Tom Dollery rang the club." There is a dinner at the House of Commons arranged for the two teams for Monday evening. A celebration for the last two county champions. "We were told we had to stay over." It is an embarrassing epilogue. On Sunday, while the Coronation Coach practises its journey down the Mall, Tom sits in a North London park with Keith Dollery and watches a scratch game of cricket. Then on Monday, while the bodies of Timothy Evans' family are exhumed from Gunnersbury Cemetery, they go to Lord's and, on another drying pitch, they watch more *processions to and from the wicket* as the Australians dismiss the MCC for 80. At the House of Commons, Tom is lucky to be sitting between two ladies who know too little about cricket to rub in his embarrassment, and Alan Townsend remembers the debate they watch from the Strangers' Gallery. "About half past ten, Sir Winston Churchill walked in with a dinner suit on, and he started cracking jokes. This poor MP was speaking about river pollution, and nobody was taking the slightest notice."

Warwickshire have lost twenty wickets in a day. Sixteen catches, three lbws and a run out. Forty-four years on, Bernie Constable inspects the scores on the Wisden page. "Look at all the noughts," he laughs. Five in the first Warwickshire innings, seven in the second. Sherry glasses arrive at Edgbaston for the duck-makers, with Wilfred Pickles' catchphrase attached. "Give them the glass, Barny." "My mother thought they were marvellous," Tom recalls. "She didn't see the other side." They remain with him still, a reminder of a day that nobody present will forget. "I doubt if anybody will ever see that kind of game again."

"Cricket, above all sports, singularly perhaps, is the one that has changed its format, its method of playing, almost totally. It's so dramatic the change. I would much prefer to see people play natural cricket. Then you get a multi-faceted game. And when you take away some of the facets, which we have done, it shrinks in its artistic form, certainly in the disciplines required, and therefore the overall product is diminished."

Tom spends the winters of his youth at Rootes Motors at Coventry, making Humber Pullmans, Hillman Minxes, Sunbeam Talbots. "Just about every motor car came through Coventry. It was exciting to work there." An industry based on a great tradition of science and engineering, but "it's been dismantled, hasn't it?"

"I'm glad I played when I did," Tom reflects. "It was a magic time. I'm just sorry I'm not still playing."

SURREY v WARWICKSHIRE

The Oval. 16 May 1953

SURREY WON BY AN INNINGS AND 49 RUNS

WARWICKSHIRE

F.C. Gardner	c Laker b A.Bedser	7	c Laker b A.Bedser		7
T.W. Cartwright	lbw b A.Bedser	0	lbw b Laker		9
Don Taylor	c Fletcher b A.Bedser	0	lbw b A.Bedser		20
+R.T. Spooner	c Whittaker b A.Bedser	16	c and b Laker		0
*H.E. Dollery	c Lock b A.Bedser	8	c Surridge b Laker		0
R.E. Hitchcock	c Whittaker b Lock	3	c A.Bedser b Laker		0
A. Townsend	c McIntyre b Lock	7	run out		0
R. Weeks	not out	0	c Surridge b A.Bedser		0
C.W. Grove	c Fletcher b A.Bedser	3	c Constable b Laker		10
K.R. Dollery	c Brazier b A.Bedser	0	not out		0
W.E. Hollies	c Laker b A.Bedser	0	c sub b A.Bedser		0
Extras	*lb 1*	1	*b2, lb 3, nb 1*		6
		45			**52**

1-3, 2-3, 3-8, 4-27, 5-30, 6-36, 7-42, 8-45, 9-45, 10-45
1-20, 2-22, 3-26, 4-26, 5-26, 6-32, 7-32, 8-49, 9-52, 10-52

A.Bedser	13.5	4	18	8	13.4	7	17	4
Surridge	6	1	17	0				
Lock	7	2	9	2				
Laker					13	6	29	5

SURREY

E.A. Bedser	b K.Dollery	5
D.G.W. Fletcher	c Townsend b Weeks	13
B. Constable	c Grove b K.Dollery	37
T.H. Clark	c K.Dollery b Hollies	2
A.F. Brazier	c Townsend b Hollies	6
G.J. Whittaker	b K.Dollery	0
+A.J. McIntyre	c & b K.Dollery	9
J.C. Laker	c H.Dollery b Hollies	18
*W.S. Surridge	b Grove	19
A.V. Bedser	not out	5
G.A.R. Lock	retired hurt	27
Extras	*lb 4, nb 1*	5
		146

1-5, 2-27, 3-50, 4-61, 5-65, 6-77, 7-81, 8-108, 9-119

Grove	10.1	3	29	1
K.Dollery	11	4	40	4
Weeks	8	1	24	1
Hollies	10	4	48	3

Umpires: L. Gray and E. Cooke

Frank Tyson

THE GOALKEEPER'S TRIP TO OLD TRAFFORD

Lancashire v Northamptonshire
August 1953
with Dennis Brookes

Dennis Brookes played for Northamptonshire from 1934 to 1959, captaining the side from 1954 to 1957. A right-handed batsman, he scored over 30,000 runs, including 71 centuries, playing in one Test in 1947/8. He stayed with the county as Second XI Captain, Coach, Assistant Secretary and President. He remembers a match at Old Trafford when Northamptonshire struggled to put out a side.

Wednesday 12 August 1953. It is another day at British Timken for Peter Pickering. Five years ago his footballing career stood on the brink of greatness. Seven penalty saves in fifty games for York City, then a seven and a half thousand pound move to Chelsea. A new British record for the transfer of a goalie. 'A magnificently built and spectacular goalkeeper,' the reference books record, 'but he lacked consistency'. By 1953 he is keeping goal for non-league Kettering Town, and working for British Timken, who manufacture roller bearings for the car industry. In summer he plays cricket, for the works side and sometimes for the county second eleven. He was hoping to be playing for the Seconds today, but he is needed in the office and another British Timken employee has taken his place.

Britain is basking in a heatwave, and today pork becomes yet another item removed from ration controls. What a summer of celebration it has been! Everest has been climbed. Queen Elizabeth has been crowned. On Saturday the final Test match will start and, if England can win, they will hold the Ashes for the first time for nineteen years. Freddie Brown, the Northamptonshire captain, is Chairman of Selectors. He has played himself in the exciting draw at Lord's, but the plan for the Oval is to set the young Freddie Trueman at the Aussies. The nation is alive with anticipation, but for the next three days the chairman must captain his county here in Manchester.

Northamptonshire. What a change there has been in their fortunes! Just nine championship victories in eight summers before Freddie Brown's arrival. The wooden spoon is theirs almost by right. The 1949 fixture card allocates them to Worthing, and the town clerk protests angrily at such unattractive opposition for their cricket week. "With regard to Northants," Sussex writes back, "somebody must have them." Then Freddie Brown, the pre-war Surrey amateur, arrives, and Northants win ten matches in one summer. They finish sixth in the table, and poor Sussex, down at thirteenth, are roundly beaten at Worthing. Billy Griffith is the Sussex secretary, and he bags a pair.

"We should have started to climb in 1948," Dennis reflects, "but we needed a captain. Freddie Brown was a man of determination and character, and of course he brought a first-class all-rounder in himself. By the force of his personality he dragged the county with him."

It is Wednesday morning, eight o'clock. The telephone rings in Dennis's hotel room, and his captain's voice comes down the line from another room. "I'm sorry, Dennis. I'm not going to play. My wrist has swollen up." He will travel down to the Oval and leave the dependable Dennis in charge of the team.

The team. What team? It is three months since they started their season with a thrilling tie with Middlesex, and only three of that eleven are still fit for duty. Livingston and Barrick lie second and third in the national batting averages, but Jock has a broken bone in his hand and Desmond a pulled leg muscle. Oldfield and Nutter, the Lancashire rejects, always relish these visits to their old county, but Buddy has a damaged thigh muscle and Albert cartilage trouble. They have not even brought a twelfth man with them. "Who can you suggest?" Freddie Brown asks, and Dennis thinks of British Timken, the company owned by the club's chief benefactor. At least they can get off work there. "There's a chap called Peter Pickering," he says. "He's had one or two games in the seconds." Freddie, the amateur captain, is also on the British Timken pay-roll. "I'll get on the blower," he says. "See if they can get him across here."

It is a quarter past nine when a voice comes over the British Timken public address system. "Would Peter Pickering report to the Chairman's office immediately." His personal secretary is standing at the door as Peter arrives. "Get in quick," she says. "It's urgent." "I couldn't imagine what the problem was," Peter remembers, "but I'll never forget the Chairman's words: 'Freddie Brown has hurt his hand. You are required at Old Trafford. There is a car in the garage being made ready. Get up there as fast you can, and Freddie can drive the car back.'" It is already a hot morning as Peter hurries home, springs the surprise on his wife and whitens his boots. With the aid of a route map, he sets off down the winding roads from Northampton to Manchester.

The sun blazes down as Dennis tosses up with Lancashire's Nigel Howard. *'How did Manchester adapt itself to its brief sojourn in the tropics?'* the Manchester Guardian asks. *'The answer is simple: it did not. It made no concessions. The habit of coat and waistcoat is ingrained. A generation ago there would probably have been more waistcoats under jackets than there were yesterday. But if a revolution is taking place it is still a slow one. A surprisingly large number of women in the mid-day sun were either wearing or carrying cardigans or jumpers. In Manchester, as in all other proper English towns, one does not really believe in summer. One expects the thunderstorm, and one prepares for it.'*

"There was no wicket there at all," Dennis recalls. "It was all scratched to bits. Lancashire were running for the championship, and they'd got a poor wicket. We tossed up, and I lost. I thought, 'Well, goodbye'." His team mate Brian Reynolds tells the same story. "They didn't cut a wicket. They picked the worst part of the square. You could put your fingers down into the cracks." "What's your team?" Dennis asks Nigel Howard before the toss. "When I started," Dennis recalls, "we had a captain, a nice fellow, he'd never ask who the side was." Lancashire have four bowlers: one quick and three slow. All the newspapers tell of a well-watered wicket taking spin from the start.

The young Frank Tyson marks out his run. "The quickest bowler I have seen," Freddie Trueman still says. This is only his ninth first-class game, and he has taken just ten wickets for 448 runs. Nought for 62 against Lancashire at Northampton. No cause for Geoffrey Howard, the Lancashire secretary, to regret that letter two years ago. 'Dear Tyson, I am sorry to say that I am afraid I cannot be of any help to you this summer.' One game in 1949 for Lancashire second eleven. Five overs, nought for 19. Now he runs in for Northants, and he bowls the Lancashire captain, Nigel Howard, for just three. 13 for one.

Tyson is one of six Lancastrians on the Northants staff, not to mention the two Australians from the Lancashire Leagues. With five Yorkshiremen and a New Zealander, a Shropshire lad and Freddie Brown born in Peru, they have rebuilt the county by recruiting far and wide. "We realised we'd got to do something," Dennis recalls, "or we'd go out of cricket." Why, even Peter Pickering, now in a car somewhere between Northampton and Manchester, is Yorkshire born.

At the other end from Tyson is Bob Clarke, and he at least has grown up in the county. A broad, barrel-chested man, he has been in the Navy in the war and he knows how to handle himself in a late-night brawl. "He bounced up to the wicket from about fifteen yards," Frank Tyson tells, "and let the batsman have it." Not for him the science of grip and body action. "Hold the ball and bowl like this," Freddie Brown tries to explain one day, "and it will swing in." Bob stares uncomprehendingly. "Oh, aar, do it?" Dennis remembers the conversation about an opposition bowler. "He bowls a lot of short ones, this fellow," somebody says, and Bob joins in. "Oh, aar, but he bowls some long hops as well." "That's how much Bob knew about the game." There is no question of his shining the ball at his end, but somehow it swings both ways in the air, and *'Edrich turned an in-swinger from Clarke straight into Tribe's hands at short leg.'* It is 30 for two.

Albert Lightfoot replaces Tyson. "I only bowled Frank in short bursts," Dennis explains. "I think that's the way to bowl fast bowlers. Five or six overs at the most." Albert Lightfoot is the Shropshire Lad. "Nice fellow, but he never reached his potential." Like Frank Tyson, he is new in the team and finding little success, two for 262 in his first five appearances. "His game oozed a rural upbringing," Frank writes. "With the get-up-and-go of an Allan Lamb, he could have been a Test player." At Taunton he bowls his first ever ball in county cricket to Somerset's Harold Gimblett, and it sails over long-on and lands in a timber yard. Here at Old Trafford he bowls to Jack Ikin, and *'a too carelessly turned shot off his toes had Ikin well caught at short leg'*. 36 for three, and the large crowd are in for a spell of dour cricket.

'Perhaps the very gravity of their situation weighed so heavily on Wharton and Grieves that it reduced them to foot-bound immobility,' Denys Rowbotham writes in the Manchester Guardian. *'They crouched, groped and prodded, and at lunch Lancashire were only 77.'* The Northants scorer reads out the bowling

figures each interval and, whatever they are, he adds the words "Well bowled" to each of them. "Tribe, eleven overs, eight maidens, ten runs, no wickets. Well bowled."

George Tribe. He was Lancashire's bowling coach, yet still they let him go to Northamptonshire. He played three Tests for Australia before migrating to England. A back-of-the-hand left-arm bowler, he changes his action in England. "He started to push it through more," Dennis says. "He bowled a chinaman and a googly, and he learnt to push one on. Then he developed two types of googly - one a very obvious one, one not quite so obvious." For eight years he will torment batsmen all round the country, 1057 wickets in all, and he will bat and catch as well. "He was a quiet, unassuming fellow. He always played for the team."

Dennis Brookes joins Nigel Howard for a separate lunch with the committee. It is very pleasant, but it is not as grand as it was in his early playing years. "Before the war at the Oval, you could have as many drinks at lunch as you wanted, and they used to have Pimms Number One. I can remember some of our senior players, they used to be a bit high by the time they went out. They stopped that later on. It was just a pint of beer or its equivalent. In the pre-war days, it was very carefree. It was really enjoyable."

Peter Pickering arrives too late for lunch. He has spent forty minutes finding his way from the outskirts of Manchester, and he has had trouble persuading the gateman that he really is a player. "Good, you're here," Freddie Brown says. "Now I can get off to London. Have a good game." His team mates feed Peter with sandwiches and tea as he changes, and he is in the field in time to see George Tribe take four wickets in the afternoon. *The batsmen did not use their feet on a wicket which took spin generously,'* Denys Rowbotham writes, *'and they were unusually fallible in their judgement of a ball's length and direction.'* Lancashire are all out for 163. It is a poor score but perhaps on this wicket not that poor.

It is August 1953. Manchester announces plans to introduce slot machines for the purchase of soft drinks. In factories and railway stations first. Then in cinemas, football grounds and cafes.

Dennis Brookes goes out to bat before tea. He walks through the Old Trafford gate, with its ever-present gateman. Dennis alone survives from those dark days of the 1930s when the county goes four years without a win. What must it be like to play so long for a team and never win? His fifth championship appearance brings victory, but he has to wait 75 more games for another taste of success. A home game against Leicestershire over Whit Bank Holiday 1939. "I always remember that match," Dennis tells. "I woke up in the morning. I'd got a stiff neck, I'd got a boil on my neck, I'd got a sore throat, and I was wretched. But in those days, if you didn't play, you didn't get paid." He takes the field in a scarf and he watches Leicester slump to 8 for five. "They'd come off a wet wicket somewhere, and they were playing back when they should have been playing forward." The boil bursts, and Dennis has 120 not out by close of play. On Monday they complete an innings victory, and the crowd swarms in front of the pavilion. They have only beaten

Leicester, but "the public demanded a speech from the captain." Five years with Freddie Brown, some inspired recruiting, and these are now folk memories.

But Lancashire and Yorkshire, the two Northern counties, rich and powerful, still dominate the little Northants. Their win at Headingley in June is the first time Northants have beaten either of them since the First World War, and they have never come away from Lancastrian soil with a victory. Lancashire have four Test bowlers in their attack - Statham, Tattersall, Hilton and Berry - and they have an awkward wicket on which to bowl at this makeshift Northants batting line-up. Statham removes Vince Broderick and Brian Reynolds while Tattersall removes Dennis. "I never worried about Brian Statham. He always used to keep the ball up to the bat, and I liked to play forward. But Tattersall bothered me. He wasn't a big spinner, he flighted it, but he used to bowl this ball that floated away, and it wasn't easy to detect." Dennis turns a quick off-spinner into the leg trap, and Northants are 15 for three.

George Tribe and Roy Tattersall. They are great spin bowlers, but in the fifties there are so many of them around the counties. In the years that have followed, where have they all gone? Dennis remembers back to the 1948 cricket committee at Lord's that introduced a new ball every 55 overs. "Gradually it went up to 65 and 75, but the damage had all been done by then. When the current crop of bowlers retired, there was nobody to replace them. Nobody had bowled the overs." Then there is the limited over game. "There's not much merit in getting people out rather than stopping them scoring. It starts at school, doesn't it? A lad comes up and bowls leg-breaks. He gives four runs away so they take him off."

Eddie Davis makes 22. "He was a peculiar sort of batsman but very effective. He made runs against good bowling sides." But it is soon 71 for six, and Peter Pickering steps out to join George Tribe. George is under instructions 'to have a slog', but Peter "just played a natural game. He wasn't waiting to see if the ball turned or popped; he just hit it. He was an amateur cricketer. He just went and played as if they were schoolboys, and he got some valuable runs." *In twenty-five minutes Northamptonshire's score jumped from 71 to 108 before Pickering was brilliantly caught at cover.'* "I kicked myself all the way back to the pavilion," Peter recalls. "I checked on my shot. If I had gone through with it, I would have been all right." In a low-scoring contest, his 22 has been well worth the trip up from Northampton.

Lightfoot and Tyson contribute one run each, it is 125 for nine, and Bob Clarke comes to the wicket with 39 still wanted for the lead. "He was frightened to death of anybody above medium pace," Dennis remembers. "He used to back away to square leg." But perhaps he is still dreaming of his innings at The Oval last August. Four runs needed to save the follow on. "Get your effing head down, Clarke, and let the chap at the other end get the runs," Dennis recalls them telling him. "Bedser was bowling. The first ball went through the covers like a rocket. And he went on like that to 50. It was incredible. He'd got that ability, but he was afraid of the ball." His 50 comes out of 54 in just 32 minutes, and he comes off to a standing ovation. How will he play this evening at Old Trafford? *'Tribe continued to hit cheerfully,'* Denys Rowbotham writes. *'Clarke provided stern down-the-line defending, and at the close Northamptonshire were nearer to grace than they had any right to be.'* 157 for nine, seven runs for the lead.

It is August 1953. Two hundred and seventy new cases of poliomyelitis have been recorded in the last seven days.

The temperature has reached 89 degrees Fahrenheit, the hottest day for years, but thunderstorms are rolling up from the South. They are preceded by high winds that raise dust storms sufficient to stop the traffic in Sheffield. 'Miniature tornado hits Barnsley' is one headline, and perhaps those Manchester folk, who *'do not really believe in summer'*, who *'expect the thunderstorm and prepare for it'*, have got it right after all.

Peter sits in the hotel, the enormity of his day sinking in. "I had achieved my great sporting ambition. To play first division football and first-class cricket."

In the morning the destination of the first innings points is settled. *'With the fighting spirit that has always been part of his cricket character,'* the Northampton Chronicle and Echo writes, *'Clarke square-drove Tattersall to the pavilion rails to relieve the pent-up feelings of all'*. George and Bob add 20 runs, and their 50 partnership is the highest so far in the match. Then the rain comes, pools of water form on the outfield, and the cards come out for poker in the pavilion. It is not the new pavilion that the Lancashire committee tried to build after the war, they could not raise the money for that, but it shows no signs of the bomb damage it suffered, the years of being a transit camp and a supply depot. German prisoners of war have painted it for a wage of three farthings an hour, light work compared with that of the British prisoners who built the Thailand-Burma railway for the Japanese. Lancashire's Geoff Edrich spent three years there, and like his brother Bill he will never want for courage on a cricket field.

The Manchester Evening News arrives, and there is no good news for Lancashire here. Surrey are piling on the runs at Loughborough while *'alarm spread through Lancashire today with the news that Japan is to be allowed to step up her textile exports to Colonial and Dominion markets.'* Could this be the beginning of the end for the county's traditional economic power?

It is a quarter past four when play resumes, and the rain has made this barely-prepared wicket quite lethal. "The ball flew all over the place," Dennis recollects. What better an opportunity will Frank Tyson have to show Lancashire what they have passed over! He is fast, and the stories of just how fast are starting to spread around the county circuit. 'Did you hear about his first ball for the county? It hit first slip before he even saw it.' 'He bowled against the Australians, and he had McDonald lbw. The poor chap could hardly hobble back to the pavilion.' 'Sussex had a few minutes to bat out on the first evening, and they were all standing up to peer over the high window ledge at Northampton to see how fast he really was. Cor, you've never seen so many heads duck down so fast.' "What power there is in bowling fast!" Frank writes when he is older. "If I had my life to live over again, I should only want to be allowed to bowl fast once more. There is no comparable feeling in the world." Within eighteen months his pace on the fast Australian wickets will give England the crucial edge in the next Ashes series, and this evening at Old Trafford, Brian Statham writes, is "the only time that I have seen him bowl at his Australian speed."

He catches the shoulder of Ikin's bat with his first ball and Albert Lightfoot at first slip, a long way back, takes the catch. There is a wind behind him and, when he bangs one in just short of a length, it flies over Geoff Edrich's head and sails ever upwards. "Brian Reynolds, behind the sticks," Frank writes, "rose to it like a trout taking a fly." He is almost forty yards back, but it is too high for him even, and it hits the sight screen on the full. "At Old Trafford, that's no mean feat," Brian says. *'From the next lifting ball Edrich should have been caught off his gloves at close fine leg.'* "It was Eddie Davis," Dennis recalls. "He wasn't a very good fielder. Freddie Brown wouldn't have him in the side." In this threadbare eleven, somebody has to field in the leg trap. "He grabbed at it and put it down." Nevertheless, the blow worsens a hand injury Geoff Edrich is carrying, and he takes more blows to the hand and body before the day is out. Tyson bowls Howard and has Grieves caught. Then Edrich is dropped again at short leg. It is 13 for three. The arrears are not yet cleared.

What if Tyson had stayed at Lancashire? What if he and Statham had bowled in tandem on these Old Trafford wickets? Would Surrey have won the titles they did? Would Tyson have lasted longer in the domestic game? Len Hutton takes him aside after one match on a slow Northampton wicket. "If you carry on playing for this side," he says, "you'll be out of Test cricket in two years. Go back to Lancashire." There are some who say that Frank's run-up and action are awkward and place too much strain on the body. There are others who tell how the Northampton pitches are deadly slow and the away ones all doctored before his arrival. Whichever way, it is a short but a legendary career.

He has had his burst, now Clarke and Lightfoot keep up the pressure. Wickets continue to fall, but Geoff Edrich - despite a third life - *played an old-fashioned type of sticky wicket innings. Two qualities served him above all: a courage which prevented him from taking his eyes off the ball, and the belief and determination that no match is beyond winning or saving until it is lost.'* He is in pain now with every judder of ball on bat, but it is not the pain of working as a six-and-a-half stone weakling on the Thailand-Burma railway and he comes off at the close with 59 not out, his team just 94 for seven. *'Edrich loves his cricket,'* Denys Rowbotham writes, *'and a man will suffer and risk much for what he loves. He may yet prove to have brought victory within Lancashire's grasp.'* On Saturday he will discover that his hand is broken. This will be his last innings of the season. Back in the pavilion, Geoff pulls off his batting gloves, and Peter Pickering still recalls the state of his hand. "It looked as though it had been hit repeatedly with a two pound hammer."

Manchester Hippodrome offers an evening with Eddie Calvert, 'the man with the golden trumpet', while at the Opera House the first Elizabethan Age is recalled with 'The Young Elizabeth'.

It is August 1953. Georgi Malenkov, the Soviet Prime Minister, reveals that his country has a hydrogen bomb.

Friday's cricket begins as Thursday's has ended. The Manchester Evening News describes the early overs. *'Tyson produced a bumper or two to add to Edrich's discomfort, and there were cries of 'Take him off' when a further bumper whizzed past the batsman's chin. Clarke knocked the bat out of Edrich's hand with one ball that lifted nastily.'* As ever, Bob runs in and bowls as fast as he can, no shining of the ball and no special grip, and he removes the tail to finish with six for 60. On the last afternoon of the season at Worcester the game will be petering out, and Dennis will approach Freddie Brown. "You know Bob's got 97 wickets," he says. But the captain is not a man for statistics. "I couldn't care bloody less," he says, and Bob does not bowl. He will never reach such heights again, and within five years he will be gone. He will become cricket coach at the Christ's Hospital School in Horsham. Dennis smiles. "I have an idea he was more groundsman than coach."

Geoff Edrich has made an unbeaten 81 and, though it has left Northants only 128 to win, *'they could not have begun more disastrously'*. Dennis may be bothered by Roy Tattersall, but on this wicket he decides to set about attacking him. A pull to square leg, a lofted on-drive. Within quarter of an hour they have 22 on the board, but "I did the unpardonable thing. I tried to hit him over the man on the boundary." Old Trafford is a large ground and, though he still remembers the game so vividly, it is not for his own contribution. He returns through the gate with just seven runs to show for his two innings.

The pitch is lethal, and in this forty-five minutes before lunch Brian Statham sets to work on it. *'All the Lancashire fieldsmen were clustered within a few yards of the bat as Statham continued to hurl down his thunderbolts, and there was no suggestion of 'Take him off' from the crowd this time.'* Eddie Davis bobs and weaves in his own ungainly style, but *'the sight of his flashing, feeling, tentative bat inspired Statham to fresh efforts'*, and Vince Broderick is caught at the wicket *'in the act of using his bat as a sort of shield'*. It is 30 for two. 98 more wanted.

Brian Reynolds comes to the wicket. He has worked his way into the side as a stop-gap wicket-keeper, but back in Northampton another Lancastrian, Keith Andrew, is serving his twelve-month qualification period. Keith will play two Test matches for England, but for many observers he will be the best keeper of his generation, better than the legendary Godfrey Evans. "He wasn't showy," Dennis reflects. "Sometimes it can act against you if you're not flamboyant. On the big occasion Godfrey turned it on. Day to day Keith was far better."

In 1953 Brian keeps to Frank Tyson. Next summer Keith will keep, and Brian will stand next to him at first slip. "It was harder than keeping wicket with gloves on." Here at Old Trafford he faces Brian Statham, and the ball leaps up from a length. "I just pushed forward at one," Brian recalls, "and it hit me just above the forehead." It is long before the days of helmets, and it is all that he does recall. Frank Tyson takes up the story. "It felled him like a log. The fieldsmen carried him off, and he was as stiff as a board. Statham accompanied the cortege as far as the dressing room, firmly convinced that he had killed him. I have never seen a more worried man - nor a more relieved one when the thick-skulled Reynolds came round." And it is back to Brian. "I remember just coming round when they shut the gate. I heard it clang as they carried me up the steps."

"It could have killed me," Brian reflects, "but it didn't. I'm too thick in the head."

The New Zealander Peter Arnold replaces Brian and, as he passes through the gate, one Lancashire member calls out to him. "Don't worry, youngster, there are plenty more stretchers where that one came from."

While Brian nurses "a very large headache", he is oblivious to the action in the middle and the roars of the crowd as the game takes a decisive shift in Lancashire's favour. Eddie Davis *'hit cross-batted in desperation'*, Peter Arnold is beaten in the air by Tattersall, and *'Statham threatened Greasley's head, shin bones, ribs and nose before finally bowling him with a yorker.'* It is 40 for five, 88 more wanted and Brian in no fit state to bat.

Peter Pickering, the 'magnificently built and spectacular goalkeeper', joins George Tribe at the wicket. He scored 22 in the first innings, and the lead was just 14. Now he takes guard in a real crisis. "Being a professional footballer," Dennis explains, "his nerves were all right." "I was able to steer a ball past gully for a boundary," he remembers, though it is *'a savage cut for four'* in the Manchester Guardian, and he and George survive to lunch at 45 for five. There is time for this battered and depleted Northants side to take stock one more time. And time for Brian Statham to rest his feet. "It was hilarious," Frank Tyson writes, "to hear Statham talking to his feet." "Come on, lads," Brian says. "Tha's not got long to go. Then tha' can have a good soak and a neet's rest."

In London queues are forming outside the Oval for the start of tomorrow's Test. Freddie Brown appears to announce that Godfrey Evans has been passed fit to keep wicket. The anticipation of cricket lovers is growing keener by the hour.

"At this stage," Peter remembers, "the morale of the side had dropped. But when George Tribe and I returned to the crease, he said to me, 'Come on. We *can* do it.'" Brian Statham is at his fastest, and Peter struggles to connect. "Are you batting on leg stump?" George asks him, ever the canny Australian. "Don't let Statham know, but move over to middle stump." The very next delivery Peter drives the ball to the cover boundary, and it runs so fast that it rebounds halfway to the middle. "It was the best shot I ever made in cricket, and it was so effortless." Peter continues to play his natural game, and in 25 minutes they add 30 priceless runs. He may only have scored 14 runs in two innings of Minor County cricket, but here at Old Trafford on a near-unplayable track against Test match bowlers he plays his shots with freedom. If he can save penalties in front of fifty thousand at Stamford Bridge, he can hook Brian Statham for four. By the time Hilton *'tempted him by fuller flight to drive once too often'*, he has made 37 out of a partnership of 51 with George Tribe, and there are only 37 more needed to win. Is there anybody in Northampton who could have travelled up on

Wednesday morning and played a more confident innings? "The trouble in cricket," Dennis reflects, "is that the professionals see something happening, and they say 'Oh you can't …'. He wasn't really bothered whether he got out or he didn't. He just played a natural game."

Peter Pickering. 22 and 37 in his only match for Northamptonshire. Tomorrow he will be back in the British Timken works team, and the opposition will applaud him all the way to the wicket. He has kept goal in the first division, and in time he will umpire first-class cricket in South Africa, but this applause will always be his most emotional moment in sport.

Albert Lightfoot joins George Tribe at the wicket, the Shropshire lad and the quiet Australian. It will not be A.E.Housman that George quotes as they meet in mid-wicket.

'Say, lad, have you things to do?*
Quick then, while your day's at prime.
Quick, and if 'tis work for two,
Here am I, man: now's your time.'

Albert is a lad of seventeen. He will play for Northants through eighteen summers, but he will never reach greater heights than his two innings against the Australian tourists in 1961. Not out innings of 80 and 57 against McKenzie, Davidson and Benaud. Then, with scores level and one ball left, a famous victory theirs for the running of a single, he stands motionless in the non-striker's crease. "It's no wonder you don't do any good," an opponent says one day about this Northants side. "You haven't got any brains in your team."

'Berry indulged Lightfoot's lunging prod and had him caught off the bat's edge at short leg.' It is 94 for seven, 37 are wanted, and Brian Reynolds returns to the battle. "If you don't go back in," he says. "You're in trouble. So it didn't unnerve me." Nigel Howard brings back Brian Statham *'in a change that was ruthless but justified'*, and his yorker traps Brian lbw. It is 108 for eight. *'Now all was an agony for fifteen minutes.'*

'Five times in one over Hilton beat Tyson's bat. In the next over he almost caught and bowled him. And all the time to Lancashire's frustration there was Tribe, now glancing a single, now turning another, waiting, waiting, waiting for the first loose ball. At last it came, and Tribe drove Hilton soaringly and crushingly to long on for four. Then Tyson drove in his turn, and this time it was caught and bowled.' It is 117 for nine, and eleven runs are wanted. *'Cricket at its best,'* the Northampton Chronicle and Echo declares. *'Fighting cricket that comes only once, if ever, in the lifetime of a keen watcher of the game.'*

"English cricket was at its best in the fifties," Dennis says, looking back across his sixty and more years at Northampton. "Things that have destroyed the game are the covering of wickets, the introduction of one-day cricket (which spoilt the skills of it) and of course the grassroots (no cricket played in the state schools). Cricket is a lifetime's job. You can't suddenly become a good cricketer at twenty-three or twenty-four. You've got to eat, drink and play it."

Bob Clarke. "When he went out down the steps," Dennis recalls, "there was a little chap always on the gate who opened and shut it for the players, and he said 'I won't bother to shut the gate. Tha' won't be five minutes.'" The consequence of this remark is picked up by the Chronicle and Echo reporter. *'Clarke closed the iron gate at the foot of the pavilion steps with an air of finality, and this gesture of his determination did not go unnoticed by the hopeful home supporters.'* Hilton's first ball to him is greeted with *'a bat dead enough for caricature'*.

Northants have never won here in Lancashire, and this is their thirtieth attempt. They have brought this most makeshift of teams, and they stand on the brink of a famous victory. At the crease are George Tribe and Bob Clarke, their first innings stand of 54 is the highest of the match and now they want just eleven more. But they have played for Northants long enough to know how often things have a habit of going wrong. Together with Dennis, they are the only survivors of that tie at the start of the season when the last three wickets fell for one run, poor Des Barrick stranded powerless at the non-striker's end. They are survivors, too, of last year's game here at Old Trafford, when Lancashire needed two to win off the match's final ball, and the wicket-keeper dropped the ball to allow an impossible second run. When games are as close as this, anything can happen.

'Statham bowled a wonderfully controlled maiden over to Tribe.' He has bowled 17 out of 21 overs from his end, and Lancashire are suffering from the want of another quick bowler to support him. Bob drives Hilton's first ball for a single, and the game reaches its crunch. *'Surely with Hilton and Tribe at grips,'* Denys Rowbotham writes, *'it must be now or never. Hilton flighted a ball never so bravely, and Tribe drove it with all the force of his square shoulders. The flight none the less had done the trick, and the ball was rising toweringly to long on. There too was Marner.'* Peter Marner, the seventeen-year-old youngster of this experienced Lancashire team. Peter Marner, only playing because Cyril Washbrook is unfit. Here is his chance of glory. *'But sickeningly for Lancashire he was not wholly deep as he should have been but three quarters deep. The ball sailed above his head and, though he clawed for it, he could not hold it.'* Then George runs a single to take strike from Statham, and there are just five to win.

"We were on the war dance in the dressing room," Brian recalls. "We were watching, but we were trying not to watch." "Someone decided that no one had to sit down," Peter explains, "so we kept perambulating around the dressing room table." Off the first ball of the over, all the planning goes wrong as Bob Clarke calls a leg-bye and leaves himself to face five deliveries from Statham. Dennis groans in despair: "There was never a dull moment playing in that team, but we didn't have many thinking cricketers." George Tribe is one of them, but what is he thinking as Nigel Howard moves Bob Berry from third slip to backward short leg and Bob Clarke waits anxiously for the next Statham thunderbolt?

Bob Clarke. In five years' time he will be teaching the boys of Christ's Hospital School how to bat and bowl, and now he must do it himself. Dennis still laughs about the evening he survived a torrid spell from Worcester's Reg Perks. "He was retreating so much the square leg umpire had to go back." Freddie Brown is not amused. "Get Clarke in the nets in the morning," he tells Dennis. But when morning comes, Bob has a hand all swollen from a late-night argument. "How did you get that?" Freddie Brown interrogates him. "Reggie Perks hit me last night," Bob replies. Dennis laughs at the memory. "He was backing away so much, the ball never got near him, but Freddie didn't know." Freddie is forever trying to catch up with Bob, but somehow Bob always seems to escape.

Brian Statham bowls an in-swinger, and poor Bob jabs clumsily at it. It cocks up towards Bob Berry at backward short leg, but somehow it eludes his outstretched arm. They scramble a single, and George is back on strike. *'Even the wary Tribe almost cocked the next ball to gully.'* Is there anybody still watching in the dressing room as he prepares for the next delivery? In a low-scoring game, he has made over a hundred runs without dismissal, and now the fate of the contest lies in his hands. *'A drive by Tribe off the toes to mid-wicket for two, a glance for a single, and all was over.'* At the thirtieth attempt Northamptonshire have come here to Lancashire and won. "The coach journey home was certainly a joyous one," Peter Pickering remembers. "We stopped at a couple of pubs and had our celebratory dinner at a fish-and-chip shop."

"It was a terrific game," Brian Reynolds recalls, "but I've played on better wickets at Old Trafford."

In the same season they have won in both Lancashire and Yorkshire. Dennis has been in charge for both outings, and at the end of the summer he will succeed Freddie Brown to become Northamptonshire's first professional captain. It is a blow for Jock Livingston, who earns a little money on the side providing cricket stories for Joe Hulme's column in The Sunday People. "A tip from the inside," Joe writes every so often. "Livingston will be the next captain of Northants."

Freddie Brown will smile when he hears the cricket score from Old Trafford, but his greater triumph will come next Wednesday. While Geoff Edrich is nursing his broken hand, his brother Bill is the rock of England's second innings as they graft their way to a decisive eight-wicket victory.

Wednesday 19 August 1953. Freddie Brown crowns a wonderful five years with this Coronation Year Ashes triumph, and he stands amid the celebrations as Len Hutton, England's first professional captain, speaks from the pavilion balcony. Sixty miles away at the Northampton county ground Raman Subba Row is scoring a fine century for Surrey, a century that will lead to his appointment as captain of Northants. In 1957 Dennis will lead this little-fancied county to second place, then he will stand down to accommodate the young amateur.

Wednesday 19 August 1953. A day of triumph for English cricket. But for Peter Pickering it will be just another day in the office at the roller bearings factory. There will never be another call to play for the county.

LANCASHIRE v NORTHAMPTONSHIRE

Old Trafford. 12, 13 & 14 August 1953

NORTHAMPTONSHIRE WON BY 1 WICKET

LANCASHIRE

J.T. Ikin	c Tribe b Lightfoot	25	c Lightfoot b Tyson		0
*N.D. Howard	b Tyson	3	b Tyson		6
G.A Edrich	c Tribe b Clarke	4	not out		81
K. Grieves	c Reynolds b Clarke	30	c Clarke b Tyson		2
A. Wharton	c Davis b Clarke	21	c Tyson b Lightfoot		4
P. Marner	b Tribe	22	b Clarke		5
M.J. Hilton	st Reynolds b Broderick	20	c Davis b Clarke		4
+F.D. Parr	b Tribe	10	c Reynolds b Clarke		10
J.B. Statham	c Reynolds b Tribe	4	lbw b Clarke		17
R. Tattersall	b Tribe	5	c Davis b Clarke		6
R. Berry	not out	6	c Tribe b Clarke		0
Extras	*b 11, lb 2*	13	*b 4, lb 2*		6
		163			**141**

1-13, 2-30, 3-36, 4-80, 5-95, 6-133, 7-137, 8-147, 9-152, 10-163
1-0, 2-11, 3-13, 4-34, 5-49, 6-57, 7-94, 8-125, 9-139, 10-141

Tyson	7	1	14	1	15	5	30	3
Clarke	15	4	34	3	21.4	6	60	6
Lightfoot	7	4	11	1	9	4	27	1
Tribe	25.2	10	53	4	5	0	18	0
Broderick	13	3	38	1				

NORTHAMPTONSHIRE

*D. Brookes	c Grieves b Tattersall	0	c Marner b Tattersall		7
V. Broderick	b Statham	1	c Parr b Statham		8
E. Davis	c Grieves b Tattersall	22	c Wharton b Statham		11
+B. Reynolds	c Edrich b Statham	0	lbw b Statham		8
P. Arnold	c Grieves b Berry	10	lbw b Tattersall		2
G. Tribe	not out	73	not out		37
D.G. Greasley	c Ikin b Tattersall	10	b Statham		2
P. Pickering	c Berry b Hilton	22	b Hilton		37
A. Lightfoot	st Parr b Hilton	1	c Grieves b Berry		3
F.H. Tyson	b Statham	1	c & b Hilton		0
R.W Clarke	b Hilton	20	not out		2
Extras	*b 11, lb 6*	17	*b4, lb 7*		11
		177		(9 wkts)	**128**

1-6, 2-14, 3-15, 4-42, 5-58, 6-71, 7-106, 8-120, 9-125, 10-177
1-22, 2-30, 3-37, 4-37, 5-40, 6-91, 7-94, 8-108, 9-117

Statham	18	2	54	3	18	4	44	4
Tattersall	24	8	76	3	13	2	40	2
Berry	10	2	25	1	3	0	9	1
Hilton	8	6	5	3	9	1	24	2

Umpires: A.E.D. Smith and W.T. Jones

Len Hutton

WHAT MIGHT HAVE BEEN AND WHAT HAS BEEN

Yorkshire v Leicestershire
June 1954
with Terry Spencer & Maurice Hallam

Terry Spencer played for Leicestershire from 1952 to 1974. A right-arm medium-pace bowler, he took 1367 wickets in his career. After he retired from playing, he became a first-class umpire. He now works for himself as a window-fitter in Leicester.

Maurice Hallam played for Leicestershire from 1950 to 1970. A right-handed batsman, he hit 1000 runs in a season 13 times. He captained the county in four seasons in the 1960s. After he retired from playing, he became cricket coach at Uppingham School.

They remember a game at Huddersfield with a dramatic last day's play.

It is a damp Wednesday morning in Huddersfield. *'A dull grey cloud hung over the ground,'* Bill Bowes writes in the Yorkshire Evening News, *'and there was a nasty light drizzle in the wind'.* Huddersfield may have been one of the original homes of Yorkshire cricket, but now it stages just this one fixture a year. Ten thousand spectators pack the ground each year for the final of the local Sykes Cup, but for this visit of Leicestershire there are barely three thousand enduring the elements as Hutton and Lowson open the Yorkshire innings.

Len Hutton. He has scored a century in four of his last six appearances here, and how he could do with a hundred today to break the run of injury and poor form that has dogged him all summer! He has travelled overnight from the Lord's Test where Khan Mohammad has bowled him for 0, and there is talk that David Sheppard will replace him as England captain for the forthcoming Ashes tour.

It is June 1954. Roger Bannister has run the first sub-four minute mile, and an eighteen-year-old Lester Piggott has won the Derby on Never Say Die. "I got away to a good start," Piggott says, "and it all went according to plan."

It is a damp morning in the North for Leicestershire. They have travelled up from Worthing, another match ruined by the rain, and, although it is only the sixteenth day of the month, the Daily Telegraph is already declaring it 'the wettest June for 37 years'. Flooding in London gets into the telephone cables while in Leicester it confines a hundred residents to their homes. *'The drizzle did not come through hard enough to force Palmer to take his men off,'* Bill Bowes writes. *'Driven by the strong breeze, it felt worse than it was.'* The wicket is quite grassy, but for Hutton *'the memory of his Test match failure'*, according to the Manchester Guardian, *'appeared to provide him with just the incentive he required'.* Like Lester Piggott he makes a good start and, with forcing drives off the back foot, he reaches his fifty with just 62 on the board.

Len Hutton may be the England captain, but he will never take charge here in Yorkshire. With the amateur tradition as sacrosanct as it was in Lord Hawke's heyday, Norman Yardley is in his seventh season as skipper. "You know," Yardley says, "if they'd give the captaincy to Len, I'd pack up tomorrow." Yorkshire are a team full of outsized personalities, and Yardley's gentle touch does not always get the best from them. "Wardle, Closey, Fred, they were always getting on at each other," Terry remembers. "'Get up there' ... 'I'm not fielding there', that sort of thing. They were an unruly sort of team, and Norman Yardley wasn't a disciplinarian." Maurice puts it slightly differently: "They were always arguing but, when you tried to argue against them, you came up against a brick wall. They were one clan, Yorkshire for Yorkshiremen." The committee will never make Hutton the offer of captaincy and, by next year's Huddersfield game, he will have retired, beaten by chronic rheumatism. "If he'd got the captaincy," a later skipper, Ronnie Burnet, writes, "I think he would have played for another seven or eight years." Though they do not know it, this Huddersfield crowd is applauding his boundaries for the last time.

'Industrial, smoky, architecturally ugly, crammed with mills and factories, Huddersfield bears the visible stamp of the Victorian age. Her buildings are of the local stone, blackened by soot, solid, unbeautiful.' So reads the 1950 Guide to the West Riding of Yorkshire. The textile industry is in decline, but other factories are springing up: chemicals, dyestuffs, tractors. Yet everywhere a greater Victorian past hangs over the modern life of the town. The gravestones of the neighbouring churchyard are visible from the square, and subscriptions are invited for a memorial to George Hirst and Wilfred Rhodes, the local men whose all-round triumphs earlier in the century still dominate every list of Yorkshire records. This Fartown ground in Huddersfield is the flattest field in all Yorkshire, they say, but, if you walk the three miles to Kirkheaton, where Hirst and Rhodes grew up, the cricket field sits on a shelf and beyond its drystone walls are undulating hills and many a mile of windswept moor.

It is a landscape vastly more imposing than the farmlands and market towns of rural Leicestershire, and the scale of the contrast is reflected in their differing cricket fortunes. Between the wars Yorkshire win twelve titles, never finishing below fifth place, while Leicestershire manage just two appearances in the top half of the table. It is much the same after the war, but in 1953 the world turns upside down. For four heady days in mid-August Leicestershire sit at the top of the table, and their final position of third is nine places above Yorkshire, the only time between 1895 and 1970 that they will finish ahead of the Northern county. Does the young Terry realise how fleeting is the glory? "Everything was fantastic to me at the time," he recalls. "I was playing local cricket one year, and I was playing for the county the next, bowling against all the great batsmen." Here at Huddersfield he and Brian Boshier bowl *with some accuracy'*, but *'Hutton, his old dominant and assertive self again, was able to hit through the covers and past long-off to his heart's content.'* Yorkshire are in the leading pack in the championship while Leicestershire languish once more at the foot of the table.

Len Hutton is the England captain, and last summer Terry came so close to joining him in the England team. A surprise choice for the Test Trial at Edgbaston, he bowled Bailey, Compton and May while Fred Trueman at the other end went wicketless. *'Spencer enjoyed a thoroughly satisfactory first appearance in representative cricket,'* Wisden records. But Fred has that extra bit of pace, and Hutton is a great believer in pace. "The wickets I took were all coming in to the bat," Terry explains. "They seemed to think the ball coming in wouldn't be such a good ploy against the Australians." He will play for twenty more years, and he will never again come so close to an England cap. 'What might have been and what has been.' Fred will carry all before him, 67 Tests and 307 wickets. "Ah, well," Terry sighs. "They made the right choice, didn't they?"

A Test trial, first place in the county table, now this most memorable of games at Huddersfield. In time he will realise what peaks these are, but for now he is happy to run in and bowl. Throughout these early glories he is on National Service, an equipment repairer in the stores at Glen Parva, and he still retains his army pay book. There is little sign of any equipment repairing in these summer months. "One year I went four months before I got back to draw my pay." Army cricket has kept him out of the Leicestershire side for the last three matches, and he returns here at Huddersfield, determined to make up for lost time. "I don't think I got a wicket in the first innings, did I?"

By one o'clock Leicestershire are onto their sixth bowler. Terry and Brian have hit the seam with the new ball, Charles Palmer the captain has tried his medium-pace floaters, and the Australians Jack Walsh and Vic Jackson have spun the ball, left-arm wrist spin and right-arm finger spin. Now it is the turn of Vic Munden, bowling slow left arm. *'Nothing seemed more certain than that Hutton would make his first hundred of the season but, having hit 60 out of 82, he was snapped at the wicket off Munden, when again attempting a forcing back shot.'* It brings Vic Wilson to the crease, and at lunch Yorkshire are 94 for one.

It is June 1954. Doris Day sings 'Secret Love', and in America the first pre-recorded tapes go on sale.

The rain clouds pass during the lunch interval, and the sun comes out. Terry and Brian try again to make the breakthrough, but it is Jack Walsh who finally removes the obdurate Lowson. *'Never had there been a time when he looked like achieving freedom or prosperity'*, and now he plays on to a chinaman, bringing Ted Lester to the wicket. "Who's the best bowler, the most difficult bowler you've ever played against?" Ted remembers Hutton asking him. "I've got to say it's Jack Walsh," Ted replies, and Hutton, never a man of many words, concurs. "Aye, not a bad bowler, is he?"

Jack bowls chinamen and googlies. "He was absolutely fantastic," Maurice recalls. "He could bowl five or six different balls." There are three googlies, one of them easy to spot, the other two for the great game of bluff and double bluff that he so loves, always that mischievous twinkle in his eye. There is an orthodox slow left arm, a seamer and a chinaman. "I could read the chinaman from slip, but not when I was batting against him in the nets. It's amazing, that four yard difference, that little bit of time." Terry fields at short leg, and he remembers the sound of the ball as it passed him. "He spun it so viciously you could hear it fizz in the air. There weren't many who could do that." Jack's fellow Australian Vic Jackson stands at first slip, and he runs to leg slip at the first sign of the chinaman. Is it really true that he caught Essex's Harry Crabtree like this one day at Clacton? "Jack bamboozled lots and lots of great batsmen," Maurice recalls. "It was always a joy because there was always something happening. It was interesting. It was great to be out there." And nobody enjoys his cricket more than Jack Walsh, his eyes twinkling in his creased and weather-beaten face.

In this summer of 1954, the Leicestershire spinners will bowl 63% of the overs. By 1996, the figure will be down to 29%, and nobody will turn it both ways like Jack. "I find it very difficult to watch now," Maurice confesses, "because it's more or less the same all day long. Seamers are on, seamers are on, seamers are on. And you think, 'My God, when are we going to see a little guile?'"

Ted Lester mis-hits a drive to deep mid-on, and tea is taken at 208 for three. The day is warm now, and Vic Wilson and Willie Watson enjoy the early evening sun. *'Driving, cutting and pulling by both men left the bowling much the worse for wear.'* Vic is a burly man, from farming stock in the East Riding, a powerful hitter of the quicker bowlers, but history books record that 'he lacked the style of Willie Watson' and that 'he never conquered his fast footedness against spin'. Yet here at Huddersfield he races to the first of four centuries that will see him a surprise choice on the boat to Australia - though it would be more of a surprise if he played for a county like Leicestershire. It is just after six o'clock when Jack Walsh traps him for 138, and the innings is declared at 351 for four. *'The bowling seemed to be there to be bent to the batsman's will.'* Terry and Brian bowl off long runs, but Leicestershire have got through twenty overs an hour and Yorkshire have got their runs quickly enough to have a short bowl at the end of the day. "That's how I was brought up," Maurice reflects. "We had to get as many as we could by six o'clock so we could declare and put them in for half an hour."

Maurice goes out with Gerry Lester, and Fred Trueman has 25 minutes of work to do. *'Trueman bowled with three slips, two gullies and three short legs in an intimidating array around the batsmen and bowled with plenty of devil.'* Maurice is just twenty-two years old, an uncapped player still seeking his first hundred. What is it like to face Fred like this? "I don't say I liked it but, with him being a bit raw, it suited me. He was a bit wayward at times so he'd give me a chance to get the old square cut and the hook in. It was the people like Brian Statham who put everything on line who were the problem children for me. But then Freddie got better and better. After about four years he could put it more or less where he wanted." Gerry Lester edges Fred to the keeper's right and sees the catch go down. The day closes at 27 for no wicket.

Yorkshire and Leicestershire. The players of the two teams mingle in the bar. Yorkshire is a vast county of three ridings, with a population of nearly five million, while Leicestershire are home to just six hundred thousand. Is it surprising that the Midland club recruits so many players from out of county? And nowhere do they find more players over the years than in Yorkshire. From 1951 to 1986 Leicestershire award 51 county caps: of these, only ten are home grown cricketers while twelve are Yorkshiremen. Here in Huddersfield in 1954 Jack Firth and Gerry Smithson are returning to the county that discarded them. "They were always dead keen to do well against Yorkshire," Terry remembers. And in four years' time Willie Watson will make the same journey, lured by the prospect of a captaincy that his professional status denies him at Yorkshire. Jack Birkenshaw, Dickie Bird, Jack van Geloven, Ray Illingworth, why do they all choose to come to Leicestershire? "I should think they knew they were going to get in the side," Maurice jokes. The teams relax over a drink, perhaps they are attracted to the happy atmosphere of this Leicester side, and nobody is happier in a bar than keeper Jack Firth. "Wicket-keepers and goalkeepers have to be slightly mad to do what they do," Terry reflects. "Jack loved his cricket, and he loved his social life, too. He was always the first in the bar and the last to leave. He used to sing popular tunes and change the words." 'Alice Blue Gown' is one of his favourites, "something to do with a little pink nightie."

"Sides got on far better together than they do now," Terry says. "You had to make your own fun in those days." Maurice agrees: "I always say that Wilson, the Gloucestershire keeper, got me into first-class cricket." It is twelve months before this Huddersfield game, and Maurice is batting at number eight, "playing absolutely terribly". "I'm playing like an idiot," he says to Andy Wilson. "Just look at the scoreboard," comes the reply, and there is twenty-odd against Maurice's name. "Keep your head. You'll be fine." He makes a match-turning 77, and "I never got out of the side from then on. And at the end of the day, it was 'Come and have a drink.'"

It is June 1954. High above Lake Geneva, in Lausanne's Olympic Stadium, the opening ceremony of football's fifth World Cup takes place, and television carries the pictures. As more TV sets are sold, the British Lion Film Corporation goes into receivership and Huddersfield's Palace Theatre closes down.

Maurice and Gerry Lester share a partnership of 58 before Maurice is bowled by Fred for 24. Maurice Tompkin replaces him, *'Trueman had a warm greeting for Tompkin, making the batsman hop with a ball which pitched on his foot.'* Maurice Hallam recalls Gerry Lester's advice on such occasions. "'Don't let them see it's hurting you,' he'd say. 'My leg's dropping off, Gerry, what am I going to do about it?' 'Don't rub it, don't rub it.' Gerry was a hard man. He'd sooner let the ball go through him than shy away from it."

Gerry is all guts and determination, and at the other end Maurice Tompkin is all grace and style. "He looked like a god," Maurice Hallam recalls. "He'd got blond hair, he was built right and he'd always got this smile and this complexion that looked right. And he played like it. His strokes were terrific. The straight drive was his forte, it was as sweet as anything you've seen. And he could run like a stag as well. There was something about the man that everybody loved. He was just a nice guy, very rarely had a cross word with anybody." Before the war he has enjoyed a brief career as a footballer here at Huddersfield, and today he returns to score *'the first century for the Hunting Shire against Yorkshire'* for eight years. *'He drove Close for six,'* and *'he welcomed Appleyard with a shot to leg that lifted the ball clean out of the ground.'* *'For just under four and a half hours he batted with charm and distinction'*, and he survives one false shot at 106 when *'Close at first slip muffed an easy chance'*. The sun is out, the wicket is true, and *'a team which fails to hold its catches may be said to have dug a pit for itself'*.

To the Manchester Guardian's correspondent, *'the Yorkshire bowlers, apart from Trueman, were not formidable'*. Trueman, Appleyard, Yardley, Wardle, Close: they are all Test match bowlers, but Gerry Lester *'was content to savour the bowling, to roll it round his palate before deciding whether he cared for it or not. It surely needed no such epicurean judgement. For the most part it was there as the batsman's delight.'* It is 183 for two when Close bowls him for 74. When Maurice Tompkin is stumped after tea for 149, it is 281 for five.

"There were more delicate shots then," Maurice reflects. "Instead of the touch players like Hutton, Compton and Graveney, beautiful drives and tiddle them round the corner, now it's either a four or nothing. They give it a big whack. We were placers. It was what I call poetry in motion. And the bowlers can't put it where they want to. But that's the way it goes."

At Ascot the young Lester Piggott rides his Derby winner, Never Say Die, to fourth place in the King Edward VII stakes. A stewards' inquiry disqualifies him, and a disciplinary hearing suspends him from riding for six months.

The sun shines on the historic Fartown ground in Huddersfield. *'In good weather this Huddersfield pitch is as docile as any in the country,'* Bill Bowes writes. Gerry Smithson is at the wicket now, the score is 315 for five, and the match has produced 666 runs for the loss of just nine wickets. It is June 1954. In the Middle East Britain is negotiating with the new Egyptian Prime Minister, Abdul Nasser, to remove its troops from the base beside the Suez Canal.

How quickly it will all change! Next year there will be no Len Hutton in this Yorkshire side. The following year there will be no Huddersfield on the fixture card. By the end of 1956 Britain will have retreated in ignominy from their attack on Egypt, and Maurice Tompkin, whose free-flowing century has charmed this Thursday afternoon, will have died of stomach cancer. Here in 1954 the crowd sits in pleasant sunshine, no thought for any of this. They have seen 666 runs for the loss of nine wickets, and Leicestershire need just 37 for first innings points.

Gerry Smithson is relishing his every run against his old team mates, reminding the crowd of those days seven years ago when they talked of him as the new Maurice Leyland. While Clement Attlee is announcing a tightening of peace-time rationing in 1947, he is stroking a career-best 169 at Leicester, and it is one of just two centuries that earn him a tour of the Caribbean. "If he'd been playing for Leicestershire," Maurice Hallam reflects, "he'd never have smelt it." Now, seven years on, he *is* playing for Leicestershire and, with the end of rationing just a fortnight away, he lofts the ball over Brian Close's head, only to see a right hand go up to take *'a lovely high return catch'*. It is a catch that transforms the contest. Five wickets fall for 13 runs, and Yorkshire gain a first innings lead of 23.

There is time for Terry to try once more to catch the England captain's eye. 'One of the best young prospects,' Hutton has called him, and this evening he takes out Lowson's middle stump, has Wilson dropped in the slips and - best of all - has Hutton himself caught behind. It is 20 for two, and suddenly it seems that there is something in the pitch for the bowler.

In the World Cup in Switzerland England go three-one up against Belgium. Stanley Matthews, Billy Wright, Tom Finney and Nat Lofthouse. This is a fine England side, but the game slips away and they manage only a four-four draw.

It is June 1954. At the Old Vic Theatre in London, Richard Burton opens as Hamlet while at the Princess Cinema, Huddersfield, the film of the Queen's Commonwealth tour is retained for a second week.

Friday brings back the clouds, and batting becomes a struggle. Terry dismisses Wilson and Watson with *'a couple of beauties'*, deliveries that pitch on the left-handers' leg stump and take the off bail. *'Absolute gems'*, Bill Bowes calls them. Ted Lester grafts a watchful 34, but Terry knocks out his middle stump. Then *'Yardley's off stump described a series of somersaults'* when Terry hits it, and the game is transformed.

Six wickets down, all six to Terry. There are no great celebrations. "You didn't get the high fives. Just a 'Well bowled'. A little confab, 'Who's coming in next?', and that was it."

Brian Boshier is suffering from sciatica, and Charles Palmer leaves Terry to bowl unchanged while he and Vic Jackson plug the other end. Vic is a bowler who resents every run scored off him. "He didn't stay on long if he were getting stick," Terry remembers. "He'd have some ache." Four years ago, while the West Indians were thrashing 682 for two at Leicester, he sat in the pavilion with a back strain. Today he bowls ten overs for 25 and gives the ball back to his captain.

Charles Palmer is a schoolmaster in Bromsgrove when he takes on the Leicester captaincy. A small man with round glasses and a quiet voice, he seems so unlike a sportsman, but cricketers come in all shapes and sizes, and his Test cap last winter in Barbados is the only one won by a Leicestershire player between 1934 and Willie Watson's arrival in 1958. In his career he will make 33 centuries, and he will rise in the game's administration to be President of the MCC, but it is his bowling that they still talk about.

Next May at Leicester, with a bad back keeping him from bowling, he will give himself an over against Surrey so that Terry can change ends. "He got a couple of wickets," Terry remembers, "and he treated it as a joke." "I'll stay on for another over now," he says. He is a slower bowler than Terry so he bowls a fuller length. "The pitch was dry," Terry explains, "apart from this dinner plate of a wet patch right on his length." After 12 overs he has taken eight wickets for no runs. "I was the only one who was caught," Bernie Constable recalls. "The rest were all bowled." Jim Laker tops the all-time list of remarkable analyses with his eight wickets for two runs at the 1950 Test Trial, and now only he stands between Charles and even more remarkable figures. Jim slashes the ball into the covers, and a sharp chance goes down. What might have been and what has been. Then Jim edges a four to fine leg, and the record books read 14 overs, eight wickets for seven runs. In the second innings he bowls 13 more overs for just one run. Bernie Constable shakes his head. "He was just a dobber really."

Then there are the donkey drops. "I was the first one involved in that," Maurice recalls. "He bowled one to Jock Livingston, and I was standing at slip. I had no idea it was coming, I just started running backwards, getting out of the road, and funnily enough he hit it straight down my throat. Everybody collapsed in a big heap." The donkey drop is responsible for "quite a few" of his first-class wickets. "They went miles up in the air, into orbit. We're talking probably twenty feet. The strike rate was unbelievable. He hit the top of the stumps, people trod on their wicket or knocked the stumps down. Colin Cowdrey played it best. He changed hands and whipped it away with a table tennis shot."

Here at Huddersfield he bowls to the left-handed Brian Close, a loose ball down leg. "It wasn't a great delivery," Terry recalls. "Close had a sweep, and I'm damn sure it hit the back of his bat on the second time around. It looped up in the air, and Firthy ran back for the catch." Forty-three years later the ball sits on Terry's mantelpiece. The seam is pronounced, the quarter cut clearly visible. C.T. Spencer, 23 overs, nine for 63. They are the best figures of his 23-year career, and in the pavilion he even gets a "Well bowled" from the England captain. Yorkshire are all out for 113, and Leicestershire need just 137 to win. They have only ever won once here in Yorkshire, and there is plenty of time to make the runs.

Terry has bowled unchanged, 23 overs in all. "He was a workhorse," Maurice remembers. "He never shirked anything." "If they have to bowl eight overs these days," Terry says, "it's a long spell. That were just starters for us. It makes me laugh. I used to do thirty overs a day. And they say they're fitter." "Well bowled", Len Hutton says, and Terry must be so close to the England team. But he is still on National Service. Tomorrow he is back out of the limelight, playing for the Army at Sandhurst, and Hutton is looking for that extra pace for the bouncier Australian wickets. Tyson and Loader, not Spencer, will be the new names the selectors announce in August, and Terry will draw the wrong conclusion. "Where I went wrong was to strive for pace instead of sticking to the way I set off. You try to bowl quicker, and your action tends to go a bit." Later in his career he will realise his mistake. "When he slowed down and put it up there," Maurice says, "it was a different ball game. He started to use his head, but it was too late. He'd missed the boat by then. Dare I say it? Perhaps he played for the wrong county."

Terry has struck for Leicestershire. Now it is time to see what Fred Trueman can do in reply. Fred is out of favour with the England selectors, the result of 'alleged incidents' in the Caribbean, where Len Hutton was captain and Charles Palmer the player-manager. "You can imagine Fred and Charles not getting on," Terry laughs, but Fred's lifelong grievance is not directed at the schoolmaster. He is having to bowl his way back into the Test side, and he is currently third in the national averages. *'Immediately Trueman struck back so that half the Leicestershire wickets were down for 29 runs.'* 666 runs for nine wickets, followed by 155 runs for twenty wickets. What an unpredictable game is cricket!

"I've never been a great watcher myself," Terry reveals. "I think I was having a stroll around the ground at one stage. Then, when the wickets started falling, I finished up running back. I didn't envisage having to bat again really, but that's the game, isn't it? That's what makes it so compelling and enjoyable."

Vic Munden and Charles Palmer restore some calm, and now the clock and the weather start to enter the equation. The finish is set for a quarter past five, and *'the rain, which drifted across in showers, did not help Yorkshire - indeed, the bowlers had to call for towels'*. Fred's new-ball strike is over, and the bowling now is in the hands of Appleyard and Wardle. Fred is third in the national averages and they are the two above him, such is the strength of this Yorkshire attack. But Leicestershire never say die, and *'we saw some courageous strokes from Palmer while Munden not only defended stubbornly but hit the ball hard as well'*. At 72 for five, there are only 65 runs still to win, and *'what was more, the scoring rate had caught up with the clock'*. Eight years ago, in only his second county game, Vic has come in at number eleven and batted out for the draw against an equally mighty Yorkshire side. Now his sights are set on victory.

The ball is wet, the wicket is losing its earlier life, and *'the rain, whipped by the wind, strengthened.'* It is the wettest June for 37 years, *'but neither side looked to the pavilion.'*

'Yorkshire have only one fixture at Huddersfield,' the Times correspondent writes, *'and more often than not most of the time is spent watching the rain fall, but when play is possible it is hardly ever dull.'* Next year will be the last first-class game here, and Gloucestershire will be the visitors. "The pitch was black," Bomber Wells recalls. "There was smoke belching from a nearby factory chimney." Bomber rubs his hand on the grass to improve his grip, and "the ball became quite black." Bomber loves to tell how Norman Yardley comes out to bat and sends him off to wash his hands. He returns to trap Yardley lbw first ball. Here in 1954, is there smoke coming from the nearby chimneys? "I don't remember that," Terry says. "The pitch was quite green." But he does remember the neighbouring churchyard. "You could see the gravestones."

Johnny Wardle bowls with the graveyard behind him. He is the latest in line of the great Yorkshire tradition of slow left arm bowlers. From Kirkheaton's Wilfred Rhodes, whose 4187 wickets will never be beaten, through Hedley Verity, who died so tragically in an Italian prisoner camp, his career average of 14.90 unmatched this century. Wardle mixes wrist spin with orthodox slow left arm, and they do not all like it around these parts. "They couldn't accept that he was different from his predecessors," Ted Lester writes. "Rhodes and Verity didn't need to bowl chinamen, so why should he? Did he think that he was a cut above them?" Johnny Wardle is the most talented of bowlers, yet always he carries the resentment at the comparison with Rhodes and Verity. The gravestones are behind him as he bowls Charles Palmer for 31.

"Wardle was a great, great bowler," Bomber Wells says. "Number one. The greatest match-winner for Yorkshire, greater than Fred even. He could bowl teams out on good pitches." Wardle one, Trueman two, Appleyard not far behind. Bomber smiles mischievously. "Boycott would be about twenty-ninth."

Now it is time for Jack Walsh to bat. "He weren't a purist," Terry recalls. "He'd just give it a whack." *'Walsh struck a vengeful six off Appleyard'*, and with Vic Munden he raises the score to 123 for six, just fourteen runs to win. *'All over bar the shouting said some of the crowd as they began to melt away.'* But there is plenty of shouting to come, and they will regret their early departures. Vic is run out by Yardley, and Jack falls victim to Wardle's flight, mis-hitting an attempt at another *'vengeful six'*. Then Wardle lures Jack Firth out of his crease, and there are still ten runs needed to win when Brian Boshier, *'limping badly from an attack of sciatica'*, joins Terry at the wicket.

Brian is six foot five, so big and solid that the masseur, with his bottle of olive oil, "couldn't get his fingers into his legs," Terry recalls. He has been unable to bowl, yet he is batting without a runner - if you can call Brian's efforts batting. Next summer he will reach mid-June before he scores a run. "He held the record for most ducks on the trot. He had them all marked on the bat." Then at Hinckley against Statham and Tattersall he will come in at 25 for nine and hit top score with 13. What would Leicester do for a few of those runs here at Huddersfield?

The clock reads almost a quarter past five, time for just one more over. Soon there will be a memorial clock for Hirst and Rhodes, but for now the Yorkshire tradition is in the hands of Johnny Wardle. Terry has taken nine Yorkshire wickets in an innings, the ball still sits on his mantelpiece; now he has to score nine runs to bring his team to victory. Somehow they scramble a couple of singles, and there are seven runs wanted off the last three balls with Terry back on strike.

Wardle bowls slow left arm. He flights it, he pushes it through, he bowls out of the back of his hand. "He was the ideal bowler for that final over. You were never certain what was going to come down. The first one he pitches up, I thought, I'm going to have a whack." *'Wardle, going all out for victory, tossed one up to Spencer in the hope of getting the batsman caught.'* "I think it was out of the back of his hand," Terry says. Not at all what Rhodes or Verity would have done, but it gives Terry the chance to execute his plan. *'Spencer crashed it for six into the cemetery.'* "I cleared the field by a long way."

The scores are level with two balls remaining, and Wardle looks down the wicket at Terry. "He was a dour Yorkshireman who didn't like being hit. He wasn't a jolly character." How does he react to such treatment? "I think there was a little clap and a 'Well hit'." "In the fifties it was absolutely a dream to play," Maurice remembers. "There was no money if you won the championship, and it wasn't so intense as it is now." But surely Yorkshire will mind if they lose here to Leicestershire? "Make no mistake. When Freddie was bowling, he wasn't bowling you little donkey drops." And, when Johnny Wardle bowls the fifth ball of the over, he *'changed his tactics by bowling a faster one on a dead line with the wicket, and Spencer was unable to turn it away for the vital glory.'*

So to the last ball of the match. Will Terry find the space to work that vital single, round off a day of personal glory in the most thrilling of victories? Will Wardle's guile outwit him and bring Yorkshire their first tie in 120 years of county cricket? Or will it all stay unresolved in the anti-climax of a draw? Only one other finish in Terry's career ranks with this moment at Huddersfield. At The Oval in 1961 he bowls to Peter Loader with Surrey wanting one to tie and two to win. The Leicestershire players are on a rolling win bonus of twenty-five pounds, and he knows how Loader backs to leg when the bowling is quick. "A yorker on leg stump, I thought." The ball grazes the outside of the stump, and a bail falls down. "Oh dear, the cheers," he recalls. A dramatic win over Surrey with the ball, does it sit in his memory next to a dramatic win over Yorkshire with the bat?

Terry meets Brian Boshier in mid-pitch, big Brian with his sciatica. "Whatever you do," Terry says, "get out of your trap quick."

'Wardle, with his hop, skip and jump, came up to deliver the last ball to Spencer. Spencer pushed it down the pitch, and he and 6 ft 5 ins Brian Boshier dashed for the run that would have meant victory.' "If I make contact, we've got to go, that was the idea, but I didn't play it as wide of Wardle as I should have done." *'Like a flash Wardle picked up, turned, and flung down the wicket at the bowling end.'* Brian is lumbering home at the keeper's end. And Terry? He is a tall man, and his paces cover the length of the pitch at speed. Never Say Die. The bails come off, and he is *'only an inch or two from the crease to which he galloped so gallantly.'* The umpire's finger is up. It is a tie. What might have been and what has been. "I was so disappointed that we hadn't won, but it probably made more headlines than if we had."

Huddersfield will never see another county game like it. A championship match in 1955 and a few Sunday League games, that is all. The last of the Sunday games will be in 1982. With British ships trying to regain pre-Suez glory in the Falklands, Terry will stand as umpire on this ground, look once more at the graveyard where his towering six landed, think again of that 'inch or two' that lay between him and a heroic victory.

The Rhodes-Hirst memorial clock suffers the attention of vandals. By the late '80s the pavilion will be a night club.

"If I had my chance again," Maurice says, "I'd go back then. I don't think I'd be too happy playing now. The beauty of it in those days was you'd got friends all over the country. Now it's get in the car and belt off to the next venue."

"I'm just pleased that I've been a professional cricketer," Terry reflects, "and I've met so many fine people."

YORKSHIRE v LEICESTERSHIRE

Huddersfield. 16, 17 & 18 June 1954

MATCH TIED

YORKSHIRE

L. Hutton	c Firth b Munden	60	c Firth b Spencer	6
F.A. Lowson	b Walsh	38	b Spencer	8
J.V. Wilson	c Palmer b Walsh	138	b Spencer	18
E. Lester	c Boshier b Palmer	33	b Spencer	34
W. Watson	not out	80	b Spencer	0
*N.D.W. Yardley			b Spencer	22
D.B. Close			c Firth b Palmer	1
J.H. Wardle			b Spencer	0
+R. Booth			c Smithson b Spencer	8
F.S. Trueman			b Spencer	8
R. Appleyard			not out	1
Extras	lb 1, nb 1	2	b 4, lb 1, nb 2	7
	(4 wkts, dec)	**351**		**113**

1-82, 2-123, 3-183, 4-351
1-13, 2-18, 3-43, 4-43, 5-82, 6-85, 7-87, 8-97, 9-108, 10-113

Spencer	25	3	70	0	23	3	63	9
Boshier	17	3	51	0				
Palmer	12	4	33	1	12	6	18	1
Walsh	20.5	0	77	2				
Jackson	14	3	52	0	10	2	25	0
Munden	23	4	66	1				

LEICESTERSHIRE

G. Lester	b Close	74	b Trueman	4
M.R. Hallam	b Trueman	24	b Trueman	2
M. Tompkin	st Booth b Wardle	149	c & b Appleyard	6
*C.H. Palmer	c Hutton b Wardle	15	b Wardle	31
V.E. Jackson	c Booth b Trueman	1	c Lester b Trueman	4
G.A. Smithson	c & b Close	25	c Lowson b Trueman	0
V.S. Munden	b Appleyard	19	run out	31
J.E. Walsh	b Wardle	0	c Hutton b Wardle	28
+J. Firth	not out	8	st Booth b Wardle	3
C.T. Spencer	st Booth b Appleyard	0	run out	8
B. Boshier	c Watson b Wardle	1	not out	1
Extras	b 8, lb 4	12	b 6, lb 11, nb 1	18
		328		**136**

1-58, 2-183, 3-216, 4-223, 5-281, 6-315, 7-315, 8-327, 9-327, 10-328
1-8, 2-15, 3-19, 4-21, 5-29, 6-72, 7-123, 8-123, 9-127, 10-136

Trueman	22	1	83	2	18	2	44	4
Appleyard	31	11	62	2	20	8	38	1
Yardley	6	1	22	0				
Wardle	44.4	18	82	4	13	4	36	3
Close	21	3	67	2				

Umpires: E. Cooke and Harry Elliott

Arthur Milton

MEMORIES ARE MADE OF THIS

Gloucestershire v Nottinghamshire
June 1956
with Bomber Wells & Merv Winfield

Bryan 'Bomber' Wells played for Gloucestershire from 1951 to 1959 and for Nottinghamshire from 1960 to 1965. An off-spin bowler, he took 100 wickets in a season three times and 998 wickets in his career.

Merv Winfield played for Nottinghamshire from 1954 to 1966. A right-hand bat, he scored 1000 runs in a season four times.

They both remember the first ever county match at Stroud.

Gloucestershire's headquarters are deep in the south of the county - that large, featureless ground in the city of Bristol. In the north they play at Gloucester's Wagon Works and in the splendour of Cheltenham College. But there are many square miles of Cotswold countryside beyond these conurbations, and in 1956 they venture out to Stroud, to the Erinoid Plastics ground..

Bill Haley and Elvis Presley feature in the Hit Parade, now expanded to a Top Thirty, but most of the people of Stroud are happier to whistle and sing along with the cheerful sentimentality of Dean Martin.

'Sweet, sweet, the memories you gave to me.
You can't beat the memories you gave to me.'

Erinoid Plastics was founded in 1912 to manufacture artificial horn for buttons, buckles and umbrella handles. By 1956 they are producing pvc for curtain rails and polystyrene for fluorescent light diffusers, and their cricket field is the best in the area. Forty years on, local man David King stands on the Dudbridge Road and looks down at the factory extension, the car park and housing estate that cover the land where in 1956 he sat and watched his sporting heroes. "I've only got schoolboy memories," he says. "In retrospect, everything means more than it does at the time."

What are the memories that the cricketers retain of Stroud?

"We had to stay in two hotels," Merv recalls. "There wasn't anywhere big enough in the town."

"The wicket used to do everything," Gloucestershire's Arthur Milton remembers.

"I was awarded my blue at Stroud," Cambridge's Richard Bernard says. "What a gloomy ground that was!"

"It's usually damp and wet here," David King explains. "This valley's like that."

Bomber's memory throws a more cheerful sunshine over it all. "It was a lovely ground. Long and narrow, with this beautiful stream running down the side of it. Just an old wooden hut for changing quarters. All rough and ready, like the old Stroud people, as good as gold. It didn't matter whether you were Tom Graveney or old Jim Bloggs, they'd treat you all the same." And that, of course, is what they say of Bomber. He could be bowling at Bradman or he could be bowling at Charlie Snook from the next village, it is all the same to him. "There *is* no difference," he says. "It's just another day."

But for Stroud, Saturday 9 June is a special day. "I was pleased when I heard that a match had been allocated to Stroud," Gloucestershire's captain, George Emmett, writes in the Stroud Journal. "It is a most pleasant ground to play on and provides a good sporting wicket." Sporting for bowlers, certainly. In the years that follow, there are games in which 200 is a good enough score for an innings victory. The Turnip Pitch, they start to call it on the county circuit.

Nottinghamshire are to be the first county to visit the Cotswold town. It is the third stop in a fortnight's tour: Gravesend, Cardiff, Stroud and Bath. After the war they are among the weakest counties, but for the last three summers their fortunes have been transformed by the arrival of the Australian Bruce Dooland. Seven wins in the three summers to 1952, twenty-nine in the next three summers. With his mixture of quickish leg-breaks, googlies and flippers, he takes 518 wickets in these three summers, no other bowler near him. With runs and catches as well, is it any wonder that they have started to call the county Doolandshire?

"He was almost medium pace," Merv recalls. "If he hit the stumps, they'd go out of the ground." His most deadly delivery is the flipper, which kids the batsman onto the back foot and scuttles through low to have him lbw. Only Jock Livingston of Northants consistently gets the better of him, but then Jock has kept wicket to him in Australian state cricket. "You're not with it today, Brucey," he says as he dances down the track.

The days are gone when half the Notts side comes from the local pits. Bruce and Alan Walker are Australians, Ken Smales is a Yorkshireman and Merv is from Lincolnshire. Freddie Stocks is the only member of this team at Stroud who has worked down a pit, and in fifty years of post-war cricket he will be the only ex-miner to win a Nottinghamshire cap.

At Gravesend Bruce takes fifteen Kent wickets in the match, and still Notts do not win. At the other end Ken Smales bowls sixty overs of off-spin for just two wickets, and it is Ken who is left on strike for the last ball. Four to win, and just one wicket to fall. *'Smales swung hopefully,'* the Times records, *'and missed.'* It is a draw, and Ken will have no moment of glory to treasure. "I'm sorry," he says, forty years on. "I don't remember playing in that game."

Then it is into the cars for the long journey to Cardiff, and Ken comes alive with the memory of his night on the road with captain Reg Simpson. "We got lost in Monmouth. I remember us having to mend a puncture. It was midnight, and the street lights had gone out." Travelling with Reg is never a restful end to a hard day's cricket. "He had a Ford Consul," Merv explains. "Very often he used to overtake on the grass verge. If it was hot and he'd got the windows open, all the hedgerows would come through the car." Later, when Merv marries, his wife will ask him who he is travelling with. "If you said Reg, it was three changes of underpants."

It is June 1956. The speed limit for heavy goods vehicles is raised to thirty miles an hour while an annual test is to be introduced for ten-year-old cars.

Spring has been dry and warm. Rainfall has been less than half the seasonal average, with temperatures well up in the seventies, so that by late May heath fires are blazing in Surrey, Dorset and Wales. Then comes the cold and the rain, just as the cricket season starts to develop. Here at Stroud, *'rain-leaden skies and a cold northerly wind this morning presented a bleak outlook.'* Barely two hundred spectators gather, and the Stroud Journal's cartoonist tells the story in a series of sketches entitled 'Erinoid Aquatics'. *'Notts elected to bat. Reg Simpson, their skipper of England fame, dived in first - but found the water too cold and soon came out.'* Reg takes a sharp single to Arthur Milton at short mid-wicket, and the stumps are thrown down at the bowler's end. It is a wonderful piece of fielding, but Bomber knows better than to join in the crowd's applause. He has shown his joy one day when Ron Nicholls takes a brilliant catch, and George Emmett soon lets him know his feelings. "He's paid to do that," he barks. "There's enough exhibitionism in cricket without your adding to it." Here at Stroud it is 12 for one, and soon the drizzle is thick enough to drive the players off the field.

It is June 1956. Third-class travel is abolished on the railways while overhead electric wires begin to replace steam trains.

Play resumes at one o'clock, and Bomber comes on for his first bowl. With his one-pace run-up, the batsmen dare not look away between deliveries. "I liked to get at 'em," he explains, and he tells of his over at Worcester, begun and ended while the clock strikes twelve. "Take your time," his bowling partner Sam Cook curses. "Take your bloody time. No sooner have I got to mid-on than I'm going back to bowl again." It is as bad for the fielders. "I'd be walking away to field at mid-wicket," Arthur Milton recalls, "looking at the boundary, and I'd hear the ball hit the bat." Bomber recalls the words of his captain George Emmett. "Do you know, you're making the game look absolutely stupid."

"You didn't realise straightaway," Arthur explains, "but later on we began to find out in the nets, everybody found it in time. When he bowled, he was so strong that the ball used to pitch that much further up to you than what you thought. People were playing back to half volleys."

"I could bowl standing still. If you're a natural, everything comes easy. You can do what you like and get away with murder. If you're coached, unless you stay in that cog, you're struggling, aren't you?"

The crowd is seldom short of entertainment when Bomber is in action, just as the cricket societies are seldom short of laughter now when he shares his memories. "I took a catch on the boundary once while I was drinking a cup of tea … Have I told you about the ball I bowled from thirty yards? … And the time

Derek Morgan chased me up the pitch to run me out. 'Now that's not fair, Derek,' I said, 'I've got pads on.' ..."

"Mind you," his team mate Ron Nicholls says, "it could be infuriating in a tight game of cricket to have him pratting about."

"It wasn't all that easy in the dressing room," Arthur Milton recalls. "George Emmett didn't tolerate him as well as he should have done."

Bomber's memories are all happy, though. "We weren't light-hearted, far from it. Old Emmett was magnificent, the greatest captain I've ever known. He was a hunter. He went out for the kill. You've got to have a certain discipline, haven't you?"

'Stir carefully through the days,
See how the flavour stays,
These are the dreams you must savour.'

Wells, Cook, Mortimore. Gloucestershire have as good a trio of spinners as any outside Surrey, and for fast bowling they have big Frank McHugh.

Forty years on, Ken Smales will retire from his job as Secretary of Nottingham Forest Football Club, and he will spend some of his new-found leisure time printing up career records for the team mates of his cricketing days. Merv spreads several pages of computer paper across his living room floor as he looks for this Stroud game. "First innings. Caught Emmett, bowled McHugh, 7," he reads. "No, I don't remember that." It is 38 for two.

Sam Cook and Bomber bowl on either side of lunch. Sam is a journeyman plumber from Tetbury, Bomber a journeyman printer from Gloucester. Sam bowls slow left-arm. "He was fantastic. He just plodded along," Bomber says. "If he ever bowled a bad ball, there'd be an inquest afterwards." Bomber bowls off-spin, with leg-breaks and all sorts mixed in. "It used to bore me to bowl more than two balls the same." But he too is accurate. They sit together at lunch. "If Sam was bowling, he wouldn't eat. I used to sit next to him purposely so I could have his lunch. He'd have a liquid lunch, a liquid dinner. I can honestly say that I never saw Sam have a proper meal." Outside, the district band tries to raise the spirits of a cold and damp crowd.

Bomber resumes after lunch, and he dismisses Giles and Poole to make it 57 for four. Ronnie Giles is in the best form of his life, high in the national averages, while C.J. Poole is always a dangerous batsman once he gets going. "CJ was a wonderful player," Merv recalls. "If he was playing in one-day games now, he'd be the Lord Mayor of Nottingham. Nobody knew where to bowl at him." Bomber knows today, it seems, or maybe CJ is not ready when he delivers the ball.

Bruce Dooland hits 22, but John Mortimore mops up the innings with four cheap wickets. As the cartoonist records,

'4.30 Sun came out (cheers)
4.31 Sun went in (groans)
4.40 Everybody went in as Notts were all out for 122 (cheers).'

It is Nottinghamshire's turn to field in the cold, but there is no early success for their opening bowlers. *'Emmett's 33 was the best innings of the day,'* the Western Daily Press declares. He makes his runs as wristily as ever in just 45 minutes, *'and it seemed an injustice that such an enterprising effort should have been ended by the ball trickling along the ground with just sufficient force to dislodge the off bail after a defensive stroke.'* He may be a disciplinarian, a gunner in the war, but George Emmett is a nervous man and he lights a cigarette as soon as he is back in the pavilion. "His hands used to tremble a lot after an innings," Bomber recalls. Between 1949 and 1951 he reached the nineties on 23 occasions, and only ten times did he complete his hundred. Here at Stroud he gives Ken Smales a slightly fortuitous wicket.

Nicholls and Knightley-Smith bat for close of play. *'There were times when Knightley-Smith was troubled by Dooland's leg-breaks, but the amateur was quick to spot the hittable ones and was responsible for the only six of the day - a square leg hit off the Australian.'* Perhaps it lands with a splash in the stream.

It is 76 for one, just 46 runs behind the Notts total, when Ron Nicholls pops a return catch back to Ken Smales, and worse follows when the dependable Jack Crapp turns Ken's off spin into Merv's hands at short leg. "Merv was very good close to the wicket," Ken recalls. Keeper Rochford is sent out but, the cartoonist records, *'it was too cold even for Gloucester's night watchman - who wouldn't stay in for double time'*. Rochford, bowled Smales, 2, and 76 for one has become an overnight 78 for four. *'Smales takes 4 for 12'* is the headline in the Nottingham Evening Post. "Ken was a very intelligent off-spinner," Merv remembers. "He wasn't flat like they are now. Nowadays you can see over the top of the ball; you know where it's going to pitch."

It could be even worse for Gloucestershire for *'Milton had a lucky escape when he put a ball through the hands of forward short leg.'* What are the memories of this miss?

"I dropped Jack Crapp off Bruce Dooland, just before the close," Merv remembers. "It flew upwards, and it didn't quite stick in the palm."

"Merv and I don't agree on this," Ken Smales reveals. "It was Arthur Milton, and it was a dolly. It went through him and hit his stomach. It was off me."

Bomber tells a more vivid story. "Bruce had Milt dropped a couple of times, then he had someone else dropped. Ken got four wickets, Bruce had four dropped."

'Smales might have had five for 12,' the Western Daily Press says.
'Memories are made of this.'

It is Saturday evening. A dance and reception are arranged in Erinoid's club room, and the local MP welcomes the teams. "I remember the food," Bomber says. "It was absolutely superb. But we were never, ever encouraged to dance. I never saw a cricketer on the dance floor." George Emmett and Jack Crapp are captain and senior professional of this Gloucestershire side. They are both forty-three now, they have lost six of their best years to the war, and they carry their ailments with fortitude. George has a gammy knee, Jack a terrible eczema that he conceals under white muslin gloves. "No one dared dance," Bomber remembers, "in case you got the wrath of Jack Crapp down your back." Jack's message is bluntly delivered in his Cornish accent: "If you can get on a dance floor at the end of a day, you haven't been doing your whack in the middle."

"You ate, slept and talked cricket. You watched, you played, you practised. Nothing else ever entered into it."

Drinking is what most county cricketers like to do on a Saturday night. "Gin was popular in those days," Bomber recalls. But not for John Mortimore, who sticks to ginger beer, and not for Bomber the teetotaller with his glass of orange squash. And not for Sam Cook, who loves his pint of ale. Bomber's eyes light up with the memory of the drinking contest at the County Hotel in Taunton. "The last one to stand up was the winner." And who is the winner? "Cooky, of course. I had to take him to the toilet to be sick. Then, when I flushed, we saw his false teeth going down."

On Sunday the golfers of the Notts side spend the day at Stinchcombe, where Merv caddies for Ken. He has nothing better to do, and Ken is his mate. They lodge together in the Nottingham YMCA, playing snooker and table tennis in their idle hours. For Merv this is his first real run of games in the first team and, apart from a century at Oxford, the runs are not coming easily.

Merv is a young man, full of hope, and it is all less nerve-wracking than his debut in 1954. A long day in the field while Peter May scores a double century, followed by two days of heavy rain. Then down to Brentwood for a dashing display by Dickie Dodds and yet more rain. Finally on his eighth day, he comes to the wicket with Eric Hollies on a hat-trick and it takes him 32 balls to get off the mark. 'More will be heard in the future of twenty-one-year-old Mervyn Winfield,' his team-mate Alan Walker writes in the Nottingham Evening Post, and his father pastes the article into his scrapbook of cuttings. Will the second innings at this Erinoid ground be the moment when the cricketing public will hear more?

It is June 1956. BBC Television broadcasts the first series of 'Hancock's Half Hour' while, over on ITV, a couple beats the clock on 'Sunday Night at the London Palladium' to win television's biggest prize yet. One thousand three hundred pounds. Enough to buy two Ford Consuls.

Monday morning brings more cheerful weather, and two thousand of 'the old Stroud people' see Knightley-Smith hit another six before offering a catch off his bat handle to give Ken Smales his fifth wicket. Then *Milton and Mortimore batted wisely, defending stubbornly and waiting for the hittable ball to come along.* Bruce Dooland goes through his full repertoire of tricks, and Arthur edges one into the slips where poor Merv spills the catch. *'Apart from this chance, the partnership prospered in the sunshine and, with a square cut to the boundary, Milton took the total to 150.'*

Arthur Milton is a back foot player with a wonderful eye for a ball. An England football international, a golf handicap of one, even his greyhounds win their races. "Gloucestershire had so many natural players," Bomber reflects. "It was amazing. They had this simple belief. If you were good enough, you played. And if you weren't, you were out on your ear." Arthur is good enough for twenty-six seasons. Here at Stroud he builds a healthy Gloucestershire lead. "Yes, that was a good innings," Merv recalls.

The new ball is taken, the century stand comes up, and the spinners are back in tandem when John Mortimore is caught off Ken Smales for 45. 198 for six, and Ken has taken all six. He has David Smith lbw second ball, and he is down to the tail. And what a tail! "Emmett believed in attacking," Bomber explains, "and you can't attack if you haven't got the bowlers." This is Gloucestershire 1956. There is no question of the bowlers working on their batting, and there is no question of them propping up an end for Arthur Milton. "It was against our union rules to stay around," Bomber says.

Wells, Cook, McHugh. Has there been a worse nine, ten and eleven? Tomorrow evening they will travel up to Sheffield, and Bob Appleyard will mop them up in one of cricket's easiest hat-tricks.

'Wickets started to tumble and Milton burst into activity to get as many runs as he could while there was still time.' Bruce Dooland is the main danger, with his assortment of leg-breaks and googlies, not to mention the flipper that shoots along the ground. Arthur takes care of him, and he leaves the others to cope with Ken Smales' off-spin. "It was the best I'd seen Bruce bowl," Bomber recalls. "He bowled beautifully." Ken remembers differently. "The pitch was too slow for Bruce. It was more suitable for finger spinners." Bomber's innings lasts three balls: dot, four, lbw. "I was shot out. I must have been about four yards down the pitch. I had an almighty swing at it, and that was it." "Bomber four yards down the pitch!" Ken laughs. "His footwork was never that good."

Sam Cook steps out to bat. With his weather-beaten face and his country gait, he is a distinctive figure in this Gloucestershire side. How strange to think that in later years, when the factory extension covers this field, he will be a machine fitter, walking in a white coat about the building, his cricketing celebrity buried in memory. Today he survives the last ball of Ken Smales' over, but, when he again takes strike, the third ball of Ken's next over, he chips back a return catch. Gloucestershire are 206 for nine, and Ken has taken all nine. Only Frank McHugh stands between him and the first ten-wicket haul for a Notts bowler since 1845.

Six days ago at Gravesend Ken needed four to win off the last ball, and he muffed his chance of glory. Forty years on he has no memory of the game. Here at Stroud there is even greater glory within his grasp. Frank McHugh plays out three balls with no difficulty, and Arthur Milton cracks two fours off Bruce Dooland. But Arthur fails to retain the strike, and Ken has a whole over to bowl at the number eleven.

Frank McHugh. How does Bomber remember his batting? "Disastrous. He couldn't hit the ball off the square." 111 innings, 179 runs. But he survives the first ball of the over, and he survives the second. Perhaps it is not going to happen after all. "Go round the wicket," Arthur suggests. "That's the best way to get him." And the very next ball breaches Frank's ungainly defence and knocks back the stumps. "You could just see it happening," Bomber recalls. "As the wickets went down, you knew it was going to be his day." From that first dribbling played-on by George Emmett through Merv's dropped catches to this final round-the-wicket dismissal of Frank McHugh, everything has gone Ken's way. "He was such a grand fellow," Merv remembers. "Everybody was delighted for him."

Ten for 66. They are the same as Arthur Mailey's figures at Cheltenham in 1921, and Arthur's autobiography is called '10 for 66 and all that'. Ken will never write an autobiography, only a history of Nottingham Forest Football Club, but he is in line for the £100 award for the best bowling of 1956. "I know a bookie in Hucknall," Freddie Stocks tells him later. "He'll give you thirty-three to one on somebody beating it. Why don't you cover yourself with a three pound bet?"

Ten wickets in an innings. In forty English summers since 1956, it has been done just four times, yet it is done four times in this one wet summer. Jim Laker has already taken ten for 88 for Surrey against the Australians, but Tony Lock will beat both Jim and Ken with ten for 54 at Blackheath, only for Jim to take ten for 53 in that never-to-be-forgotten Test at Old Trafford. Nineteen out of twenty wickets in one match, and a Test match against Australia at that. Surely this is one record that will never be broken.

Jim Laker drives home at the end of it all, and he stops for a sandwich and a bottle of beer near Lichfield. He sits unrecognised in the corner of a bar while the regulars talk about his nineteen wickets. "Going far?" the landlord asks him with a bored politeness, then returns to the main conversation. "It was a transport caff," Bomber says. "Jim told me personally. We all lived in transport caffs on our away matches. So cheap and reasonable and plenty of it. He was sat at a table with these two drivers, and they were watching the wickets on the television news. 'Go on, Jim,' they were shouting. No one gave him a second look."

Pub or transport café, it is Jim who picks up the season's bowling prize while Ken collects ninety-nine pounds from the bookmaker at Hucknall. He is not as successful as Colin Ingleby-Mackenzie in 1958. Colin hits a fast century in May and lays down twenty-five pounds on its being beaten. Then in June he beats it himself and collects two lots of a hundred pounds.

Here at Stroud Gloucestershire have a first innings lead of 92, but Reg Simpson soon clears the arrears with 'easily the best innings of the match'. Frank McHugh has a long spell from the changing hut end. "He was a big, handsome lad," Bomber recalls. "Very tall. Black hair. Strolled around as if he owned the place. The girls used to fall over backwards." He bowls fast cutters, but nothing seems that fast when you bowl at Reg Simpson. "He was the best player of fast bowling there's been," Merv says. "Probably ever. He just used to have so much time." Only a month earlier Reg has faced the lightning-quick Frank Tyson on a green wicket at Northampton. He is struck near the heart by a lifting ball but he barely flinches, and he makes 150 before tea. "The best innings I've ever seen. He hardly played and missed." He takes off his shirt to reveal a massive weal. Here at

Stroud, *'Simpson made some grand square cuts and also drove powerfully.'* John Mortimore bowls Giles, and Merv joins his captain. It is soon 111 for one on the Stroud scoreboard, Simpson 70, and Notts are back in the match with a lead of 19.

Reg Simpson is not a man of many words at the wicket. He lets his batting do the talking, and Merv still remembers with pride the one time he outscores his captain, against the great Surrey attack. "Well played," Reg says, and the rarity of his praise makes it all the more special in Merv's memory. On this Monday evening at Stroud Reg is at his imperious best. *'Then Simpson was caught in the slips by Emmett, who held the ball at the second attempt.'* 111 for two.

It is June 1956. Teddy boys fight in a Paddington cinema, and housewives are warned not to be 'lured into overspending' in the new self-service shops.

Frank McHugh bowls to Cyril Poole. He is not the Lord Mayor of Nottingham today as his stumps go cartwheeling back for a duck. 111 for three. In half an hour the game is transformed. Four more wickets fall, and 111 for one becomes 126 for seven at close of play. Merv plays correctly, but his 24 not out has little chance of turning into a major score with all the main batting blown away. Frank McHugh's late spell nets him five wickets for just nine runs.

Frank McHugh is thirty years old, but he is playing the best cricket of his life. At Sheffield in the next match he will take eleven wickets against the mighty Yorkshire. "He was just coming in to be one of the great bowlers," Bomber recalls. Little does anybody here at Stroud suspect that he is in his last week of county cricket and that his great frame will soon be laid low by tuberculosis.

Bomber and Merv sit in the bar. Perhaps they reminisce about their National Service days at Chilwell, near Nottingham. "We had this commanding officer, Major-General Lee-Cox," Merv tells. "Bomber used to call him Genny. He'd wave the staff car down with the General in it, ask him for leave to play cricket. Then the General would let him into his garden to take some fresh vegetables home." This is Bomber's way through life. "He was a Gloucestershire man, see," Bomber explains. "Basically, he gave me a leave pass for the whole summer."

Bomber and Merv. In four years' time they will be team mates at Nottingham. "I filled the gap between Bruce Dooland and Gary Sobers," Bomber likes to boast. He and Merv will record their highest scores on the same day at Swansea. Merv will bat five hours for 134 while Bomber will hit five sixes in a half-hour 55. At breakfast the next morning a Trent Bridge secretary rings Merv with congratulations. "Oh, thank you," he says with surprise. "I had a little luck, but ..." "No, no," she says. "Your wife's given birth."

'Some grief, some joy.
Memories are made of this.'

Notts are 32 runs ahead with seven wickets down, and only a small crowd gathers for the final day's play. Sam Cook bowls Alan Walker, *'then trouble came for Smales.'* Is he ready as Bomber bowls? *'He played back to a ball from Wells.'* Is he another one misjudging Bomber's length? *'There was a confident appeal, and he was out lbw.'* There is a knack in getting that umpire's finger up, and the good humour of Bomber and Sam here in Gloucestershire wins more lbws in 1956 than the belligerent competitiveness of Tony Lock and Johnny Wardle, great bowlers though they are. 'Coaching manuals issue all sorts of advice to batsmen and bowlers,' Bomber writes in his autobiography, 'but not many of them inform the young cricketer not to annoy the umpire.'

Poor Merv has batted nearly three hours for his 27. '*Winfield had made a valiant attempt to find someone to stop with him to make a recovery.*' Now there is just Eddie Rowe left to keep him company. When Tyson is firing on all cylinders at Northampton, Eddie is deputed to pad up as night watchman. "His knuckles were white, hanging onto the window ledge," Merv recalls. "Bruce scored nought not out in 40 minutes, and Eddie shook him by the hand as he left the field. 'That's the finest innings I've ever seen,' he said."

For lovers of stylish batting, Stroud's first match has not been a memorable one. Seventies by Arthur Milton and Reg Simpson, a cameo by George Emmett, now this dogged effort by Merv. It is a 'sporting wicket', and the rain has made it even more sporting. Is this what the 'old Stroud people, all rough and ready' want to watch? "People were gentler then," Bomber says. "They had time. They'd sit and watch the game and appreciate it. It's like a football crowd now, isn't it?"

Merv consults the computer paper spread across his living room floor. "Second innings. Caught Rochford, bowled McHugh, 27. I think I might have been last man out." Notts are all out for 137. Their last nine wickets have fallen for 26, and Gloucestershire need only 46 to win.

It will be three years before a batsman truly masters this turnip pitch. Warwickshire will be left 318 to win, and Mike Smith will score 182 of them. "I've never seen an innings like it," Arthur Milton recalls. "Mike was a great batsman," Bomber says, "but he was a bit of an on-side Harry, wasn't he?" Bomber is playing for the second eleven, and he meets Sam Cook back in Bristol. "Christ, Cooky, 180's a good score *for a side* at Stroud. What went wrong?" "The ball was wet," Sam replies. "We couldn't grip it properly. We kept having to fetch it out of the brook."

"When Bomber came to Nottingham," Merv tells, "everybody thought he talked a load of rubbish. But he always turned out to be somehow right."

Here in 1956 '*Emmett wasted no time, attacking the bowling in a determined manner.*' Knightley-Smith is caught at the wicket, but '*Emmett ran out to Smales and drove quite furiously to the boundary.*' A two through the covers, a single to square leg and it is all over by one o'clock. Gloucestershire have won by nine wickets. Ken Smales may have the lifelong glory of taking ten wickets in an innings but, like Bruce Dooland at Gravesend, he leaves the ground with no victory to show for his triumph.

"We bowled to take wickets," Bomber says. "Now they'll give you a single to stop you getting any runs. Everything that gets into sport nowadays is defensive-minded." It is not easy to be defensive on wickets like this. "Since the pitches have been covered," Bomber reflects, "players haven't served a proper apprenticeship, have they? That's half the battle." Sam and Bomber may be journeymen in their trades, but they are master craftsmen with the ball, and in this summer of 1956 they take 272 wickets between them. But would there be a place for their skills in the cricket of the nineties? "Limited over cricket," Bomber reflects. "Neville Cardus said to me, it's like trying to play Beethoven on a banjo."

'All in all,' the Stroud Journal declares, 'this was a memorable match and, it is to be hoped, the forerunner of many on this delightful ground.' Within ten years the grass will be concreted over. Now there is not just a factory and its car park but a housing estate, too. Near the site of the old wooden changing hut is David King's house. A name plate hangs by the front door, 'Smales Pitch'. There will be few among the young families around the cul-de-sac who understand the reference. On the other side of the estate, the brook still runs, a gentle stream in a damp valley.

"It all fades away in the memory, doesn't it?" Ken says. "I've had people come up to me and say, 'I was there that day at Trent Bridge when you got ten wickets'."

"It still comes up in quizzes," Merv says. "Who was the Nottinghamshire bowler who took ten wickets in an innings? He'd never have done it if I'd held that catch."

"I could have taken all ten wickets in my debut match," Bomber says. The sun still shines in his memory. "Do you want to hear that story?"

GLOUCESTERSHIRE v NOTTINGHAMSHIRE

Stroud. 9, 11 & 12 June 1956

GLOUCESTERSHIRE WON BY 9 WICKETS

NOTTINGHAMSHIRE

*R.T. Simpson	run out	5	c Emmett b McHugh	70
R.J. Giles	c Rochford b Wells	30	b Mortimore	18
M. Winfield	c Emmett b McHugh	7	c Rochford b McHugh	27
C.J. Poole	c Nicholls b Wells	2	b McHugh	0
F.W. Stocks	b Cook	14	c Milton b McHugh	4
E.J. Martin	lbw b McHugh	24	c Emmett b McHugh	1
B. Dooland	b Mortimore	22	b McHugh	0
A.K. Walker	b Mortimore	1	b Cook	1
K. Smales	not out	8	lbw b Wells	8
A. Jepson	c & b Mortimore	0	run out	1
+E.J. Rowe	c Crapp b Mortimore	1	not out	0
Extras	b 4, lb 1, w 1, nb 2	8	b 5, nb 2	7
		122		**137**

1-12, 2-38, 3-51, 4-57, 5-71, 6-112, 7-112, 8-114, 9-114, 10-122
1-50, 2-111, 3-111, 4-122, 5-123, 6-124, 7-124, 8-127, 9-137, 10-137

McHugh	22	9	27	2	26.2	11	41	6
Smith	7	0	12	0	2	1	8	0
Wells	18	7	27	2	18	4	33	1
Cook	10	2	27	1	22	10	18	1
Mortimore	10.2	5	21	4	12	4	30	1

GLOUCESTERSHIRE

*G.M. Emmett	b Smales	33	not out	31
W. Knightley-Smith	c Rowe b Smales	34	c Giles b Stocks	8
R.B. Nicholls	c & b Smales	15	not out	6
J.F. Crapp	c Winfield b Smales	0		
+P. Rochford	b Smales	2		
C.A. Milton	not out	70		
J.B. Mortimore	c Poole b Smales	45		
D.R. Smith	lbw b Smales	0		
B.D. Wells	lbw b Smales	4		
C. Cook	c & b Smales	0		
F.P. McHugh	b Smales	0		
Extras	b 5, lb 5, nb 1	11	b 1	1
		214	(1 wkt)	**46**

1-45, 2-76, 3-76, 4-78, 5-95, 6-198, 7-200, 8-204, 9-206, 10-214
1-29

Walker	25	8	50	0	3	0	7	0
Jepson	8	3	20	0	2	0	6	0
Dooland	29	13	67	0				
Smales	41.3	20	66	10	4	2	14	0
Stocks					3.4	0	18	1

Umpires: K. McCanlis and L.H. Gray

Roly Jenkins

ROSES IN DECEMBER

Worcestershire v Yorkshire
July 1956
with Martin Horton

Martin Horton played for Worcestershire from 1952 to 1966. A right-hand bat and off-break bowler, he did the double of 1000 runs and 100 wickets in a season twice and was in the Worcestershire side that won the championship in 1964 and 1965. In 1959 he played two Tests for England, and from 1967 to 1984 he was New Zealand's national coach. He remembers a match against Yorkshire from the days before Worcestershire became one of the leading counties.

"You declared at the end of the first day or earlier," Martin recalls. "Unless there was rain. It was absolutely unheard of that you batted into the second day of a three-day match."

Brilliant sunshine beats down on the small Kidderminster ground. A local nursery has decorated the pavilion with flowering plants and wrought-iron work. "There was always a festival atmosphere at Kidderminster," Martin remembers, and the Yorkshire team arrives in town on the same day as Fossett's Circus and Zoo, whose posters advertise Candy, the baby elephant in Max Bygraves' latest film. It is two shillings adult admission to the cricket. In the local department store, a pair of hard-wearing pyjamas are on sale for 19/11.

This is Kidderminster's big match of the season. It is July 1956, and the carpet-making town is under pressure from the government to provide overspill housing for the Birmingham area. With a crowd of three and a half thousand, every seat on the ground is occupied by lunchtime.

Kidderminster is a small club ground. *'One cannot recall the geometrical name for such a ground,'* Tony Goodridge writes in the Manchester Guardian. *'It contains distant lateral boundaries, but the press box is within conversational distance of deep mid-on.'* England and Australia are assembling at Headingley, and among the England team are Peter Richardson, the Worcestershire captain, and Yorkshire's Freddie Trueman. This latter selection 'eased the worries of the Kidderminster committee,' according to the Kidderminster Shuttle. 'After a report by one member who saw the fiery Yorkshireman in action at Lord's, there was talk of building a plank walk across the railway line and tunnelling through the old pavilion so as not to impair his run up.'

Roly Jenkins, Worcestershire's stand-in captain, wins the toss, and he sends out Don Kenyon and Laddie Outschoorn to build a commanding total. Don Kenyon, the man of few words, only he has scored 2000 runs in each of the last six summers. "He was such a good player," Martin says. "If you partnered him, you never had to force the pace." With a first move back and a stance more like a golfer, he plays magnificently through the covers, always across to the ball. At the other end Laddie Outschoorn is quite a contrast, "more of an eccentric player." He rocks back to cut at almost anything, half-volleys even, or he jumps out of the crease to make full-tosses of good length balls. "He got stumped quite a few times but he'd come back with all sorts of excuses."

Ladislaus Outschoorn, born in Colombo, Ceylon. In September 1918, he says, but as with so much of his life nobody is quite sure. He never speaks of his years as a prisoner of war on the Burma Road, but he exercises with his dumb-bells at the start of each day, and he sings away, accompanying himself on the guitar, "the same note ad infinitum". He takes the team to his favourite curry houses. And he writes letters to a big fan club of girls. "I get very lonely," he tells them. "Would you write to me?" He will never marry, but he is forever writing letters.

Bob Appleyard opens the bowling for Yorkshire. His bowling arm whips through so hard that he straps padding to his left thigh. "He was very accurate and just moved it a little bit." Too accurate for Laddie on this hot July morning. He is lbw Appleyard for 10. Bob Appleyard is one of only three bowlers since the war to take 200 wickets in a season and he does it in 1951, his first summer. 'He was established as a match-winner,' Don Mosey writes, 'and thus required to serve no apprenticeship of modesty and humility.' Tuberculosis robs him of two summers, but he returns to be one of the hard men of this Yorkshire team.

Yorkshire try several new-ball bowlers in 1956, and at Kidderminster it is the turn of Peter Broughton. "A big, fair-haired bloke." Don Kenyon drives and pulls him, and he is replaced by Johnny Wardle, another of the hard men. At the Test selectors' meeting the previous weekend the bowling averages show Johnny Wardle at the top with Tony Lock in second place. But Wardle loses his place to Lock, the pitch at Headingley favours spin, and the summer of Laker and Lock begins to capture the popular imagination. Meanwhile Wardle is left to toil on an unresponsive Kidderminster wicket. It is a long hot day, and he bowls 36 overs.

It is July 1956. Kenneth More is Douglas Bader in the film 'Reach For The Sky', and Elvis Presley has hits with 'Heartbreak Hotel' and 'Blue Suede Shoes'.

Bob Broadbent lasts an hour for four runs, *which hardly added much to the general interest of the proceedings'*. Bob Broadbent plays hockey for the county. On his day he can slog like the best of them, but he is often defensive. One game at Bristol he is so slow that a spectator brings a deckchair to the wicket during his innings. Afterwards the Worcester players go for a drink in a local pub, and they hear the Gloucestershire supporters at the bar. "They didn't know we were cricketers," Martin explains. "In those days you didn't wear smart blazers." Two of them join in the supporters' conversation. "We were there. It was awful, wasn't it?" they say. "That fellow Broadbent, how *does* he get his place in the Worcester team?" Bob looks at them daggers from the table, but he cannot say anything. It is 71 for two at lunch.

Don Kenyon eats well, "he liked his food", but the meal is fairly ordinary. "Martin took his own sandwiches for a while," his wife Margaret remembers.

George Dews hits 57, and the score reaches 201 for three at tea, Don past his hundred. Padgett hurts his hand on a difficult chance at extra cover when Don is 60, and Binks and Close combine to put down an easier one at 68. Yorkshire bowlers do not like to see catches dropped. Martin recalls a phenomenal effort one game by Philip Sharpe, jumping high to get his fingertips to a Don Kenyon slash off Freddie Trueman. Philip is the country's best slip, but "Just my bloody luck," Freddie curses. "They haven't caught a thing off me all season." Ray Illingworth recalls the young Mick Cowan apologising for dropping a sharp chance off Johnny Wardle, only to be interrupted with icy bitterness. "It's my own bloody fault for putting you there." *'Appleyard bowled tirelessly and accurately in his own splendidly rhythmic manner, but without the best of luck.'* He is another who does not forgive his fielders easily.

It is July 1956, seven years since Yorkshire's last championship but they have run Surrey close the previous summer, 21 wins out of 28 and still only runners-up. Currently they are fourth in the table. 'There was really an awful lot of talent in that dressing room,' Ray Illingworth writes. 'Sadly there was not a lot of camaraderie.' By contrast, Worcestershire bump along in the lower half of the table. They lie ninth as this match starts, and from '52 to '60 that is as high a position as they will finish. "Wherever we were in the table," Martin recalls, "we always tried our hardest. We were a very happy side."

There are runs galore in the evening session. Dick Richardson hits six fours in a quick 27. They say of the Richardson brothers, the farmers from Hereford, that Peter has five shots and plays three while Dick has six shots and plays eight. "Peter used to odge here and bodge there, but he'd got the ideal temperament. Dick looked good but he got himself out." Dick will join Peter in the England team next summer, and Wisden will say of his 33 that 'he left no doubt as to his promise'. But he will never get a second Test, his game will become even freer, and he will find still more ways of getting out.

It is July 1956. There are no signs of cancer in hamsters fed on tobacco smoke, and a Surrey doctor thinks heavy doses of aspirin cause polio.

Don Kenyon, on 138, edges Appleyard to slip, and this time it is Wardle who drops the catch. Martin joins Don at the wicket, and *'a glorious summer's evening was truly brightened for all save good Yorkshiremen by 130 runs that came at a rate considerably above a run a minute.'* Martin's share is just 34. "Don was so good at keeping the bowling. He'd go outside the off stump and work one away to leg. Or he'd open the face a bit and run one down to third man." Don is not a man of many words. His team-mates are all called 'matey', and he might come down the wicket to say "Cor, can you see that bird in the pavilion, matey?" Perhaps to Martin this evening he says, "Keep getting ones, matey, and I'll get the fours." The Kidderminster Shuttle records, *'He was given a fine ovation when he came in at close of play'*. It is his second double century against Yorkshire, and Worcestershire have 369 for four.

It is a seven o'clock finish, and the players share a drink in the bar. It has been a long hot day for the Yorkshire team, and they are not cheered to hear that

Surrey's Tom Clark has hit 190 at The Oval. Still, the Kidderminster ground is a small one. There will be declarations, and they will be chasing runs for victory on Friday afternoon. A coach pulls up to take the home side back to Worcester: the players, the gate men, the kitchen staff. Laddie's suitcase with his dumb-bells is heaved in, and the cards come out at Martin's table. They travel everywhere together on this coach. "It was good for team spirit, though you could be too close to people when you'd been on the field with them all day."

The players lobby the committee to be allowed to use cars, and late the next summer there is an experiment. They go to Lord's on Tuesday evening, a four-hour journey. "You had to get through High Wycombe, which was terrible in those days." At the ground on Wednesday morning, they are greeted by a news placard, 'County Cricketer Spends Night in Jail'. Bob Broadbent has stopped for a drink and demolished several bollards in West London. It is back to the coach for a few more years.

"We were a very happy side," and the coach adds to the fun. Laddie plays the one note on his guitar, and Martin sits at the card table. In time Jack Flavell and Ron Headley will join the team, and their differences will liven up the Solo Whist group. "That's it," Jack will say, when Ron's ace sets up Martin's king, and Jack will throw the cards out of the window, "I'm not playing again." But of course he does, and it is not the last pack to finish scattered along a roadside. Then there is the trip to Swansea one year. "I suppose you've all got your passports?" Don Kenyon asks, and Jim Standen comes awake. "What? What's this?" "Don't tell me you've forgotten, matey." Jim is a professional footballer, he keeps goal in West Ham's FA Cup winning team of 1964, but for all that he agrees to spend the next twenty miles hidden in the boot with the baggage. "You're all right now," they say, and he emerges, choking and spluttering. It is the mid-sixties before Bristol Street Motors provide three sponsored cars for the senior players.

Back in Worcester, Martin returns home to Margaret. "We never talked cricket at home," she recalls. "I wouldn't know whether he'd scored a hundred or none. I know a couple of the wives went through it ball by ball. We always tried to treat the cricket as a job. There was none of this 'Daddy's a cricketer'. It was just 'Daddy's gone to work'."

Roly Jenkins returns home to Olive, and he spends the evening with his Wisdens, worrying whether to declare. He looks up the Kidderminster game for each season. In 1955, *'the occasional ball kept low on the second day'*. In 1954, *'rain threatened to make the pitch difficult for batsmen on the last day'*. In 1952, *'on a pitch sparsely covered with grass, Surrey's spin bowlers held the key to victory'*. He is a great worrier, a great theorist. "He was the first person I knew who dabbled in the stock market," Margaret recalls. Perhaps he should bat on and push for an innings victory.

Roly Jenkins is a funny man but also a complex man. He is full of witticisms, but he is prone to crises of confidence. "I've seen him take eight wickets and then go straight out to the nets." His name is Roland, but Roly captures his strange crab-like run-up. He always wears his cap as he bowls semi-round-arm, a lovely flight, and he turns the ball both ways prodigiously. He is the great success of the 1948/9 tour of South Africa, but he only plays four more Tests. "He was a very good bowler, but he was temperamentally a bit unsound. He was a real worrier about everything. He used to phone Jim Laker at The Oval and say, 'I've lost my mechanics, Jim, I can't bowl', and Jim would say, 'What do you expect me to do, Roly? I can't see what you're doing wrong from a hundred miles away.'"

There are so many Roly stories. The previous year in Glasgow he bowls an over to the Reverend Jimmy Aitchison, and he beats the bat with all six balls. Leg breaks, googlies, the lot. "They tell me you're a vicar," he says. "With your luck, you'll finish up Archbishop of Canterbury." But later he sits down in the middle of the pitch, tears streaming down his face. "I can't bowl anymore," he wails. He goes home on the train with the twelfth man, and he does not play for a month.

He writes an article for a magazine on spin bowling, and he meets R.W.V. 'Cock' Robins, formerly Middlesex captain and a pillar of the establishment. "That was a very good article you wrote, Jenkins. Who wrote it for you?" "I wrote it myself, sir," Roly replies, and quick as a flash he bounces back, "Who read it for you?" One innings he is run out by R.E.S. Wyatt, another influential figure in the game. "Say something," Roly says with exasperation, "even if it's only goodbye." "I'll see you at lunch, Jenkins," comes the stern reply.

He sits all evening contemplating his decision. "He could never play any game just for fun. He always had to delve into it. I used to play skittles with him. He would still worry about his bowling for nine pins. People would say, 'We've only come for a night out, Roly,' and he'd say 'If you got your hand here and your shoulder there …'" The decision is taken. Worcestershire will bat on.

Next morning another full house gathers. The Yorkshire players arrive at the pavilion. They are smart dressers, not like Worcestershire. "At Worcester we used to go in in coloured shirts," Martin recalls. "I remember Locky saying, 'What the hell's this? A bloody rodeo?'" Johnny Wardle sits in his suit, reading the newspaper and smoking a cigarette. One report has it that the later Yorkshire batsmen are planning a pre-lunch visit to the local pub. "You'd better get changed, Johnny," Roly says as he passes him. "You're still in the field, you know." "Bugger off," Johnny replies. "You're not having me like that." And he continues to read his paper. "I'm not declaring, I'm telling you," Roly insists. "You go and ask the umpires." When the penny drops, the swearing really starts.

It is the only occasion in 1956 when a county bats on after a full first day. 'It is against the best interests of sporting cricket,' Hampshire's Colin Ingleby-Mackenzie writes, 'to go on after your side has totalled 350.' In the coming years some will advocate an enforced declaration at 250 or 300, and there is even a 65-over experiment.

"As luck would have it," Martin laughs, "or maybe it was ill luck, I was facing the first over of the day." Inevitably Johnny Wardle is to bowl it. He marks a longer than usual run, he comes in quicker, and he bangs the ball down almost at his feet. It sails like a tennis ball over the batsman's head. "What's going on here?" Martin thinks. "Is he trying to shock me into something?" But the second ball is identical, and the third. They are not no balls, and umpires rarely call wides. "It was obvious what he was doing. 'We won't let them get any more runs,' he was thinking, 'we'll just bowl maiden overs'." All six balls bounce harmlessly over Martin's head. "Thanks very much, Johnny," his captain Willie Watson says. It is Johnny Wardle's only over, and the game goes on.

71 runs are added in an hour and, when Don is finally out, caught at mid-wicket, Roly declares. The statisticians have a field day. 259 is the highest individual score against Yorkshire this century, still is. It is the highest score ever made on the Kidderminster ground. Don passes 20,000 runs in first-class cricket, and he equals 'Doc' Gibbons' county record of 44 centuries. *I imagine that if groundsman Bert Allcock ever needs a reference,* the Shuttle's sports editor writes, *'he will only have to mention Kenyon's name. Quite a few people commented on the quality of the wicket.'*

It is July 1956. The National Coal Board is considering recruiting immigrant labour to keep up with home demand. And the GPO Midland Region announces that, for the first time, more people hold television licences than radio-only ones.

Worcestershire take the field, half a morning left to bowl. "We'll show these buggers," the Yorkshire batsmen mutter, and they go out determined to smash the ball everywhere. Len Coldwell takes the first over. He is known as Crash because he arrives for a trial the previous summer, having crashed his friend's car on the way up from Devon. He insists on continuing the trial, bowling with his boots full of blood, and he makes enough of an impression to be offered a contract. It is the beginning of twelve years of Flavell and Coldwell. For this match Jack is resting his Achilles tendon and Len shares the new ball with Laddie, who bowls four overs of gentle out-swingers. In 346 first-class games Laddie takes just 33 wickets, but one of them is Ken Taylor. *'Taylor,'* the Guardian records, *'played an impetuous, undisciplined hook shot that would have sent a chill down the spine of all traditional Yorkshire opening batsmen.'* "You didn't hook in Yorkshire cricket," Ken explains. "The bounce was too unpredictable so you didn't hook and you didn't cut." By lunch Yorkshire are two down.

Bob Berry takes over and bowls his flighted slow left arm. He has come down from Lancashire and in time he will become at Derbyshire the first cricketer to win three county caps. He has a terrible stutter. His winter job is to ferry cars for H.A. Saunders Limited, and one day he is hitching back from Somerset with the trade plates. A lorry driver winds down his window. "W-w-w-where you going?" the driver asks, a stutterer himself. "W-w-w-worcester," Bob replies. "B-b-bugger off," the driver shouts and drives away at speed.

After lunch, the wickets fall thick and fast. Padgett, missed twice in two balls at slip, *'tempted providence once too often and was caught at deep square leg'.* Close *'stepped out to Berry and missed the ball by a foot for an easy stumping'.* At least Worcestershire are a better fielding team than they were in 1951. Roly likes to describe his old cover field: Bob Wyatt, who had turned fifty, Reg Perks who was forty and could not bend down, and Dick Howorth who was forty-two.

"Non-movers, all of them". The county chairman tells the supporters' association that 'today we have a team which is young and virile'. Bob Broadbent, Dick Richardson, George Dews, they all catch well close to the bat. And Roy Booth, the Yorkshire keeper who comes down to Worcester to take over from Hugo Yarnold, dear old Hugo with his leg iron and no kneecaps. This is Roy's first summer. A real fighter with a lovely sense of humour, he fits so well into this 'young and virile' Worcester team.

Yorkshire fight back from 79 for five. Watson and Illingworth add 54, but George Dews takes *'a nice catch low down at slip'* to dismiss Watson. Bob Berry worries the batsmen with his subtle variations of flight, and Illingworth soon runs out of partners as *'the rest just came and went in entirely undistinguished fashion'*. Yorkshire are all out for 163 in just three and a quarter hours. They follow on, 277 runs behind. *'Jenkins,'* declares the Birmingham Post, *'managed the attack with the keen judgement of an old campaigner.'*

It is July 1956. Marilyn Monroe arrives in London with her new husband, Arthur Miller. "One day," she says, "I'd like to play Lady Macbeth."

Roly has good and bad days in the field. He is brilliant off his own bowling but not always in the outfield. One week at Dudley he drops a dolly off Bill Edrich and sees him make 175. Then in the next game there he drops another sitter, this time the Reverend David Sheppard who goes on to 239. "I'm not going close to the wicket," he says, taking himself to the boundary. "The ball looks like a bunch of confetti coming at me."

Don Kenyon's funeral in 1996 is a sombre occasion, full of grief and tears, but at Roly's in 1995 the aisles shake with laughter. "It was the most super funeral I've ever been to," Margaret Horton reflects. "It was so Roly." "We are given memories so that we can have roses in December," is one of his favourite sayings. "He was full of these lovely sayings," Martin recalls. "Of course, they do wear on you if you get the same ones all the time, week after week."

"There was no sitting down and planning how to get everybody out. We'd get on the field and everybody would go automatically to the same places." This Worcestershire team in 1956 is happier to invent little jokes among themselves. They pretend that there is a spot on the square and they circle round it, staring intently, till the batsmen and the umpires are looking, too. "Silly, infantile things, really, but, if you're together for four months, you need that sort of outlet."

Yorkshire *'made an ominously determined start to their second innings'*, according to the Worcestershire handbook. Ken Taylor clips a full-toss from Martin to silly mid-off, but *'Lowson and Wilson went on without further setback in a way that showed that the hardships of the first innings had been both self-inflicted and unnecessary'*. They reach 69 for one at the close, and there is the prospect of some tough cricket on the third day.

It is July 1956. Gas lamp standards are giving way to concrete electric ones, and in Stoke a man chains himself to a lamp post, protesting 'against all the beautiful things in this country being destroyed'.

Yorkshire have largely got over their morning anger. Worcestershire are a happy team, nobody wants to fall out with them. Bob Berry has a repertoire of party tricks in the bar. One of them involves balancing a tray, the outside of a matchbox and a raw egg on top of a pint of beer. He flicks the tray so that only the egg falls into the beer, then he drinks the beer and eats the egg. "He'd delight in showing his gums with bits of egg shell sticking out. Then somebody'd say, 'Bob, I didn't see that', and he'd do it again."

Bob Berry ferries cars in winter. Don Kenyon, 'an astute fellow', works at Dudley Iron and Steel. The Richardsons are farmers. Martin works in the indoor cricket school that the county has created from a disused furniture store. But Roly does not do much. "Why should I give it all to the taxman?" he asks, and he studies the share prices in the newspaper. And Laddie? "He went down to London. He had some job at Smithfield Market. Later on, he'd turn up with a car boot full of packages of meat. 'Do you want to buy some steak?' he'd ask. We never quite knew what he was doing." Somerset's Ken Biddulph knows more. "I used to knock around with him," he says. "You could write a book about what Laddie got up to in the winter."

It is July 1956. Only one household in twelve owns a refrigerator.

Altogether a record 7,500 attend the three days at Kidderminster, and the receipts total a healthy £416. County membership is up by 780 in 1956, and there is enough money for improvements to the Worcester changing rooms. Bar takings at Kidderminster are good, too, and the only blot is the second break-in in three weeks to the club tea room, though nothing of value is taken.

On Friday morning Roly bowls himself in tandem with Martin. "Spin for Roly," he says as he releases the ball. "Spin for Roly." *'Not so long ago,'* the Guardian reflects, *'nothing would have been more certain than a drawn match in such circumstances.'* Wilson swings at Roly and is caught ankle-high in the leg trap by Bob Broadbent. There are no high-fives as Roly celebrates with a clap and a skip, and soon the wickets are tumbling. Lowson shuffles across a straight ball from Martin. Padgett gives Roly a return catch, and Close, having dispersed the field with some hefty blows, a pull for six off Martin, holes out trying to repeat the shot. *'Wardle hit out in a similarly reckless mood before being caught at long on.'* Binks is snapped up by Dick Richardson at short leg, no shin pads or helmets for the crouching fielders. "Dick was brilliant. I wasn't the most accurate spinner, and the ball would fly past his head. He just used to grin." But the Guardian is more positive about Martin's control. *'Jenkins, with his richly rolling gait and air of truculence, tried everything in the way of flight and spin, and the more precise Horton, keeping an extremely tidy length, bowled equally well.'* Martin takes five for 64, and, with Appleyard nursing a septic toe in the pavilion, Yorkshire are all out for 183 at a quarter past one. *'One cannot recall two such inept batting displays from a Yorkshire side as has been seen in this match.'*

"It was always a thrill to beat Yorkshire, particularly after the way Wardle and one or two of them had created. But there wouldn't have been any special celebrations. We had thirty-odd games in a season."

On the radio, Rex Alston, John Arlott and Michael Charlton describe the second day's play at the Test match. Lock and Laker are spinning the Australians out for 143. The rest of the season will show Tony Lock at the top of the bowling averages while Johnny Wardle will slip away to eleventh place.

Seventeen of the nineteen Yorkshire wickets fall to spinners. The pitches are uncovered in the fifties, more games are played on each pitch, and the bowlers get through so many overs that it is easy to hit a length straightaway. Martin's double in 1955 comes from 910 overs and 62 innings. "Finger spinners turned the ball more in those days. We were attacking bowlers so we got our fair share of wickets. Over the last twenty years, because of the advent of one-day cricket, spin bowlers have become flatter and flatter."

Roly's decision to bat on has been vindicated, and Worcestershire climb level with Yorkshire in the championship table, though neither will sustain a challenge to Surrey. Five of this Yorkshire team will have left the county by 1959 when they will bounce back with the first of four titles in five years. But in '64 and '65, they will be displaced by Worcestershire. Flavell and Coldwell will be at their peak, Tom Graveney and Basil D'Oliveira will add class to the batting, Ron Headley will be at short leg, Norman Gifford will be spinning his heart out, and Don Kenyon will preside unflappably over all his mateys. Bob Berry, Bob Broadbent, George Dews, Laddie Outschoorn, they will all have left or retired, but the seeds of this later success are being sown during their years with the county.

Roly will be working in a beans processing factory. "How much do you earn, Jenkins?" a bigwig from London asks him. "I earn three thousand a year, sir." "What, what?" the bigwig splutters. "I earn three thousand but you only pay me one." He takes up umpiring in the local leagues. He is at the bowler's end in the last over of a vital cup match, five runs wanted off four balls and both teams tense with nervous concentration. Roly steps out to stop the game. "Do you realise," he says to the bowler, "you're getting very square on. You need to get your shoulder more round here."

Laddie will be crippled by arthritis, but Martin will see him one last time at the indoor cricket school at Lord's. He hobbles along on his sticks, and he shakes Martin's hand, a twinkle still in his eye. "My hips have gone, my eyes have gone, but my middle wicket is as good as ever."

"It's easy to say we enjoyed it more than they do now," Martin reflects, "but we did." In forty years' time, will today's players look back with the same pleasure? "We're given memories so that we can have roses in December."

WORCESTERSHIRE v YORKSHIRE

Kidderminster. 11, 12 & 13 July 1956

WORCESTERSHIRE WON BY AN INNINGS AND 94 RUNS

WORCESTERSHIRE

D. Kenyon	c Close b Taylor	259
L. Outschoorn	lbw b Appleyard	10
R.G. Broadbent	b Wardle	4
G. Dews	c Binks b Wardle	57
D.W. Richardson	lbw b Appleyard	27
M.J. Horton	b Taylor	43
J. Lister	not out	20
*R.O. Jenkins		
+R. Booth		
L. Coldwell		
R. Berry		
Extras	*b 8, lb 8, nb 4*	20
	(6 wkts, dec)	**440**

1-18, 2-55, 3-172, 4-239, 5-383, 6-440

Broughton	23	1	93	0
Appleyard	34	9	79	2
Wardle	37	13	78	2
Taylor	18.4	5	44	2
Illingworth	18	2	71	0
Close	20	10	55	0

YORKSHIRE

F.A. Lowson	lbw b Coldwell	18	lbw b Horton	47
K. Taylor	c Coldwell b Outschoorn	0	c Jenkins b Horton	28
J.V. Wilson	c Booth b Berry	37	c Broadbent b Jenkins	13
D.E.V. Padgett	c Horton b Jenkins	12	c & b Jenkins	9
*W. Watson	c Dews b Horton	45	c Broadbent b Jenkins	7
D.B. Close	st Booth b Berry	4	c Lister b Horton	41
R. Illingworth	not out	22	b Jenkins	8
J.H. Wardle	c Dews b Berry	8	c Broadbent b Horton	17
+J.G. Binks	b Berry	0	c Richardson b Horton	5
P. Broughton	b Berry	12	not out	5
R. Appleyard	c Booth b Horton	3	absent hurt	0
Extras	*w 2*	2	*b 1, lb 1, w 1*	3
		163		**183**

1-2, 2-32, 3-63, 4-67, 5-79, 6-133, 7-146, 8-146, 9-160, 10-163
1-39, 2-87, 3-91, 4-102, 5-135, 6-153, 7-173, 8-173, 9-183, 10-183

Coldwell	15	4	35	1	9	2	31	0
Outschoorn	4	0	14	1	5	1	11	0
Berry	26	9	49	5	14	8	13	0
Jenkins	7	0	32	1	22	4	61	4
Horton	10	3	31	2	25	11	64	5

Umpires: Harold Elliott and W.T. Jones

110

Tony Lock

HERE COMES THE SUN

Kent v Surrey
July 1958
with John Pretlove

John Pretlove played for Kent from 1955 to 1959. A Cambridge Blue, he was a left-hand batsman, who scored over 1000 runs in 1957. He is now a marketing and public relations consultant within the construction industry. He remembers an exciting game at Blackheath against richer and more successful neighbours.

What a wet summer is 1958! 'Two years ago,' Wisden's editor writes, 'I recorded that 1956 was the wettest season in memory and now I have to state that last summer was even worse.' The touring New Zealanders lose 174 hours of cricket, little more than half of all county games produce a result, and attendances fall by half a million. With damp, uncovered wickets, 1958 is certainly not a summer for making runs, and the final first-class averages show just three batsmen in the forties with Peter May out on his own at 63.74.

It is July 1958, and at Blackheath a Saturday crowd of five thousand gathers for the annual encounter of Kent and Surrey. "It was good cricketing weather," John says. "I remember the ground being pretty hard." It is indeed hard and fast for Surrey's new ball bowlers, but *'rain drenched the pitch in the third over,'* the Times records, *'not only causing a hold-up of two hours but making conditions favourable to A.V. Bedser, Loader, Lock and Laker.'*

Bedser, Loader, Lock, Laker. A bowling line-up that hardly needs favourable conditions, they are together for the first time this summer. Loader, Lock and Laker are regulars in the England Test side while Alec Bedser has missed May and June with pneumonia. Yet still Surrey top the championship table, though their four-point lead over Hampshire suggests that a seventh successive title will involve a tighter contest than their record 94-point victory last summer.

Kent's John Prodger is in his first full season, and he waits anxiously on nought as the rain clears and the pitch dries. For two hours he waits in the cramped pavilion, the building that also serves the neighbouring Blackheath rugby club. "He looked such a good player," John recalls, "but he never seemed to relax. He was such a worrier. All the time that he played it was a test of his gut and his nerves." It is 1.40 when he again takes guard, and it is 2.40, *'amid thunderous cheers'*, when his nought on the scoreboard finally rolls round to two. Then the two increases to four before Tony Lock has him caught in the slips. It is 26 for one, and the time is approaching three o'clock.

On the BBC Light Programme Brian Johnston tries to maintain a sparkle in his voice; he would pass to John Arlott at Gloucester but, alas, it is raining there. How many listeners are re-tuning to the Home Service for 'Hancock's Half Hour'?

Kent versus Surrey at Blackheath. Like Essex, Kent play their cricket all round the county, eight grounds sharing their fourteen championship games. "We had these great Luton vans carting the seating round," John recalls, "but some of the facilities were pretty terrible. The first two years I was at Canterbury, they only had cold showers." The lime tree inside the Canterbury boundary, the rhododendrons in flower at Tunbridge Wells, the sight of the sea at Folkestone, each of the grounds has its special charm, and here at Blackheath they venture deep into urban territory, right to the border of their rich South London neighbours. It is the traditional venue of their meetings, almost a home game for both teams. Back in the Golden Age of Kent cricket, they called Blackheath 'Surrey's graveyard', but the wheel of fortune has turned and for many years now it has been a graveyard for Kent.

It is July 1958, the first week of parking meters in London. Back in 1934, when pedestrian crossings were new, the Blackheath crowd applauded Frank Woolley's 130th century, saw him share a 219-run partnership with the nineteen-year-old Arthur Fagg as Kent scored 414 for a brilliant victory. Twenty-four years have passed since that day, and the Blackheath crowd has seen just one further Kent win over Surrey.

Frank Woolley. There are many in these parts who will tell you that he was the greatest county cricketer ever. Only Jack Hobbs has scored more runs, and even he did not thrill the crowds like Frank. "To see a century by Woolley," Yorkshire's Bill Bowes said, "would keep you going for years." With over two thousand wickets and a thousand catches, a career lasting from Kent's first championship year in 1906 to the tail-end of their glory days in 1938, his tall, erect frame casts a shadow over the humbler efforts of his successors. "The shadow of gloom, old Frank," John recalls. "The whole side was sick and tired of people talking about the great days."

Arthur Fagg, the teenager who has played his early years with Frank, becomes in time the county's senior pro, a gruff no-nonsense man who regularly passes on the Woolley wisdoms. "Never buy a drink at the bar," he says. "Frank Woolley would say to me, 'Never put your hand in your pocket, son.'"

Here in 1958 the runs come a little easier for a while and, when Bob Wilson is caught in the slips for 44, the total has reached 78 for two and the stage is set for Kent's young captain, Colin Cowdrey. He is fresh from a fine century at Trent Bridge, and the crowd perks up in the hope of some attractive strokeplay. Alas, it is not to be. *'One over from Laker had him in such straits that at the end of it he took stance with his bat handle downwards in laughing acknowledgement.'* He manages two scoring shots in 35 minutes before he is caught by Micky Stewart at close short leg. Godfrey Evans fares no better, and it is soon 106 for five.

Godfrey Evans the batsman. Six years ago Tom Crawford, the second eleven captain, offered him odds of twenty to one against his reaching 1500 runs in the summer, and he scored 1613. "You've got to do it again next year," Godfrey says when he collects his winnings. "I'm not made of money," Tom replies, and Godfrey's tally never again reaches even a thousand.

At the beginning of the week Jim Laker and Tony Lock have mesmerised the New Zealand Test team with combined figures of nineteen for 109 in 112 overs. They have been to Swansea where they have taken ten more wickets in 119 overs. Now their week is ending here at Blackheath with another long spell of bowling. *'Prodger, Cowdrey and Evans, fend and wriggle as they might, all succumbed in the end,'* the Sunday Times reports, *'and the truth is that the New Zealanders are not the only ones vulnerable to Lock and Laker in these conditions.'*

It is July 1958. Cyprus is on the brink of Civil War, and the British Embassy is burnt down during an army coup in Iraq. The government sends 300 policemen to Cyprus and 2000 paratroopers to Jordan.

John is joined by Jack Pettiford, the last of the recognised batsmen, and slowly the pitch begins to ease. They survive till the end of the 65th over and the taking of the new ball. Then John hits Loader for three fours in an over, and *'soon the two were hitting with an abandon that bordered on contempt,'* H.A.Pawson writes in The Observer. *'It was some time before the bowlers could bring them back to a proper respect.'* Tony Pawson has been one of the many amateurs to dip in and out of the Kent team in the first years after the war, making his debut at Canterbury in 1946. As he steps out to bat for the first time, he hears a disgruntled voice among the members. "It's ridiculous, the committee allowing untried youngsters to play in Canterbury week."

How the amateurs come and go in those years! And what an unsettled side Kent becomes! Captains change, one even sacked during Canterbury week, team selection loses any thread of consistency, and the county discovers depths to the championship table that they have never previously known. Derek Ufton is Godfrey Evans' deputy through these years, joining the side each time there is a Test match, and he remembers the atmosphere. "Playing away from home, the lads were looking to see what time the train was at tea-time on the second day."

Kent is the county of Lord Harris and Frank Woolley, of Canterbury Week and the Band of Brothers. In Victorian times, you could ride your horse and carriage to the boundary's edge at Canterbury, and Kent still provide space to watch from cars. And in 1958 the Band of Brothers celebrate their centenary, a wandering team that preserves the true amateur spirit of the county. When John arrives, he is invited to join them and he fills out his application form. Six weeks later, there has been no reply. "I filled in the form for the BB," he says, "but I haven't heard a thing." There is an embarrassed pause. "I'm sorry, John, but your father's in trade." He may have been to public school and Cambridge, he may be playing for the county, but there is more to membership of the BB than that. Surely Henry the Fifth at Agincourt was less choosy about his men.

> *'We few, we happy few, we band of brothers;*
> *For he today that sheds his blood with me*
> *Shall be my brother.'*

Never is the atmosphere worse than when John makes his debut at The Oval in 1955. One of three new players joining the team from the Varsity match, he has been taken on by Kent as Assistant Secretary. It is a device several counties have adopted for paying their amateurs. John displaces Alan Dixon, and it does not go down well with the pros. Alan has a wife and three children, and he cannot afford to lose his match fee. John has played for Surrey Second Eleven; "here comes the traitor," the fielders growl when he walks out to bat. A traitor to Surrey, an unwanted amateur to the Kent pros, is it any wonder that the game is lost in the shadows of his memory? Here at Blackheath, he and Jack Pettiford raise the score to 198 for five by close, and the scene is bathed in bright sunshine in his memory.

"Locky was at his sharpest and most aggressive," John recalls. "The bounce suited his extra pace, and every now and then he'd let one go, a yorker into the block hole. I was pretty pleased with myself, and old Jack stuck it out and played some good shots."

'Old Jack' Pettiford. In Wisden his birth is listed as November 1919 but, John recalls, "I think he'd probably forgotten his age by four or five years". He is a tough and solitary man. "I think he'd been engaged once, and the bride-to-be died of an illness." He retreats into his books and his classical music, and he does not appear to mind if people think him anti-social. Other counties have found Australians to transform their fortunes: George Tribe at Northants, Jack Walsh at Leicester, Bruce Dooland at Nottingham. 'Old Jack' is not in their class, but he can match them all in the bar. Down at Taunton last year he was delighted to find Somerset playing three compatriots: Alley, McCool and McMahon. "We're going to have a drink with the lads," he says, and John finds himself swept along. "By the time it reached my round, I'd still got three full glasses." Jack may enjoy his Beethoven symphonies, but "he'd clear saloon bars and hotel lounges quicker than anybody with his Australian language. I loved old Jack, but you really didn't want to get in the way of him when he'd had a few."

It is July 1958. Kenneth More stars in 'A Night To Remember' while on television 'The Black And White Minstrel Show' begins its first series.

On Monday morning John and Jack return to the middle *'on a field patched with sunshine and shadow'*, and John sets about Tony Lock's bowling. "I'd been a bit of a poker and pusher, but I'd changed my style. I took to using a long-handled bat and whacking the ball straight back over the bowler. I remembered what my schoolteacher used to say: 'It's the most undefended area of the ground'." *'Pretlove hit three boundaries in one over by Lock and then was caught on the long-on boundary in his next.'* By lunch Tony Lock has picked up all the remaining wickets, eight in the innings, and Kent are all out for 291.

Colin Cowdrey leads his team into the field after lunch. Dave Halfyard takes the new ball, a big man and a big-hearted man, too. "Old Halfers was an amazing bloke," John remembers. "Never stopped trying, that chap. Went round the whole circuit in those days on a Vespa scooter with his bag tied to the back. And underneath the bag was a hi-fi player." This week's issue of the Kent Messenger brings it to the attention of the Blackheath crowd. *'Dave Halfyard is very keen on making model boats and radios. He has constructed a fine record player, supplied some excellent records for all tastes, and it is a great source of entertainment in the dressing room.'* "We used to go out to field with some very jaunty tune. One of those funny Spanish songs in English, a really lively number that was supposed to perk us up." The England team of 1996 goes out with Winston Churchill's speeches ringing in their ears, but the Kent team of 1958 has a lighter step. "I suppose we were the first to get into psychological training."

Something is stirring here in Kent. A settled team, a cheerful spirit and an unlikely fourth place in the latest table. Colin Cowdrey may be just twenty-five, but his infectious bonhomie is creating a happier atmosphere. "Colin was good at letting the air in," John says. "He got things going. He brought some sunshine."

The sun is out as Surrey's Tom Clark 'showed the way with some splendid strokes'. But he crashes a ball to leg and 'from the stand, it seemed to have disappeared into the white figure of Leary at forward short leg; it was a catch many would have been glad to avoid'. It is 30 for one, 30 for two when Fletcher is run out without facing a ball, and Peter May strides to the wicket. "He always closed the gate after him," John remembers. "It was a sort of psychological thing. He always had these very big pads and he was tall as you know, but when he was walking nearer and nearer I used to think he was getting physically bigger."

Peter May is at the height of his powers in 1958, and his arrival at the wicket can turn any game. "He was the best post-war English batsman by a parish," John says. "He'd start his innings - forward, back, forward, back, in the arc, not trying anything. Then after two or three overs he'd hit it a bit harder off the back foot. Then it was WOOF, all along the ground. The really worrying moment, when you thought 'Oh my god, he's here for a time', was when he played this whack through mid-wicket. It went off like a bloody rocket." 'With sturdy elegance he scored 50 in 80 minutes. Shortly after four o'clock he lost Stewart, but with Constable he took the score to 122 for three at tea.'

Peter May and Bernie Constable. They are very different characters, but they love batting together. Peter is a tall, powerful man, playing classical shots, while Bernie is a small, dapper man, happy to accumulate the singles. "I used to bat a lot with Peter," Bernie recalls. "He used to drive it back so fiercely, you had to be ducking out of the way. They used to come back like rockets." "Bernard," Peter writes, "was one of those unspectacular players on whom most sides rely more than is usually recognised." For Peter, Kent are the opponents he most enjoys meeting: six centuries and an average of 72.94 in his career. But for Bernie, "I didn't get many runs against Kent." And what was it like coming down to play at the little Blackheath ground after the grandeur of The Oval? "Any ground was a good ground for me if I got runs, and I never got any runs at Blackheath." Here in 1958 they add 82 to take the score to 177 for three, Peter 'confident, aggressive and entertaining', Bernie unspectacular and unnoticed. It is half past five when Peter faces Jack Pettiford with one run wanted for another century against Kent.

Jack Pettiford the bowler. Now that dear Doug Wright has retired, he alone carries forward the great Kent tradition of leg-break bowling. The tradition of 'Tich' Freeman, who stood more than a foot shorter than the great Frank Woolley, 'Tich' the only bowler ever to take 300 wickets in one season. The tradition of 'Father' Marriott, the Dulwich schoolmaster who appeared in his summer holidays and took eleven wickets in his only Test match. And the tradition of Doug Wright, the greatest leg-spin bowler England ever produced, according to Don Bradman. Doug Wright, the artist who bowled every ball to take a wicket, the man with 'the Enigma Variations'. He sits here at Blackheath, composing his column for the Kent Messenger. *'There are no flashy or frilly bits attached to Peter May's batting,"* he writes. *"His approach to the game and his attitude at the crease reminds me of Sir Don Bradman.'*

Jack Pettiford may be in the Kent tradition of Freeman, Marriott and Wright, but he is not quite in their class. The golden age of wrist spin has passed now, but Colin Cowdrey is not one to let it go without a fight. As a thirteen-year-old schoolboy, the youngest cricketer ever to play at Lord's, Colin took eight Clifton College wickets with his leg-breaks, and he yearns for the magic of this lost age. Next May the Kent team will start their season at Lord's, and John still remembers Colin's talk to the team: "we've got to bring back the leg-spinner". By half past twelve Old Jack is wheeling away, and he is still bowling at tea time. "We came off," John recalls, "and Jack sat down with a fag and a light ale. We all went, had a shower, had a couple of drinks in the bar, came back, and Jack was still sitting there with his fag and his light ale. He absolutely seized up." It is nine days before Old Jack bowls again. "And this was Colin's great plan."

Here at Blackheath 'Old Jack' bowls once more to Peter May, just one run away from another century against Kent. In the Daily Telegraph, he is *'attempting a hook'* and gives *'an easy catch to square leg'*. In the Times, he is *'trying to sweep'*. To Doug Wright in the Kent Messenger, he is *'trying to push a single. The ball either popped or stopped, and he was caught at short leg'*. Whichever way, he is out for 99. "A very classy innings," John remembers. "Typical PBH." Jack Pettiford and the off-spinner Colin Page set to work, and in half an hour 177 for three becomes 211 all out, a first innings lead of 80 for Kent.

By close of play, John Prodger is out for 21, a brighter knock than his first effort, and Dave Halfyard the night-watchman is negotiating Bedser and Lock. It is 25 for one, a Kent lead of 105, and there is all to play for tomorrow.

It is July 1958. The National Health Service is celebrating its tenth anniversary while Hugh Gaitskell, the Labour Party leader, says that it is his party's policy to provide a grammar school education for all.

All the talk in the cricketing world is of the forthcoming tour of Australia. Peter May is to be the captain, and MCC has just released their short list of 23 players. Cowdrey and Evans from Kent; Laker, Lock and Loader from Surrey. With Johnny Wardle so deadly on the bouncier overseas wickets, will there be room for both Laker and Lock? It was on this ground four years ago that they heard the news that neither of them had been selected, and the twenty-one-year-old Colin Cowdrey recalls passing through their dressing room on his way to the car park. "The atmosphere in there could have been cut into cubes and sold as solid fuel." 'There are a number of shocks in the MCC party for Australia,' he hears on a stranger's car radio, and he loads his cricket bag into his boot and waits for the full news item behind the headline. No Trueman, no Lock, no Laker.

117

These are certainly shocks, but the greatest shock of all comes when he hears his own name. Why, he is yet to score a century in the county championship! It is four years on, and he and Peter May are now the cornerstones of the English batting.

Colin Cowdrey and Peter May. In Australia they will be captain and vice-captain, two charming young gentlemen who are in charge now of their neighbouring county sides. Peter has inherited Stuart Surridge's great Surrey team while Colin strives to bring back the sunshine to a struggling Kent. "Peter gave the appearance of being this lovely, old Carthusian, 'what a smashing bloke'," John reflects, "but he was gruesomely hard, much harder than Colin. He hated losing." In truth Peter has had little experience of losing: not for Cambridge, where the team bristled with Test players in the making, not for Surrey or England. Poor Colin by contrast has had three years at Oxford without a single victory and now he has inherited this Kent side from Doug Wright.

"Dear old Doug," John sighs. "I see him sitting there, thinking 'we're off the field, thank God for that, I hope the batsmen don't make a cock of it'. A wicket would fall, and you'd get your bat and gloves and off you'd go. There was never any 'I don't want you getting out till close of play.' He just used to look up and say 'Good luck'. Colin tried to keep it light, but he got people focused. And of course he brought in Les Ames as manager." Les is the great wicket-keeper-batsman from the days of Frank Woolley and 'Tich' Freeman, and his partnership with Colin builds a bridge from one golden age to another - though, in 1958, the names of Knott and Underwood, Luckhurst and Denness, Asif and Shepherd are still locked up in the future.

"I think Colin's captaincy was at its best in those early years," John says. "He had so many ideas." By the mid-sixties, he will be infected with the democracy of the age. "In the end he's asking the twelfth man, the groundsman and the colts, 'What do you think? Shall I bat or bowl?'." Still, it works in 1970 when he drags the side from bottom place at the end of June to their first title since 1913, their triumph sealed at the Oval headquarters of a now-less-mighty Surrey. Edward Heath, who has won the General Election against similar odds, is there to cheer their victory, and back in Kent Frank Woolley's clear blue eyes sparkle with delight. In Frank's long career, Kent's triumphs come in his youth and are never repeated. For Colin, "having survived a number of years in the grey of the tunnel, before the light of the sixties started to open up and bring us all so much fun", the triumphs are the sweeter for coming so late.

It is 1958. It is the year of the first American satellite in space and CND's first Aldermaston march. Debutantes are presented to the Queen for the last time, and the Church of England comes out in favour of family planning.

Dave Halfyard the night-watchman steps out to bat on Tuesday morning, and immediately he is flailing the ball to all corners of the ground: *a furious assault which advanced Kent's score by 48 runs in the first 25 minutes*. It is too good to last, alas, and Tony Lock is soon among the wickets again. With Colin Cowdrey failing again, the Kent tactics switched to *simply sticking it out to reduce Surrey's time at the wicket,* the Times correspondent writes. *'It was a job for a time and motion expert.'* John again contributes valuable runs, 29 to add to his 78 in the first innings. He looks with pleasure at the page in Wisden. "Well, I got 100 runs in the match against them," he says, "and they had their full bowling attack. I might have been a better player than I thought."

Surrey have their full bowling attack, but Alec Bedser is forty now and only just recovered from pneumonia while Peter Loader is nursing a damaged shoulder in the pavilion. It is down to Laker and Lock to work through this Kent batting line-up, and between them they have bowled over 350 overs in the last ten days. Jim's spinning finger is swollen and sore, and he is not in the mood today. "He used to put his fingers in friar's balsam every night," Bernie Constable remembers. "He used to pickle them when they split. The actual joint used to get bigger." Jim is a sensitive man, not raw and combative like Tony Lock. "Jim used to think about it all. Locky didn't think, he just bowled." And if Jim's finger is aching and he is not getting wickets? "He used to come it sometimes when he wanted a rest." Today it seems that he wants a rest, and it is left to Tony Lock and Eric Bedser to take the wickets. Kent all out at lunch for 171, Tony Lock fifteen wickets in the match.

"I don't think you were trying to bowl them out," Peter May will tell Jim back at the Oval, and the fall-out from the remark will last for weeks. The nation will reel from the news that Yorkshire have sacked Johnny Wardle, the Daily Mail will publish long, bitter articles by Wardle, and MCC will withdraw his invitation to tour Australia. Yet all the while, behind the scenes, Jim will be withdrawing his own name, and only an intervention by Denis Compton and a 'forget I ever said anything' from Peter May brings the affair to a conclusion. It is a fortnight before Jim and Peter take the field together again, and Jim is soon among the wickets once more.

Surrey need 252 to win, and they have from ten past two to five o'clock. Hampshire have won in two days at Portsmouth, and Surrey need this victory to stay at the head of the table.

Colin Cowdrey may be an amateur, but there is something more professional about this Kent side now. They may step out to field to the sound of a jaunty Spanish song, but they are starting to gell as a team and focus on their cricket. Yet the combativeness of Surrey and Yorkshire is still not a part of their game, and Derek Ufton winces when he remembers how some of the Kent committee used to speak. "You're playing for Kent. We're nice people, enjoy your game and jolly good turnips." A trip to Yorkshire would provide the starkest of contrasts in approach. "And you'd say, 'Skipper, how come we're so nice and we get beaten in a day and a half?' But it was very difficult to be like Yorkshire if you weren't brought up in that sort of way."

Dave Halfyard takes the ball. "He was what they call a raw cricketer," Bernie Constable recalls. "He bowled the way he bowled, and that was it. Like a bloody farmer he was." Halfers is the greatest trier of them all. "He had one ambition each year," Somerset's Ken Biddulph remembers. "To take a hundred wickets. He didn't care how many overs he bowled or how many runs it cost him as long as he got a hundred. He used to count them all." When Peter Richardson arrives at Kent, he nicknames Halfers The Machine. As Ken Biddulph walks to the crease at Maidstone in 1960, the loudspeaker announces Dave Halfyard's 500th first-class wicket. "He only wants one more," Peter tells Ken. "One more for what?" "For 501." Here at Blackheath the wicket is dusty, better suited to spin, but untiringly he runs in from the Charlton end, over after over. He spent two years on the Surrey Seconds, and he never got a first team game. This is his chance to show them. Micky Stewart's off stump goes back, and Dave Fletcher's follows soon after. It is 54 for two after the first hour, The Machine has taken his season's tally to 76, and Peter May joins Tom Clark at the wicket.

"Hereabouts I must have been getting rather above myself," Peter May writes. "I was experimenting with setting myself up to play a certain shot to the next ball if it was of a reasonable length. If all went well, I was waiting for it. I remember driving Dave Halfyard straight for six as my first scoring stroke." *May got off the mark by hitting his third ball from Halfyard into some tennis courts over mid-off and made 14 in the over.'* He and Tom Clark add 51 in just 25 minutes before Clark, too, is bowled by Dave. 147 to win, seven wickets to fall, and 85 minutes remaining. With Peter May in such imperious form, the time is not a problem, but wickets are falling and Kent are not without their hopes.

Colin Cowdrey has stuck to his seam bowlers for 26 overs, and Surrey are 121 for three. "We've got to bring back the leg-spinner," he will say at the start of next summer, and here he takes his courage into his hands and entrusts the ball to 'Old Jack' Pettiford. Dave Halfyard is still going strong at the other end. "He never liked coming off," John recalls. So 'Old Jack' wheels in, and his first ball slips out of his hand, a leg stump full toss that Peter May swings at. Not at all the ball that Colin had in mind when he turned to spin. Does it land on the pavilion roof? The Band of Brothers marquee? No, it knocks back the leg stump, and *'once again, Kent took a vital wicket and the pendulum swung back to them'.*

Bernie Constable and Eric Bedser both fall to Dave Halfyard, and the score is 148 for six when Tony Lock arrives at the wicket. He has bowled 73 overs and taken fifteen wickets, and now he has to bat with 104 runs still wanted for victory. Little Arthur McIntyre at the other end hits six fours in 14 minutes. *'His favourite shot is the lap,'* Doug Wright writes, *'and he will play this to almost any ball, irrespective of where it drops.'* But he, too, is bowled by Dave Halfyard. Then Tony Lock sets about Old Jack's leg breaks, hitting him for five fours in an over. "They weren't slogs," John remembers. "He had a go at it, got his timing right, and he was away." He sets about Dave Halfyard, too, with another five fours, and he survives a life to Godfrey Evans.

Godfrey is so often there in those Greatest Test Teams of all time, but he would be on nobody's list of Greatest County Keepers. "Godfrey was a genius," his deputy Derek Ufton says, "but he found it difficult to relate to the ordinary county game." Derek tells of the game at Canterbury when he is playing as a specialist batsman, fielding at short leg, while Godfrey spills a couple of chances. He is chattering away cheerfully to everybody, and he asks, "What time are we on television?" "Half past twelve to one," Derek replies, and during that half hour Godfrey takes three superb catches. "It was the way it happened to him in life. Nobody else would have had the opportunities to catch them."

Sussex are looking for a new keeper, and they approach Derek. For ten years he has understudied Godfrey, this is his third offer from another county, but "I don't regret not having left. I wanted to prove that I could get into that Kent side." Sussex put Jim Parks behind the stumps, and within three years he is in the England side. "Derek was certainly a better keeper than Jim," John thinks. "But he stayed loyal to Kent. I don't like the way the loyalty factor has gone out of the modern game."

'Cowdrey bravely kept Pettiford on', and Jim Laker skies his first delivery from Jack for a catch for Godfrey to reduce Surrey to 188 for eight. But Tony Lock brings up his fifty, *'the innings not of a bowler called upon to bat but of a batsman at the top of his form'*. Though there are only two wickets to fall, the runs required are down to 37 in 25 minutes when finally Dave Halfyard ends his marathon spell. He is a heavily-built man with a long run, but he has bowled 22 overs without a break and he has taken his season's tally to 80. Colin Cowdrey at last turns to Colin Page. Colin bowls quickish off-spin, and he clicks the fingers of his left hand as he delivers the ball with his right. "It took me nearly a season as a naïve amateur," John says, "to understand what was going on." Tony Lock adds six more runs, then he tries to force a shorter, faster ball and edges a catch to Godfrey Evans. *'Once again, just as things seemed to be getting out of hand, Kent took the vital wicket.'*

Alec Bedser takes a single off Jack Pettiford, and it is left to Peter Loader to maintain the chase for the last 30 runs. Everybody on the circuit knows how Peter hates the quick stuff - "He was about as brave a batsman," John recalls, "as he was a horror as an opening bowler; he used to whistle off to square leg." - but how will he set about Jack's leg-breaks? In the first innings John has caught him in front of the pavilion, sweeping Colin Page's off-spin, "I remember the great roar of the crowd", but this time *'one leg break from Pettiford was enough for Loader, and a fine match was over.'* John stares in disbelief at the Wisden page. "I could have sworn I caught Loader to win the match. That's a bit of a shaker to the old memory." Kent have won by 29 runs and, while Surrey slip to an unfamiliar second place in the county table, Kent rise to an even more unfamiliar third place. It will be several years before they touch such heights again.

"To win against that Surrey team was unbelievable," John recalls, "but I can't remember anybody saying, 'Come on, we'll have pints, not half pints'." For one thing, there is the small matter of a journey to Worcester to negotiate. Within minutes, Dave Halfyard is on his Vespa, with his bag - "He never let anybody else take it" - and his home-made record player. "You never stopped on those rotten roads, weaving in and out." This is before the building of the motorways. "Later on, he went up a level - from the Vespa to a bubble car." In four years' time, he will set off from Canterbury to Weston-super-Mare in the bubble car, and he will have an accident so bad, will break his leg so terribly, that he will never shake off the limp. His season's tally will come to a halt on 98. "I don't suppose I'll get 'em now," he will grumble as they wheel him into the operating theatre. But he will not give up, and twenty years later at the age of 51 he will still be bowling for Cornwall. Indeed, he will be bowling leg-breaks in Devon cricket at the age of sixty-four, driving around France in a caravanette and still building his model boats and aeroplanes. Only Shackleton, Jackson and Lock take more wickets than him in this summer of 1958.

So who is driving to Worcester? At least Arthur Fagg, Kent's ever-gruff senior pro, has retired now and will not be giving John a lift. "I got suckered on a lift from Maidstone to Worcester once," John remembers. "I hadn't got a lift, and Alan Dixon suggested I go with Arthur. A nice Ford, immaculate inside. Bloody marvellous. We got to Worcester, and I could hear a bit of giggling going on. 'How much do I owe you, Arthur?' I asked. 'Hang on a minute,' he said, and he got hold of all this railway information from the office. He charged me the train fare, and not just the ordinary train fare. As an amateur, I had to pay the first-class ruddy train fare. The boys had stuffed me out of sight."

Kent versus Surrey at Blackheath. It is a fixture rich in history, and this rare post-war Kent triumph will linger in the memory of the five thousand spectators who have found time on this Tuesday afternoon to fill the temporary seating on this little ground. Colin Cowdrey is off to Lord's for the Gentlemen-Players match, and his place is taken in this Kent side by a nineteen-year-old Brian Luckhurst, making his county debut. When Kent next beat Surrey here in 1963, Brian will score his maiden championship century. Then in 1970, Kent will win again. Surrey, nine wickets down, will need twelve runs off just two balls to bring scores level. Pat Pocock will connect beautifully, sending the ball high and hard to the long-off boundary. In the gathering gloom Kent's Asif Iqbal will run forty-five yards, throw out a hand and bring about a sensational victory. It is the defining moment of Kent's title-winning summer, and it is the last ever moment of the long history of Kent versus Surrey at Blackheath. The modern game is fussier about its wickets and facilities, and there is too little room for all the cars to park.

"Everything has got faster and faster," John reflects. "The crowds want instant potted entertainment now." There are twenty thousand people here at Blackheath for the three days of this game, and they have seen an absorbing contest with a thrilling finish. John looks with contentment at the names on the scorecard. "I wouldn't want to replace my five or six years at Kent with anything else. I would sincerely hope that all the people who play county cricket now would have as much fun and make as many good friends as I was lucky enough to, but I'm not so sure they're able to."

Twenty years on, John will find himself playing golf against the Band of Brothers. "We've just been having a discussion," they will say to him. "It's quite ridiculous that you're not a member of the BB." But John is not interested. Life has moved on, and Kent cricket has moved on, too.

"Colin was good at letting the air in," John says. "He got things going. He brought some sunshine." Derek Ufton agrees: "Colin deserves all the accolades."

KENT v SURREY

Blackheath. 12, 14 & 15 July 1958

KENT WON BY 29 RUNS

KENT

R.C. Wilson	c Fletcher b Laker	44	c A.Bedser b Lock	10
J. Prodger	c Stewart b Lock	4	b Lock	21
S.E. Leary	c & b Lock	26	c & b Lock	39
*M.C. Cowdrey	c Stewart b Lock	6	c May b Lock	5
J.F. Pretlove	c Clark b Lock	78	b E.Bedser	29
+T.G. Evans	c Lock b Laker	1	c & b Lock	10
J. Pettiford	c Fletcher b Lock	63	c Stewart b Lock	12
D.J. Halfyard	c Clark b Lock	10	c May b Lock	30
G. Smith	c Fletcher b Lock	26	b E.Bedser	0
A. Brown	lbw b Lock	0	b E.Bedser	8
J.C.T. Page	not out	0	not out	1
Extras	*b 16, lb 16, nb 1*	33	*lb 6*	6
		291		**171**

1-26, 2-78, 3-88, 4-99, 5-106, 6-233, 7-244, 8-284, 9-284, 10-291
1-24, 2-56, 3-73, 4-82, 5-130, 6-144, 7-162, 8-162, 9-170, 10-171

Loader	23	8	54	0				
A.Bedser	18	6	24	0	12	4	35	0
Lock	44.2	16	99	8	29	11	83	7
Laker	38	14	64	2	16	5	35	0
E.Bedser	8	2	17	0	6.5	3	12	3

SURREY

T.H. Clark	c Leary b Brown	20	b Halfyard	50
M.J. Stewart	c Leary b Page	24	b Halfyard	10
D.G.W. Fletcher	run out	0	b Halfyard	10
*P.B.H. May	c Prodger b Pettiford	99	b Pettiford	36
B. Constable	c Cowdrey b Page	38	b Halfyard	10
E.A. Bedser	c Brown b Page	4	c Prodger b Halfyard	12
+A.J. McIntyre	b Page	0	b Halfyard	25
G.A.R. Lock	st Evans b Pettiford	5	c Evans b Page	57
J.C. Laker	b Pettiford	0	c Evans b Pettiford	4
A.V. Bedser	not out	8	not out	3
P.J. Loader	c Pretlove b Page	8	b Pettiford	0
Extras	*lb 5*	5	*b 1, lb 4*	5
		211		**222**

1-30, 2-30, 3-91, 4-177, 5-182, 6-182, 7-191, 8-191, 9-195, 10-211
1-26, 2-54, 3-105, 4-121, 5-129, 6-148, 7-181, 8-188, 9-221, 10-222

Brown	12	4	26	1	8	0	31	0
Halfyard	14	2	48	0	22	3	102	6
Smith	9	4	17	0	5	1	19	0
Page	20.4	6	78	5	1	0	6	1
Pettiford	14	6	37	3	10.3	2	59	3

Umpires: A.E. Pothecary and R.S. Lay

Colin Ingleby-Mackenzie

THE GLORIOUS UNCERTAINTY

Derbyshire v Hampshire
August 1958
with Malcolm Heath, Harold Rhodes & David Green

Malcolm Heath played for Hampshire from 1954 to 1962. A fast-medium bowler, he took 126 wickets in 1958 and was a member of the Hampshire side that won the championship in 1961.

Harold Rhodes first played for Derbyshire as a sixteen-year-old leg-spinner in 1953 against Oxford University, and he returned in 1975 for one game against the same opposition, but his main career fell in the years from 1958 to 1968. A fast bowler, he took 100 wickets in a season three times and appeared for England in two Tests in 1959. His father also played for Derbyshire and, like him, Harold became an umpire when he retired.

David Green played for Derbyshire from 1953 to 1960. A right-hand bat, he played for Cambridge University from 1957 to 1959, captaining the team in his final year. He left cricket to pursue a career in teaching.

They all remember an extraordinary match at Burton-on-Trent.

"You came in on the first day," Malcolm remembers. "You took your tie off, and you stuck it on the peg. And there was this glorious uncertainty of not knowing what was going to happen."

It is August 1958. Derbyshire versus Hampshire. Dour Derbyshire and Happy Hampshire, the phlegmatic Northerners and the cheerful Southerners. They play their cricket differently, but they enjoy their meetings. Derbyshire have won the championship in 1936, and they often finish in the first six. Hampshire have one third and one fifth place to show for 53 years in the competition. Yet a week earlier, with 20 out of 28 games played, it is unfancied Hampshire who sit on top of the table, a lead of 22 points over Surrey. "We almost got the feeling that we might be able to do it," Malcolm recalls. By the start of this game, their lead has shrunk to four points, but they are on a ten-day tour - Burton, Clacton and Eastbourne - and they are keen to rediscover the momentum of their earlier form. *'The championship pennant,'* the Times writes, *'may be lowered from above the Oval pavilion and forwarded to Southampton. Down in the South, the very idea of succeeding to Surrey's title has everyone in a state of high excitement.'*

Happy Hampshire. Colin Ingleby-Mackenzie, a flamboyant Old Etonian, twenty-four years old, is in his first summer as captain, inheriting the side that Desmond Eagar has built up in the last twelve years. With his indefatigable energy Desmond has combined the jobs of Secretary and Captain. "He and Arthur Holt the coach did so much for Hampshire cricket after the war," Malcolm remembers. Like Colin his successor, he is a Southern amateur. "He used to play in a Harlequins cap, but only South of Birmingham."

The summer of 1958 is, in the words of Wisden, *'one of the worst seasons for weather in memory'*. The Glorious Twelfth of grouse shooting falls on the day before the Burton game, and *'in execrable conditions of driving mist on sodden moors'* only two shooting parties venture out in Derbyshire. *'Continuous rain has stunted the heather and killed multitudes of birds,'* and the Duke of Devonshire abandons shooting for the whole season. The Times' weather forecast for Wednesday is for its *'becoming cloudy with occasional drizzle, perhaps some bright periods in the afternoon'*.

Tuesday's game at Portsmouth has gone to the last over, and the Hampshire players start the long journey north to Burton. The Prices from Eastleigh join the party. Millionaires from their bakery business, each year they choose this ten-day tour for their holiday, and they set off in their two Rolls Royces. Malcolm travels with Colin Ingleby-Mackenzie, the inveterate gambler who loves to race his motor up the winding A-roads of pre-motorway England. "What time do you finish serving dinner?" he asks the hotel on the telephone, and, whatever the reply, he assures them, "We'll be there." "I was the only one who would go with him," Malcolm explains.

"Dreadful machine, Malcy," Colin curses. "I've got to get something faster than this." Malcolm sits upright in the passenger seat, and "the old telegraph poles go VROOM, VROOM, VROOM". At East Ilsley, they are going uphill behind a lorry, and Colin gets up close behind it. At the first sight of the petrol station, he rams down the accelerator, swings round the petrol pumps and emerges in front of the lorry. "I've never driven with anyone quite like Colin when he was in form."

It is August 1958. The Litter Act clamps down on the debris left by picnicking motorists while London introduces its first parking meters.

Burton is a town full of breweries, and the air smells of beer and marmite as a good crowd assembles for the town's big match. Stands have been brought down from Derby, deck chairs fill the grass in front of the pavilion, and a beer tent sells Ind Coope. Down the length of the road a long sheet of canvas protects the ground from prying eyes. Burton in 1958 is a town full of bicycles and, when the factory hooters go, the roads are like China. They park their bikes against the railings and stand on the handlebars to peer over the canvas. "That's one of my memories of the ground," David Green recalls. "There were probably as many people peering over the canvas as there were paying customers."

Colin is last into the dressing room in the morning. "And now to the serious business of the day," he says, turning to the racing page of the paper. "There were always twelve of us," Malcolm says, "and we were never quite sure who he was going to leave out." He emerges from the toilet. "I fancy High Fidelity for the 2.30 at Sandown," he says. "Sorry, Vic, it's not your turn today." Vic Cannings is the third seamer, and perhaps by tomorrow afternoon Colin will regret this decision. Under grey skies, he wins the toss and asks Derbyshire's Donald Carr to bat.

In 1958, wickets remain uncovered throughout a match. It is only the ends where the bowlers land their feet that are protected. A pitch can alter dramatically during a game, and a batsman has to learn to play on all kinds of surfaces. "I'd like to see them come back," Harold Rhodes says. "Batsmen play on too many wickets where the ball does nothing. When they get on a wicket that seams or turns, they haven't got the technique. A complete player can play on all kinds of wickets."

"Nowadays," Malcolm says, "the most important thing is to get the hundred overs in. It never seems to be about bowling the other side out. We've got to do something about encouraging spin bowlers, encouraging batsmen to use their feet, and trying to bring in a little skill, see who can play on uncovered wickets and who can't."

That wicket at Burton, does it really support their argument? "A tremendous game of cricket," Malcolm says. "It's stood in people's memories, whereas games today don't." "I've played quite a bit of golf over the years with the Hampshire team," David says, "and they all remember the game at Burton-on-Trent." "You were playing that day, weren't you?" they recall. "And your father was the bloody groundsman."

Jack Green works as full-time groundsman for Ind Coope and Allsopp's Brewery, and each season there is one county match on his square. Walter Goodyear, Derbyshire's groundsman, comes down to advise him on the preparation. "The instructions were always to prepare a green top." At the Oval, the wickets suit the spin of Laker and Lock. In Derbyshire, they suit the seam of Jackson, Gladwin and, in 1958, the young Harold Rhodes. "The classic was Northampton," David tells. "One end was prepared for Frank Tyson, the other for George Tribe. At one end the ball was flying up off a green top; at the other it was turning square." Malcolm remembers differently. "It was a reddy colour, like the bricks. Frank used to moan and groan about it being too slow."

Colin leads the Hampshire team onto the field. Not for him the long pre-match instructions. "Come on, boys," he says, clapping his hands. "I want you to show them. I want some electrical fielding, please pay particular attention to anything in the air, and I want lots of buckets and no fuck-its."

It is the moment of truth for Jack Green, his pitch mown and rolled. "He got very nervous about his wickets," David says. "I wasn't so aware of that then as I am now." In the days before the game, he goes quiet at home and leaves for work each morning at four. It has been a dreadful summer, a groundsman's nightmare, and he watches anxiously the first deliveries.

Charlie Lee and Jim Brailsford open the Derbyshire batting, and Derek Shackleton takes the new ball. Derek Shackleton, the one Northerner in this South Coast side. The immaculate Shack, never a hair out of place, hardly an emotion shown as he bowls and bowls all season. A catch going down in the slips, he just tut-tuts, hitches up his trousers and goes back again to his mark. He is not fast, but he seams and swings the ball, and he hits a length with unnerving accuracy.

Malcolm still recalls the box of six balls they take one day into the Southampton net. Shack takes three of them and, with a short run, he bowls them to knock down first off, then middle, then leg stumps. "Shack, I've seen everything," Malcolm says. "No, you haven't," he replies, he replaces the stumps and, with the other three balls, he knocks down leg, then middle, then off stumps. Malcolm looks on in amazement. "I'm glad I've seen that, Derek," he says.

Thirty years later, in a contest to resolve a rained-off Nat-West tie, Derbyshire's bowlers aim at all three stumps, and they score one hit out of ten. "Shack will bowl till he drops dead," Somerset's Harold Gimblett says, "but he'll drop dead on a length." Eighth in the all-time list of wicket-takers, he is the most economical of them all. 2.01 runs per over in a career of more than 26,000 overs. Every summer for twenty years he takes a hundred wickets, from 1949, when milk is rationed to two pints a week, to 1968, when Carnaby Street is in full swing.

At the end of the first over, Malcolm receives an unblemished ball. Six balls later, Shack tut-tuts. "What the bloody hell have you been doing with this?" Shack is always the first to work out how to bowl on the wicket, and many is the time he says to Malcolm, "What are you trying to do? Use your loaf." But 1958 is proving a good year for Malcolm, and he has 90 wickets at the start of play.

Charlie Lee drives the ball to Colin at mid-off, and the captain's first chance to show electrical fielding ends in three runs to the batsman. "Ee, he's fused," says Shack, still showing his Yorkshire vowels. *'Before the effect of the roller had worn off,'* Denys Rowbotham writes in the Manchester Guardian, *'Shackleton and Heath were making an occasional ball lift just steeply enough to be awkward.'* In the day's seventh over, Lee gives a bat-pad catch to short leg, and Derbyshire are 8 for one.

It is August 1958. At the Radio Show 'high fidelity' stereophonic radiograms are on display. In America the moonshot planned for the weekend is given a one-in-ten chance of success.

It is David's turn to bat. *'The presence of David Green,'* the Burton Daily Mail reports, *'the Cambridge blue and old Burton Grammar School cricketer, will be a matter of great interest to local cricket enthusiasts.'* He is still Jack Green's lad and, as he makes his way to the middle, *'the drizzle that has been falling for some minutes became a heavy downpour.'* "I don't think I even took guard." The forecast is for mainly dry weather, but the downpour persists and, by a quarter to three, play is abandoned for the day. The weather has favoured Hampshire several times during the summer, "but," Colin says sadly as the puddles form, "the old jinx seems to have gone for the moment."

For the Hampshire side, there is a conducted tour of the Ind Coope brewery. "We drank a few Double Diamonds," Malcolm remembers, "thoroughly enjoyed the entente cordiale and went back to the old hotel." For a while they drive the Prices' Rolls Royces round town, waving at the girls they pass. "Rolls are two a penny in London now, but in those days people took a second look." Then in the evening the Prices take them to the cinema. "No expenses spared," Mervyn

Burden jokes, and at the interval they all get bought an ice cream. At least it is not a repeat of the evening at Hove when a restaurateur promises 'everything on the house'. They work through the starters, the a la carte, drinks galore, "a wonderful night", only to be presented with a massive bill.

It is August 1958. The Everly Brothers top the Hit Parade with 'All I Have To Do Is Dream', and Alfred Hitchcock's 'Vertigo' opens in Leicester Square.

'A fresh drying wind' springs up after play is abandoned, and in the morning *'a hot sun beat down mercilessly'*. The Times is forecasting it to be *'mostly dry at first, with some rain later'*. Against all expectations, play starts promptly at eleven. "I fancy Golden Future for the five o'clock at Beverley," Colin announces, and Jack Green once more watches anxiously as his son finally takes guard.

David Green, the amateur. They still introduce him like that at the old players' golf. He is the groundsman's lad, he has grown up with Jim Brailsford and with Harold, but his mother has persuaded him to stay at school and now he is studying History at Cambridge. He cannot afford to play cricket all summer, but in 1958 his university status requires him to be an amateur. At grounds like The Oval and Old Trafford, he changes separately, and he eats grand lunches in the committee rooms. "How was the caviar, Greeny?" Harold jibes. "We had chips." There is no such distinction at Burton, but "I did feel it." Like all the university players coming back to their county sides, he is aware of the professionals who have lost their places. "It was a bit of extra pressure batting that I could have done without." In the season's last game he will run out John Kelly, and everybody knows that the professional needs a big score to retain his contract. "I felt so awful," he says with feeling, almost forty years later. "I can't afford to play cricket this summer," he tells Will Taylor, the county secretary. "I ought to get a job on a farm." "That's all right, David," comes the reply, and, unknown to his team mates, David Green the amateur is paid.

"Plenty of buckets and no fuck-its," Colin exhorts, and Jim Brailsford is caught at slip in Malcolm's first over. David manages a score of 6 before he fences at a lifter and is caught in the leg trap. "Derek was unplayable. He was so accurate, and the ball seamed so much. Most of my runs were edges." Morgan, Hamer and Johnson soon follow, and Derbyshire are 35 for six. Yet the benevolent effect of the heavy roller is only now wearing off. *'Some desperate remedies clearly were necessary.'* The ball *'kicks with vicious spite'*, but Donald Carr, *'with a brave hook or two'*, and George Dawkes, *'with some bold driving and cutting'*, add enough runs to see the final total to 74. Shack and Malcolm have bowled unchanged for 33 overs, and Malcolm has figures of six for 35. Shack is the cab horse, Malcolm the wonder horse. 'Cab' and 'Wonder', Colin calls them. Perhaps the championship is going their way after all.

Derbyshire are a bowling side, though, and they take the field with confidence. "We got 74," Harold explains. "There would definitely be a feeling that they won't get as many as that." Malcolm knows what he means. "On that wicket," he says, "the two people you'd least have wanted to meet were Les Jackson and the young Harold Rhodes."

Shackleton and Heath, now Jackson and Rhodes, what riches of bowling talent! *'The best of the four,'* according to Michael Melford in the Daily Telegraph, *'was the tall, young Rhodes, who dug the ball in from his considerable height and moved it off the pitch either way.'* Later in his career two Chesterfield schoolteachers will time him with stop-watches at 91 miles per hour. "It was a bit Heath Robinson, but that was into the keeper's gloves so it was already slowing down." The young Harold may not bowl at 91 miles per hour, but his speed on this crumbling Burton wicket will be no fun for the batsmen.

Roy Marshall opens the batting with Jimmy Gray. Roy Marshall, the youngest player ever to play first-class cricket in the Caribbean, he has played four Tests for the West Indies and now he has settled on the English South Coast. There are few more exciting cricketing sights in the fifties than his assaults on the opening bowlers. "I'll get at them before they get at me," he says, and his mercurial batting is a key component of Hampshire's new-found success. "I used to lie awake," Somerset's Ken Biddulph tells, "the night before I had to bowl at Roy."

Today he faces up to Les Jackson. Where Shack delivers the ball with an immaculately high arm, Les comes right next to the stumps and brings his arm over in a low slinging action that has the ball leave his hand above the middle stump. Every delivery the seam travels upright through the air, and he pitches it at fast-medium at that awkward length that on Derby's green-topped wickets leaves the batsman in a quandary. "If you played forward," David explains, "you got hit on the knuckles. If you played back, you got hit on the chest. You couldn't win."

Les Jackson is a miner till the age of twenty-seven. One of his brothers was killed in the Whitwell pit disaster, and he knows that long days of bowling are easier than an underground life with pick and shovel. He bowls with niggling groin strains, he bowls with bleeding blisters in his boots, and he never complains. "Les, what's this?" Donald Carr says in the dressing room. "Why didn't you say something?" "It's just a blister," comes the phlegmatic reply. "In my opinion," Freddie Trueman writes, "he was the best six-days-a-week, day-in and day-out paceman in county cricket since the war." In this summer of 1958, he takes 143 wickets at 10.99, the lowest average for 100 wickets this century. Only Harold Rhodes, 11.04 in 1965, has come close. "Aah," they say, "it's all those green wickets they prepare." But 100 of his 143 wickets that summer come outside the county.

Les Jackson is another Shack as he bowls all day without complaint. "He was a lovely chap," David says, "but he did have sworn enemies." One is Dick Spooner, the Warwickshire keeper. On a boat to India, Dick makes a derogatory remark about coal miners, and story has it that Les picked him up and cursed him as he held him over the side of the boat.

For eleven years he has led the attack with Cliff Gladwin. For this Burton match Cliff has a stomach upset, and Harold, who is playing his first full season as third seamer, takes the new ball. Jackson and Gladwin, they are a mean machine, but there the similarity ends. Les takes it all quietly while Cliff throws his weight about as senior pro. "We were all scared of Cliff," David says, and he still recalls the rollockings. The time he tries to execute a run out by kicking the ball. "You bloody fool, that's the new ball." Or the time he does not walk in a Sunday match. "Now look here, son, we don't play our cricket like that in Derbyshire."

Not even Donald Carr the captain is spared Cliff's strong-minded views, as he discovers when he tries to declare one day. "You can't declare now, skipper," Cliff argues. "You'll give it away. Les and I don't bowl all day to throw games away like this." But Donald is unmoved. "No, I think I'll do it. I'll go to the loo and, when I come out, I'll call them in." So Cliff wedges a chair against the loo door, "I'm sorry, skip, one of the bags has dropped down. We're having a job pulling it away." It is nearly quarter of an hour before the declaration comes.

Dour Derbyshire. For Les and Cliff, every run scored is resented. And Cliff counts them all, too. He knows the grip for every delivery he has bowled and what has come of it. In Harold's debut match, Donald Carr brings him the morning's bowling figures. "Cliff is the senior pro," Harold protests. "Shouldn't he see them first?" "Oh, no, he knows." "Bowling is a percentage game," Cliff always says. "It's no good going for four, five, six an over, you'll not win many for your side like that. But two or three, you've got a chance. Keep 'em quiet, and at some stage they're going to take risks." This is the Derbyshire philosophy. At the end of their careers, Les will have conceded 2.17 runs an over, Cliff 2.24 and Harold 2.28. Not as good as Shack, but Freddie Trueman will stand at 2.58. They are not the easiest of bowlers for Roy Marshall to get at.

'The heavy roller scarcely seemed to produce any soothing influence,' Denys Rowbotham writes,' for four balls in Jackson's first two overs rose nastily enough to make Hampshire's plight only too plain. Then Marshall tried to force an out-swinger pitched barely short.' George Dawkes, the Derbyshire keeper, flings himself 'flat to his right to hold the ball inches above the ground'. It is 'a superb diving catch', and with just 4 runs on the board Derbyshire have got the wicket they most want.

Exit Roy Marshall, enter Henry Horton. It is a moment of great disappointment for all those looking for entertainment. Ken Biddulph still recalls the only time he captured Roy for a duck. "I was like a cat with ten tails. I'd got Roy Marshall out for nothing." Fielding at third man, he hears the click of the turnstile behind him. "I say, Marshall's out," comes an indignant, upper-class voice. "I've come all the way from Southampton to see Marshall bat, and some silly bugger's got him out." Henry Horton, a big, hard man. A centre half at Southampton in the days when the mud is thick and the ball a heavy lump of leather, he is as strong as an ox. A tiny backlift, bat and pad almost glued together, he is not the prettiest of sights, but "dear old Henry had the right attitude," Malcolm says. "I'm out there for Hampshire." He never flinches as the ball rears off a length. Roy Marshall will score thirty-five thousand runs, Henry just twenty-one thousand, but "I'd love to see who spent longer at the wicket."

131

Derbyshire, all out 74, but *'Hampshire's elation soon turned to disappointment,'* the Times writes, *'as their batsmen fell like leaves in an autumn bluster.'* *'Where Shackleton and Heath at medium-fast had succeeded on this difficult wicket,'* Denys Rowbotham writes, *'it was not likely that Jackson and Rhodes at fast-medium pace would fail. They found the right length at once, and scarcely once did they lapse from it.'* Gray, Pitman and Barnard fail, and it is 12 for four when Colin Ingleby-Mackenzie comes to the crease. He has recorded the season's fastest century against Kent in 98 minutes, then beaten it with one in 61 minutes against Somerset. But his swashbuckling style is not at home on *'this brutish wicket'*. Three times Harold raps him on the knuckles, and the third time, as the ball falls harmlessly to ground, he cries out in anguish, "For God's sake, somebody, catch it." He retires for repairs and, by the time he returns, Les Jackson has yorked Henry Horton. "I always thought I couldn't play," Henry says wearily as he throws his bat onto his bag. "Now I know I can't." Lunch is taken at 17 for five. "It was very quiet," Malcolm recalls. "There wasn't much said."

It is August 1958. At Highclere Castle Prince Philip scores 33 in a charity match while at Lord's Clifton College's victory over Tonbridge School is not enhanced by a score of nought by J.M.Cleese.

'The watcher could, with a stretch of imagination,' Michael Melford writes in The Daily Telegraph, *'have pictured himself standing up to Shackleton and Heath this morning. Nobody without a suit of armour could have been other than appalled by the thought of facing Jackson and Rhodes.'* "The top went," Harold explains. "Once the top has gone, it's difficult to put it back down. Once it's unstable, the ball will come off at varying heights. With the greater pace of Les and myself, that was the vital difference." It is *'a drying wicket of devilish behaviour'* in the Times, it has a *'brutish waywardness'* in the Manchester Guardian, and Michael Melford judges it *'as unpleasant as anything I remember since Trueman and Cowan massacred Surrey one evening at Headingley a few years ago'*.

It is August 1958. Southern Television, describing itself as 'the first truly local television station in Britain', is all set to go on the air on the 30th. – in time for Hampshire's last fixture, the return game against Derbyshire. Will they film celebrations as the championship pennant is hoisted above the pavilion? *'Only trouble is,'* the Everly Brothers sing, *'Gee wizz, I'm dreaming my life away.'*

'The resumption proved even greater thrills, and in less than twenty minutes Hampshire were all out for 23.' There are more heads than ever peering over the canvas as word spreads about the brewery town. Colin slashes a catch into the gully, and the last four wickets fall on the same score. "I was glad to get out," Malcolm confides. "I remember somebody came back into the dressing room, and he said, 'The first one just missed my ear, the second one went past my toe, the third one I heard a lovely rattle.'" Les Jackson finishes with five for 10 in 8.4 overs. "Les was the quickest bowler off the wicket that I ever saw," Malcolm says. "I'd hear this 'Well, bowled, Les,' and I'd still be halfway through the forward defensive." *'In their first innings,'* the Daily Mirror tells, *'Hampshire were shot*

out for 23. And the men who did it were pace bowler Les Jackson and spinner Harold Rhodes.'

Hampshire are the championship leaders, and their 23 is the lowest total since the war, the lowest total ever against Derbyshire. It will be twenty-five years before Surrey beat it, all out for 14 at Chelmsford. But Surrey will save that game with good second innings batting. For Derbyshire and Hampshire at Burton in 1958, the batting ordeal is not over. Hampshire's innings has lasted less than 17 overs, and by a quarter past two Shack and Malcolm are back in action. 'Cab' and 'Wonder', they set to work again, and Derbyshire are soon 40 for four.

Eight for one overnight, 40 for four now. How many of the heads that appear above the canvas will assume that the start has been slightly delayed, that Morgan and Carr are building a first innings score? "Second innings," they repeat with disbelief. The smell of beer and marmite hangs in the air, and the crowd looks on in amazement. This is history in the making.

The afternoon's racing has begun. "Colin was no mug, he was a very astute captain, but we never really felt he was 100% with us after two o'clock." In the next game at Clacton, he lands a winning treble, and the messages run by the twelfth man provide a nice story for The Daily Express. 'Colin's Hat-Trick' is the headline, and it leads to a roasting from one of the county's vice-chairmen. Today at Burton, is the cricket dramatic enough to hold his full attention?

Jim Brailsford attempts to drive Malcolm, and he is caught for 14. He will have just three chances to secure a spot in the Derbyshire batting line-up, and this will be his highest score. Perhaps on a better wicket he might have made a century. Perhaps he might then have made a career in cricket. Instead, he demands a pay rise of two pounds from the secretary and, when he is refused, he joins his brother's business in Chesterfield, hiring plant to the National Coal Board. In time he will become a millionaire. "He had a Rolls Royce," Harold tells. "He had an aeroplane. He had all sorts." Then the pits begin to close.

David Green is caught off a ball that jumps up at his gloves, and he sits for a while with his father on the edge of the sight screen. "He was almost in tears." At least for a while before tea, they can settle to watch a partnership develop. Derek Morgan and Donald Carr. "Derek was very quiet," Harold remembers, "but what a fine cricketer! You look at the likes of people who play for England today, and he never smelt a chance." *'Their experience in knowing what to play and what to leave alone was a big factor in their favour.'* "It was about four o'clock in the afternoon," Malcolm remembers. "I was tiring, and I heard Derek say to Donald, 'Skipper, I think the wicket's easing out a little bit now.' The very next ball, Shack comes up, with his immaculate action, Derek plays a textbook back-foot defensive shot, and the ball hits him right in the middle of the forehead." Amazingly, it is the only time a batsman is hit on the head, and it is off Shack, the slowest of the four main bowlers.

"Derek was a gutsy player," Harold says. "He always got runs against fast bowlers. And the pitch wasn't unbattable. It was a matter of getting stuck in and grinding, waiting for the bad ball." Derek's 46 is twice the Hampshire first innings total.

The bowler's run-ups are marked out with sawdust. "I was so busy running up, looking at the dotted line," Ken Biddulph recalls, "I used to go cross-eyed." "No, I don't think I had that problem," Malcolm says. But they all say of Malcolm that he could have been a nastier bowler if he had had the killer instinct of, say, Freddie Trueman. "I would have loved Fred's attitude, but I was very safety-conscious, you know. I still am. I always felt that cricket was a game to be enjoyed."

It is a long day, and Hampshire's third seamer, Vic Cannings, is on twelfth man duties. Colin may have his money on a Golden Future at Beverley, but for now his bowlers have twenty-two yards of crumbling Derbyshire earth to master. There is no change of bowling, and the batsmen start to profit from the occasional loose delivery. "I was weary," Malcolm reflects. "I wasn't getting the lift. I don't suppose I was following through anymore." Finally he traps Donald Carr l.b.w., his hundredth wicket of the season, and Shack has Derek Morgan caught at mid-wicket. Their stand of 54 is more than half the final total of 107 as *'hereafter the procession started all over again'*. Malcolm the Wonder Horse bowls Dawkes and Smith, and he has Harold caught in the leg trap by Peter Sainsbury. "Peter," Malcolm remembers. "He was the best all-round fielder I've ever seen. When he was a boy, his grandparents took him to Beale's in Bournemouth. 'What would you like, Peter?' they asked. It was a great big department store, and do you know what he said? 'I'd like a ball.' That's all he ever wanted."

Hampshire require 159 to win - or ninety minutes tonight to survive, in the hope that tomorrow will be another day. Even the forecasted rain fails to materialise as they face the prospect of another battle on a wicket long past help from the heavy roller. "159," Harold reflects. "That was a mountain to climb."

Malcolm and Shack have bowled 31 overs each by a quarter past five, and their only break is for the catastrophe of the Hampshire first innings. Malcolm has match figures of thirteen for 87. They will remain the best figures of his career, but will he remember them as part of a glorious victory or as a side show in a day of disaster? It is down to Hampshire's batting to provide the answer, and Colin tries to raise the spirits. "Come on, boys. We can still win this. You can show them, Roy." "Colin could never care less what other people were doing," Malcolm remembers. "It was what we were doing that always concerned him."

Once more it is Les Jackson to bowl to Roy Marshall. All round the circuit they talk about Les. What is his secret? "When Jacko has his fingers together," Yorkshire's Brian Close reckons, "the ball cuts back at you. When he has his fingers apart, it cuts away." Ken Biddulph reckons to have observed the same. But it is not what Harold says. "He held it the same for every ball." "I don't know what happens to the ball," Les says. "It's in the lap of the gods what it does up there. If I don't know, they don't know." George Dawkes behind the stumps never believes him: "Les knows what he's doing," he says. But, if he does, he never lets on. "It's how the seam hits the ground," Harold thinks. "I can't do it as I want to,

I wish I could. Anybody who does is kidding themselves, unless they're spinning it or cutting it." And the great Freddie Trueman? "He's a lovely chap," Harold says, "but the way he talks now, you'd think he never bowled a ball that went straight on in his life."

It is August 1958. A Burton headmaster calls for parents to ration their children's television viewing.

'Hampshire needed 159 to win,' Michael Melford writes, 'but it might just as well have been 1000 once Marshall had been lbw first ball. Jackson brought one back off the pitch at a normal height when Marshall had been expecting it to lift.' Poor Roy, his 2118 runs is the third highest aggregate of 1958, but just nine of them come in his four innings against Derbyshire. Henry Horton's defences are breached for a duck, and Jimmy Gray scores just one single to add to his pre-lunch nought. Les's precious new ball has taken the heart out of the Hampshire innings. Harold recalls the day at Wellingborough when Frank Tyson pitches his first delivery halfway down the track, and it rises and rises till it strikes the sight screen. "Just look at that," he says with wonder, and Les sits unimpressed beside him. "What a waste of a new ball!"

Hampshire are 13 for three. The factory hooter goes, and new heads appear along the canvas. "How many did we make?" some ask, and they gasp at the news that this is the fourth innings. "And I were planning on coming tomorrow," someone mutters.

Les Jackson has two Tests to show for sixteen summers of bowling, one in 1949 and one in 1961. When the 1950 tour party to Australia comes on the radio and the Cambridge University amateur John Warr clinches a place ahead of Les, there is a stunned silence among the Derbyshire players. But Les downs his pint of beer, and he never complains. He has known the coal dust, the bent back as he hacks the face with a pick, and he knows that this life of sunshine and hotels is better. He will go back to the Coal Board when he retires, but this time he will stay above ground, chauffeuring the top brass in comfortable cars.

At twenty-five to seven, the unthinkable happens. Hampshire are 40 for five, and Donald Carr makes a bowling change, the first of the day. "I was tired, to be honest," Harold says. "It was my first season. It was the mental strain of having played in four innings in a day. Many's the time I've bowled more overs." He has match figures of seven for 41 in 17 overs, and it is enough to see him presented with his county cap at the end of play.

Derek Morgan is Derbyshire's third seamer. How Hampshire would have welcomed him into their attack at three o'clock. With the extra half hour claimed, he takes three wickets, and the game is all over by a quarter past seven. Thirty-nine wickets have fallen in less than seven hours, the most in a day this century, and Hampshire have lost by 103 runs. The championship leaders have been dismissed for 23 and 55. An acute case of vertigo? "We were very despondent," Malcolm admits. "It was a desperately sad day. If we'd won that, who knows what? But what a wonderful game of cricket it was!" Malcolm has taken thirteen wickets in a day, not many have done that. It is the greatest performance of his career. "Were you there that day at Burton?" people will ask him over the years, and sometimes his eyes will glaze over. "Yes, I think I was," he will say vaguely.

"Racing tomorrow at Newbury, Malcy," Colin says wearily. "Shall we pop in on our way to Clacton?" 'Newbury,' Malcolm thinks. 'Will that mean another dash through the petrol station on East Ilsley Hill?'.

"I remember," David Green says, "there were a hell of a lot of people in the beer tent after the game. There was tremendous discussion about the proceedings. You couldn't wish to play in a more memorable game."

"Since then," Colin writes, "I have always thought of this disastrous match when I have drunk Ind Coope's beer, and a Double Diamond always seems rather bitter to me." Forty years later he will be President of the M.C.C., and "he hasn't altered," Malcolm says. "He still gets on well with everyone."

By the return game at Bournemouth, Hampshire's championship challenge will have slipped away. David Green will run out John Kelly, Les Jackson will take eleven for 65 in 43 overs (and not on a Derby green top), and at the end of the second day Derbyshire will need just ten runs with five wickets in hand. The teams enjoy the hospitality of the Yacht Club tent and in the autumnal dark they walk back across the square. On the dusty, uncovered wicket, they stand in a line and they all have a pee. "County cricket," the young Harold thinks, "this is the life for me. I always remember that." After a pause, he continues. "Mind you, I don't know what would have been said if we'd all been bowled out the next morning."

In three years' time, another autumnal game at Bournemouth, Hampshire will again be pressing for the championship, and Derbyshire will once more stand in their way. It will be Harold's father who raises the umpire's finger when Henry Horton is lbw to him, and the crowd will be calling out, "How's that, Dad?" for the rest of the day. Then Harold will be batting for the draw on the final evening, another marathon bowling stint from Shack to survive. "Your lad's going to stop us winning the championship," Colin says to Harold's dad. "He isn't, you know," comes the reply, a twinkle in his eye, and he doesn't. The unthinkable happens, and happy Hampshire pip mighty Yorkshire to win their first ever title. The newspapers talk of Colin's 'wine, women and song' approach. Certainly it is not Double Diamond that they drink as the celebrations last into the night. "All I ask," he tells one reporter, "is that my players are in bed before breakfast."

"We were always good friends with Hampshire," Harold remembers. "They played the game the right way."

"When you walked in to bat in those days," David recalls, "everybody was totally friendly. You actually felt at home. It was a pleasant environment, how the game should be played."

But uncovered wickets? Would more days like this one at Burton-on-Trent really improve our national game?

"I still maintain that it was a golden age," Malcolm reflects. "A game like that, people never forget it."

DERBYSHIRE v HAMPSHIRE

Burton. 13, 14 August 1958

DERBYSHIRE WON BY 103 RUNS

DERBYSHIRE

C. Lee	c Horton b Shackleton	8	c Horton b Heath		6
F.C.Brailsford	c Barnard b Heath	4	c Horton b Heath		14
D.J. Green	c Sainsbury b Heath	6	c Barnard b Shackleton		4
A. Hamer	c Pitman b Heath	5	c & b Heath		7
D.C. Morgan	c Horton b Shackleton	3	c Marshall b Shackleton		46
*D.B. Carr	c Burden b Heath	12	lbw b Heath		19
H.L. Johnson	c Harrison b Heath	4	c & b Shackleton		6
+G.O. Dawkes	c Burden b Heath	19	b Heath		0
H.J. Rhodes	b Shackleton	0	c Sainsbury b Heath		2
E. Smith	not out	6	b Heath		0
H.L. Jackson	b Shackleton	4	not out		0
Extras	lb 2, w 1	3	lb 1, nb 2		3
		74			**107**

1-8, 2-13, 3-24, 4-27, 5-27, 6-35, 7-52, 8-56, 9-68, 10-74
1-21, 2-25, 3-25, 4-40, 5-94, 6-100, 7-100, 8-106, 9-107, 10-107

Shackleton	16.4	8	36	4	18.2	4	52	3
Heath	16	5	35	6	18	4	52	7

HAMPSHIRE

R.E. Marshall	c Dawkes b Rhodes	4	lbw b Jackson		0
J.R. Gray	b Rhodes	0	c Dawkes b Rhodes		1
H. Horton	b Jackson	5	b Jackson		8
R.W.C. Pitman	run out	0	c Carr b Rhodes		11
H.M. Barnard	c Morgan b Rhodes	5	c Carr b Jackson		16
*A.C.D. Ingleby-Mackenzie	c Lee b Rhodes	2	b Rhodes		4
P.J. Sainsbury	b Jackson	4	c Dawkes b Jackson		4
+L. Harrison	not out	2	c Jackson b Morgan		0
D. Shackleton	c Lee b Jackson	0	c Jackson b Morgan		1
M. Heath	b Jackson	0	b Morgan		4
M.D. Burden	b Jackson	0	not out		0
Extras	nb 1	1	lb 6		6
		23			**55**

1-4, 2-5, 3-7, 4-12, 5-17, 6-17, 7-23, 8-23, 9-23, 10-23
1-1, 2-1, 3-13, 4-23, 5-32, 6-46, 7-47, 8-47, 9-55, 10-55

Jackson	8.4	5	10	5	15	8	16	4
Rhodes	8	3	12	4	9	1	29	3
Morgan					5.3	3	4	3

Umpires: J.S. Buller and H.G. Baldwin

Trevor Bailey

WE'LL HAVE A RESULT

Essex v Gloucestershire
August 1959
with Arthur Milton and Richard Bernard

Arthur Milton played for Gloucestershire from 1948 to 1974, captaining the side in 1968. He scored 58 centuries in his career, and, as a brilliant close fielder, he held 63 catches in the summer of 1956. He played six times for England, scoring a century on debut.

Richard Bernard was a Cambridge University blue who played occasionally for Gloucestershire. A great-grandson of E.M. Grace, W.G.'s brother, he maintained the family tradition by pursuing a career in medicine.

They remember an exciting finish at Leyton.

"Cooky wasn't the worst with the bat," Arthur remembers. "He'd try for you. He didn't just have a whack at it." Cooky may not always be the worst at Gloucestershire, but there are few other counties in the fifties where he would not be an automatic number eleven.

Cecil Cook. Sam they call him. A slow left-arm bowler from Tetbury, his wartime service was in the RAF. "He made a hundred when he was in the raff. At a place called Bulawayo. He always used to talk about his hundred at Bulawayo."

Sam Cook. A plumber by trade, a vegetable gardener at home, a lover of good beer. It is August 1959, he is in his 14th year in this Gloucestershire side, and they are pushing for a title they have not won since the heyday of W.G. Grace. Sam is within a week of capturing his 1,500th first-class wicket but, when he takes guard at Leyton on Friday afternoon, he has barely 1,600 runs to his name. And victory depends on his adding one to that tally.

Cook, C., Gloucestershire, 1946-64. Career batting average, 5.39. At Leyton he faces Essex's Barry Knight with one run wanted for victory, two minutes left on the clock. "A wonderful match," Arthur remembers. "Essex always played a good game." Essex's Doug Insole returns the compliment: "A game played in a great spirit. Gloucestershire were a very jolly lot." Alas, Sam Cook is no longer alive to relive that last ball.

It is August 1959. Bank Holiday Monday is at the start of the month, and it falls during Leyton's cricket week. A record 12,582 spectators pay £1,447 to watch the three days of the Worcestershire game, and they see a double century by Martin Horton. Now the crowds flock in for Gloucestershire.

Leyton Cricket Ground. This is Essex's deepest incursion into London. In 1959 the county has no headquarters, and the team travels with their scoreboard on the side of a bus. It is Gloucestershire's tenth visit to Essex since the war, and they have played on eight grounds. They have played everywhere except

Chelmsford. "The outfield was like lumps of rock at Leyton," Arthur recalls. "I think it was a local authority ground." "There were football pitches on either side of the square," Doug Insole explains. "The groundsman only really worked on the square itself."

"Unquestionably, Leyton was our ugliest ground," Trevor Bailey writes. "But the old stone wall and old style pavilion did give it a certain gnarled charm." "A ramshackle pavilion," Richard Bernard calls it. "The Essex players always put their shoes on to avoid splinters." But Leyton has its place in cricket history for it was here in 1932 that Holmes and Sutcliffe scored 555 runs for Yorkshire's first wicket.

On a gloomy morning Doug Insole wins the toss and decides to bat. Barker is soon caught at short leg, but this only brings forward the arrival of Brian Taylor. "Tonker Taylor," Arthur recalls. "We played at Moreton-in-the-Marsh once, and he got fifty-odd. The ball went everywhere, not once where he aimed it. The first time he middled it, he holed out." Here at Leyton his batting brings kinder words from Denys Rowbotham in the Manchester Guardian. *To the end of his innings he never stopped cutting, hooking, driving and sweeping, and beautifully solid, compact, crisp and confident shots they all were."* He scores 74 out of 85 before he falls to Gloucestershire's sixth bowler of the morning, David Allen.

Off-spinners. Why does Gloucestershire have so many? The great Tom Goddard plays till pneumonia stops him in 1952. Then Bomber Wells turns up, six wickets in his first innings. "He was just a boy from the sticks," Arthur recalls. "He strolled in, changed, came out. Nothing worried him. And he kept getting people out." Then John Mortimore, who last winter flew out to Australia to play three Tests, now David Allen. With Sam Cook's slow left arm, it is quite a job to know which one to bowl. Gloucestershire's captain Tom Graveney is not one for too much theory: "I worked on the principle that the first chance went to the best bowler of the previous game." But Tom has a broken finger, and Arthur the senior pro is in charge for this Leyton game.

David Allen is in his first full season, and already he is on the shortlist for the coming West Indian tour. Gubby Allen and R.W.V. Robins, chairman of selectors and tour manager, are on their way to Leyton as David has 'Tonker' Taylor caught at cover point. It is 101 for two, and Les Savill has barely twenty to show for his morning's efforts. *'It was not perhaps wholly surprising that, when Allen did make an off-break nip, Savill should be trapped in the middle of a grooved, forward shot and caught off the edge at short leg.'* Allen, two wickets for six runs, and the Chairman of Selectors settling into his place. *'The moment of illumination had surely come'.*

"David was a big spinner," Arthur recalls. "Slightly more aggressive in his outlook than Morty." Allen and Mortimore are among half a dozen candidates for the Test space left by Jim Laker. No sooner does the Chairman arrive than David Allen splits his spinning finger while fielding, and he bowls no more in this day. The distinguished visitors are left to watch their fellow selector, Doug Insole, with the bat. The Times speculates about Insole's recall but concludes, *'He is probably content to have finished with Test cricket'.* "1959?" Doug reflects. "No, I was over the hill by then."

Bright sunshine dispels the morning gloom, and Doug Insole's batting has the pens of the pressmen flowing with praise. *'I have never seen him play better,'* Michael Melford writes. *'Very few, I imagine, have.'* *'Insole was irrepressible,'* Denys Rowbotham writes. *'Bailey could afford to be his Sancho Panza, but this was Insole's day for tilting at windmills. Tilt Insole certainly did.'* *'The Essex captain,'* the Times notes, *'reached a landmark by scoring his fiftieth hundred.'* "I probably played as well as I can play," Doug reflects. "He was a beautiful timer of the ball," Arthur explains. "Nothing to look at, but look where the ball went." Here he plays *'a number of fantastic, almost Comptonesque strokes for which no field could have been set.'*

It is August 1959. Barclays Bank has just put its customer accounts onto a computer.

For Charles Williams it is his fourth game of the season for Essex. It is a hot summer, most of July has seen temperatures in the eighties, and he endures the heat of a stuffy office, working for British Petroleum. Now he has leave to resume his amateur cricket career. At the Parks in 1955 he hits a *'beautiful'* century off Cook and Mortimore. The same summer he matches Insole run for run in a 200-partnership at Leicester. But at Leyton in 1959, he is bowled Brown 3, just eight runs in his last five innings. "It was my last shot at Essex," he recalls with sadness. "A very bad year for me. I was just playing down the wrong line." Joe Milner, a young South African from the nearby Walthamstow club, is out soon afterwards for 6. Their dismissals are hardly noticed beside Doug Insole's magnificent, three-and-a-half hour display.

Richard Bernard. "He bowled these little in-duckers," Arthur recalls. 13 overs for 67 runs. "I didn't know where to bowl at Insole," he confesses. "If I bowled at his off stump, he whacked me through mid-on. If I bowled at his middle stump, he whacked me through mid wicket. And if I bowled outside the off, he cut me." He turns to his captain in despair. "Where do I bowl at him, Milt? He's batting so wrongly." "Just bowl straight and bowl a length," comes the reply, and he is more discouraged than ever. He takes to bowling down leg, giving Doug a single every ball. Bowling at Trevor Bailey is less dispiriting, and he has the consolation of having him caught behind for 50.

"Insole was such a good on-side player," Arthur says. "He'd play the off-spinners, no problem." Mortimore, nought for 82, there will be no place for him on the boat to the Caribbean. Allen, two wickets for six runs and an injured finger, he avoids the Insole treatment and he becomes the find of the winter. Cook, 20 overs, nought for 38. "Cooky was the other side. Doug didn't have quite the same armoury on the off side." Sam bowls round the wicket. "I don't think I ever saw him bowl over like they do these days, into the rough. There wasn't a slow left-arm bowler who would lower himself to bowl into the rough. Because it's negative. You can't really get anybody out."

"The off-spinners used to bring you forward," Richard says. "You'd think 'Ah, a half volley', and it used to dip. That doesn't happen now. The whole art of flight has gone because of heavy bats and people like Botham. It doesn't matter if they haven't got their feet quite to the ball; they can still whack it for six. So the dart-playing off-spinner has come into fashion."

There are no long run-ups in this Gloucestershire side. Brown and Smith stand at first slip and peel off their sweaters to bowl. With over an hour left to play, they have bowled 118 overs and Essex have enough runs to declare. 364 for six, Insole 177 not out, and *the crowd stood and cheered him in*. "For God's sake, take longer to bowl your overs," Martin Young curses as he pads up. "I'm forever going in to bat at six o'clock."

Martin Young is a dapper ex-public schoolboy, a charming man, and he is having such a good season that there is talk of his making the England side. "Martin was a good player, orthodox," Arthur recalls. "He didn't like the real quick boys, though." His strategy against them is to be extra-courteous in the pavilion. "I'll give him wife and kids," Surrey's Peter Loader mutters with menace after one such exchange. This evening the young Barry Knight bowls him, and it is 31 for one at close of play.

Out for 14 in front of the Chairman of Selectors, the edge is taken off Martin's evening out with Sam Cook. The public school charmer and the Tetbury plumber. "They were an incongruous duo," Richard remembers. "They used to disappear I know not where at close of play." "You're too young," they tell Richard, "to accompany us old men." For the rest of the team there is a meal together. "Mostly it would be steak places, Berni Inns," Arthur recalls. "But the boys were beginning to get into Indian and Chinese food. Barrie Meyer, Smithy. Not Morty."

It is August 1959. Tom Graveney has been out for a month. His deputy and predecessor, George Emmett, is also out of this game. Tom will survive only one more season, then the amateur Tom Pugh will be catapulted into the job. By his second season the team is playing good cricket, but the committee replaces him with Ken Graveney, Tom's brother, returning after a twelve-year retirement. "Oh dear," Arthur sighs, "we had a few in those days."

Tom Graveney and George Emmett, their batting is missed at Leyton. Jack Crapp has retired, too. John Frederick Crapp. Among Gloucestershire cricketers they say 'John Frederick', not 'Crapp'. When Arthur steps out on Thursday morning with Ron Nicholls, he looks down at the rest of his batting order. Not one of them will average 20 for the county. "If Ron and I had gone early, we'd have been right in the John Frederick."

Milton and Nicholls will give Gloucestershire 52 years of service between them. With Smith and Meyer, they make up a quartet of professional footballers. Milton and Nicholls, is there a pair on the circuit better at taking the quick single? "Ron loved his cricket," Arthur says. He will be playing for Cheltenham when he

142

is 60. "The boys said he was a better player than when he played for the county." He will still be playing two days before he dies.

'Morning sunshine passed into gloom, and Gloucestershire's batting, which began brightly, slumped into dull mediocrity.' It is 133 for two when Ron is caught just before lunch. The bowler is Alan Hurd, Richard's Cambridge colleague. He is another off-spinner who flights the ball, but his fielding, Richard remembers, "would be poor in any club side. There was no question of him swooping down or running sideways to stop it." Here at Leyton he even manages to let one through his legs for four.

'Milton in Sombre Mood' is the Times headline. *'Milton, who was evidently suspicious of the batting capabilities of the rest of his side, decided to dig in.'* It is 238 for four when Essex take the new ball, and Arthur is one run from his seventh century of the summer. With his first delivery Knight gets a little bounce, "I think I was looking for it to come in to me a bit more than it did", and a high gully catch sends him back to the old style pavilion. "In those days they had a tie for people who made 99."

Arthur is a crossword man, the Daily Telegraph. He sits in the pavilion and studies the clues. 'Seven across, Such easily acquired wealth would make my donor feel poor.' There is no easily acquired wealth for county cricketers. He is staying with his mother-in-law in Muswell Hill, saving his three pound lodging allowance, and Richard is taking lessons in how to fill out his expenses claim. 'Money for old rope,' Arthur writes. "The professionals were serfs," Richard says. "They were paid a pittance, then they had a benefit."

Richard is next in. He has played without a break all summer, zig-zagging about England on Cambridge's ten-match tour, then joining the county circuit. "It was a gigantic adventure, a great lark," he reflects, "but I was getting very tired by this Essex game." He makes his Gloucestershire debut at The Oval the previous week, going out to bat at 31 for five in each innings. "Don't worry, Richard," they say to him in the next game at Bristol. "It won't be as bad this time." He looks up at the scoreboard as he walks to the middle, and it is 16 for five. He makes 65 at The Oval, but it is a success he will not repeat. "We never did any practising. Nobody ever had a net. It was one of the reasons my form deteriorated so rapidly." 'W.G. Grace's relation fails', they like to write in the local papers. At Leyton he is caught at second slip off Bailey's out-swinger, Brown and Smith fall to Knight's in-swing, and it is left to David Allen and Barrie Meyer to cheer up proceedings with a 50 partnership that lasts just 35 minutes. *'They had passed a woeful indictment on the rest'*, and Essex have a first innings lead of 35 runs.

With a pitch like Bristol's, is it any wonder that Gloucestershire batsmen under-achieve? Tom Graveney moves to Worcester when he loses the captaincy, and it is the making of him. The shadow of the great Wally Hammond still hangs over all their efforts at Bristol. "It was so slow and low, you really couldn't play back on it," Arthur remembers. "They used to put sand on it. We had lots of two-day games." Worcestershire's Roly Jenkins looks incredulously at the sand at the start of one game. "I'd have brought the family and the deck-chairs if I'd known," he says. Worcester, by contrast, is pacy and bouncy. "It brings you up to concert pitch," Arthur says, "a wicket like that." Or Taunton. Between '51 and '68, Arthur makes seven centuries in eleven games there. "If I'd played for Somerset, I'd probably have scored twice as many runs." He is forever pleading with Bernie Bloodworth the groundsman, but the reply is always the same. "Wally could play on it."

At the end of 1966, the under-groundsman David Bridle takes over, and Arthur is 39. "Are you going to give up?" Morty asks. "No, I'm playing on," he replies. "The wickets will be better." The next summer he hits seven centuries and is the leading run scorer in the country. The chairman manufactures kitchen utensils in Lydney, and he offers a prize for every hundred. "It filled our kitchen."

Les Savill and Joe Milner open the Essex second innings, and they both fall to Tony Brown before the close. Essex are 23 for two, a lead of 58. "For a time," Charles Williams remembers, "it was between Les and me who should be in the side. I had a slight guilt feeling that I as an amateur was depriving a professional of his match fee." Les is in and out of the Essex team from '53 to '61, and this is the one season when he makes 1000 runs. He lacks Charles' stroke play, but he works hard at his game and on this Thursday evening at Leyton Doug Insole awards him his county cap. Joe Milner, the South African, has a shorter career but, though he does not know it when he walks back to the old pavilion, he will have one more chance of glory in this game.

It is August 1959. In the Leyton High Road, the Essoldo Cinema closes, television blamed for falling attendances. "It will not last," a spokesman says. "People will return to the cinema one day."

A good crowd arrives for the final day, and what excitement is in store for them! It is the injured Ken Preston's benefit match, and the game lives up to its occasion, *'fairly bubbling with excitement'*. But, as Denys Rowbotham writes, *'it began as most excitements do - quietly.'* Gloucestershire's seamers gain life from a wicket *'from which it was now possible to extract occasional lift'*. Tonker Taylor misses a full toss, and Roy Ralph is bowled. Trevor Bailey faces up to Richard Bernard's in-duckers, and Arthur edges closer at short leg to catch him. "A brilliant catch," Richard recalls, one of 632 championship catches that will give Arthur the post-war record. "You have to be in a position where you don't have to go down," he explains. "You watch the bat, you don't move till you see the ball, then you just do it." Alan Hurd is in the ramshackle pavilion, and he is well-placed to pass on to his friend Richard what Trevor Bailey says on his return. "Fancy getting out to that piss-hole bowler not once but twice in the same game." Though Trevor will soon forget, the words still echo in Richard's memory.

Charles Williams is surprised by the lift from a Smith delivery, and he is caught behind for one. At the end of the game, he will ask Doug Insole to drop him. It is his last first-class innings, and he will return to his hot B.P. office a sadder man. By the 1990s, he will be the author of a biography of Sir Donald Bradman, and he will be Lord Williams of Elvel, a key figure in Tony Blair's

Labour Party. Essex's Dickie Dodds laughs: "He didn't seem very Labour in those days in his Harlequins cap."

Arthur, with 32,000 runs behind him, the last man to play both football and cricket for England, will retire in 1974 and become a postman. "I didn't have any money," he explains. "But the Post Office, that turned me right round. Serving somebody else, it did me the world of good." John Mortimore will retrain as an accountant while Arthur will think back to his schoolboy prowess at Maths and the university place he never pursued. But he has no regrets. "It was born in me to play cricket, and they were wonderful days in the sun. The days were never long enough."

Essex are 83 for six, just 118 ahead, and Doug Insole, *'once again in superlatively good form',* comes to the rescue with a powerful 90. *'He contrived even to make his edged shots look like intended deflections.'* Bill Greensmith stays with him, and by lunch the lead is 211 with 170 minutes left to play. "I liked Doug. He was the sort of chap I could have played for," Arthur says. "Very nervous. He was always biting his nails." In the Essex dressing room Doug debates the declaration with Trevor Bailey. "Shall we give it away now or shall we go on for ten minutes?" Arthur may have left his Maths at Cotham Grammar School, but he is the shrewdest calculator in the game. He joins them, and he makes his offer. "You declare now, and we'll go all the way. We won't block at all at the end. We'll have a result." Doug looks surprised. "Don't you have to phone the club or anything?" he asks. "We're in charge when we're here," Arthur says, and Doug makes his decision. "Okay, done. It's a deal." 212 to win, two hours fifty minutes to get them in.

It is August 1959. Tommy Steele performs in Red Square, Moscow, to a crowd of three hundred gaping Russians, and price inflation stands at 0.0%.

Nought for one. Trevor Bailey gets some lift to send back Martin Young, his prospect of an England cap receding further. "Trevor was a great bowler," Arthur says. "If you're going to be an all-rounder playing for England, you've got to be good enough at one of them." Once more it is Milton and Nicholls, dashing their quick singles and taking the score to 61 for one after 55 minutes. Arthur is not long out of the England team, but "I was quite happy, it wasn't my scene. I liked to play with the lads I knew."

"Ron and Milt were footballers, very fast on their feet," Richard says. "I wonder how they'd look now. It's hopeless comparing one generation with another, but I suppose they'd be very ordinary in the modern game." Comparisons are invidious, but we all like making them. "Take Walsh out of the Gloucestershire side," Richard thinks, "and I suspect, unlike any other sport, my side of 1959 would beat the 1996 side."

'Then the match turned its first somersault.' Arthur pushes the ball into the covers and sets off for *'a too brisk single'*. Ron sends him back, and he slips and lands on his backside in mid-pitch. The Times carries the picture: *'Milton watches helplessly as he is run out'*. So central is Arthur to this makeshift batting

line-up that *'Gloucestershire's innings was immediately attacked by nerves and desperation.'* Morty appears and tucks straight into a Ralph over with three fours. Alas, his fourth effort finds Charles Williams on the square-leg boundary, and the score is 73 for three. Ron Nicholls is caught at mid-wicket, and Carpenter and Smith each drive fours, only to fall next ball trying to repeat the shot. Richard is out for one, 'W.G.'s relation fails again', and, when Allen plays back to a half-volley, it is 131 for eight. 81 wanted in 50 minutes. "We were right in the John Frederick," Arthur reflects.

Seventeen across, 'Accuse a club-room organisation - of being unperturbed?' 'Cool as a cucumber,' Arthur writes, and he leaves his Daily Telegraph to watch the final overs.

"We won't block at all," Arthur has promised. "We'll have a result." So Tony Brown has no choice but to play his shots. "He was a good driver," Arthur says. "He never got as many runs as he should have done." He lofts the leg-spinner Greensmith for six, he sweeps him *'with rare authority'* for four. He drives Knight *'with the blow of a sledgehammer'* for another six, a third six comes from four overthrows, and he lofts Greensmith over long-on for a fourth. *'It seemed too good to last, yet it did.'*

At the other end is the keeper Barrie Meyer. "He was a good batter in these circumstances," Arthur says. "He was always quite reliable." *'Meyer, as placid a number ten in a crisis as could be wished,'* Denys Rowbotham writes, *'helped Brown by pushing singles almost every time he faced the bowling.'* Michael Melford goes further. *'The powerfully built all-rounder Brown was supported by Meyer with a phlegm and efficiency which could put him among the great number tens of all time.'*

"Barrie wasn't really a natural wicket-keeper," Arthur remembers, "but he got better the more he played. Our best keeper was Bobby Etheridge. He was a damn good cricketer, a natural, but he didn't give two monkeys for anyone. He hit Wardle into the stand at Cheltenham once. Wardle was astounded. I said, 'He wouldn't even know who you are, Johnny.'"

"I'd worked out that we were going to lose," Richard recalls. "So I had a long, leisurely shower. Twenty minutes, half an hour. I was aware of an awful noise going on, but I hadn't twigged we were going for it." 193 for eight. "Good heavens," Richard thinks, standing beside his packed bag. "We're going to win this game." Doug Insole - is he chewing his nails? - finally withdraws his leg-spinner. Greensmith, eight overs, two for 65. *'Singles and twos brought the 200 and the new ball.'* Brown drives and sweeps Knight for two fours. 209 for eight, just three runs to win. *'It was now that Bailey took a great risk. He dug an out-swinger in hard and short. It lifted. Brown tried to cut it and was caught off the edge at the wicket.'* He has scored 91 in 90 minutes at the crease. It will be seven years before he betters this score.

Arthur Milton watches from the press box where Keith Miller is covering the game. The Australian has the paper open at the racing page, but so enthralled is he that he forgets to bet on the last races at Newmarket. It is school holidays, there are always plenty of boys at Essex games, but *'the clamour from the small boys died as Cook came in and took guard'*.

Dear Sam Cook, at least he won't be running between the wickets with Bomber Wells. "They got so fed up with us," Bomber tells, "that we were on a half crown fine for each run out." "For God's sake, call," Sam cries out during one debacle, and "Heads" comes back Bomber's reply.

And he won't be running with old Tom Goddard. "I'll never forget the day at Lord's," Arthur says. "It was a bloody pantomime. Of course Goddard was always trying to be in charge, he was six foot three and he really fancied himself with the bat. Well, Sam calls Tom for a run. He gets halfway up the wicket and sees he's got no chance so he turns and beats Tom back to his own end. You should have heard them when they came in."

It is August 1959. 'Thousands, yes thousands, of winning Premium Bond holders could have bought a new car,' the advert tells, 'and still had money over from their winnings. This is the new way, the exciting way to save.'

209 for nine, two to tie, three to win. Trevor Bailey runs in to bowl to Sam Cook. That familiar leap in the delivery stride, how does Neville Cardus describe it? 'Like a man at a bus that is nearly leaving him behind.' He digs in another out-swinger, hard and short, and he watches the ball curve towards the slips for a wide. "Cor, you should have seen his face," Arthur recalls. "He could have cut his throat, couldn't he?" 210 for nine, one to tie, two to win.

The over is survived, and Barrie Meyer prepares to face Barry Knight. He cuts the first ball cleanly, and it runs down to wide third man. It bobbles across the bumpy football pitch outfield, and he has to decide. Should he take a comfortable single, make the tie safe and trust in Cooky? Should he push for the second, force the fielding error as the ball bumps across the ground? Or should he stay put and wait for a more certain two? He runs the first, and he watches the fielder closing on the ball.

Who is it down there? Is it Les Savill, feeling on top of the world in his new county cap? Or is it Charles Williams in his Harlequins cap, in his last moments as a first-class cricketer? "I can't help you there," Lord Williams confides. "I've got no memory of the game at all. I'm afraid it's lost in neurotic oblivion." "It was my friend Alan Hurd," Richard reveals. Alan Hurd, who has already once let the ball through his legs for four. "He had the most dreadful lobbing throw; it only went about thirty-five yards. It was an easy two." In the excitement, Richard bellows "Run two, Barrie," but they settle for one and Richard's heart sinks. The tie is secure, but it is down to Sam Cook to score the wining run.

Sam Cook. Here is his chance to capture the headlines in the Bristol Evening Post - as he did that day at Taunton. What did they write? "Cook gritted his teeth, swung his bat purposefully and connected somehow, running up the pitch in the same motion like a scalded cat. Only by the narrowest of margins can he have got home." When you bat at number eleven, it is always death or glory.

There are five balls left in the over. *'Insole, without hesitation, surrounded Cook with two slips, a gully and three short legs.'* Cooky, he scored a hundred at Bulawayo and he has just one run to score now. He almost squeezes the next ball through the three short legs, but *'Williams, with the spectators shrieking in excitement, scrambled along the ground to cut it off'*. Four balls left. *'Cook carefully played back the following ball.'*

Three balls left. Knight bowls a perfect in-swinger, it lifts a little and catches the glove. It flies low to Joe Milner's left in the leg trap. "If I remember right," Arthur says, "he was quite an athletic sort of lad." He flings out his left arm as he dives across the turf and, with every breath in the Ilford ground stopping for a second, the ball lodges in his outstretched palm. It is all over. A tie. The first one in county cricket since 1955. There will not be another for eight years.

It is *'the catch of the season'* in the Daily Mirror. He is *'Jumping Joe'* in the Herald. *'As Milner sprung up off the turf,'* the Walthamstow Guardian describes, *'he did a passable imitation of a South African war dance.'* "I don't think it was quite as good a catch as that," Arthur recalls, "but it makes a good story, doesn't it?" The clock shows two minutes to five. "I'm surprised when you tell me that. The time factor didn't raise its ugly head. It was always going to be a result."

There are drinks in the bar. "Oh, Barrie," Richard laments. "Why didn't you go for the two?" There are six points for the tie, but there were six more there for the taking. At the end of the season it is as runners-up that they enjoy a celebration dinner with the Duke of Beaufort. "Well, fellah," Sam says to Martin, still the incongruous duo, "you enjoy this. It won't happen again in your lifetime." "They were convinced it was a fluke," Richard says.

From Leyton the Gloucestershire players make their way down the A4 to Bristol. Arthur and Tony Brown drive The Bounty, the dormobile full of kit, and they stop at Reading for fish and chips. Tomorrow it is off to Cheltenham for festival week there, and Arthur will score another century. "Wonderful days in the sun," he says. "The days were never long enough."

ESSEX v GLOUCESTERSHIRE

Leyton. 5, 6 & 7 August 1959

MATCH TIED

ESSEX

L.A. Savill	c Brown b Allen	25	b Brown	10
G. Barker	c Mortimore b Brown	6	b Brown	6
+B. Taylor	c Brown b Allen	74	b Brown	6
*D.J. Insole	not out	177	c Cook b Brown	90
T.E. Bailey	c Meyer b Bernard	50	c Milton b Bernard	10
C.C.P. Williams	b Brown	3	c Meyer b Smith	1
J. Milner	c Milton b Brown	6	c Meyer b Brown	11
B.R. Knight	not out	17	c Meyer b Smith	0
L.H.R. Ralph			b Bernard	13
W.T. Greensmith			not out	28
A. Hurd				
Extras	lb 5, nb 1	6	b 2, lb 2, nb 3	7
	(6 wkts, dec)	364	(8 wkts, dec)	176

1-16, 2-101, 3-114, 4-289, 5-305, 6-325
1-21, 2-22, 3-32, 4-59, 5-82, 6-83, 7-109, 8-176

Smith	23	2	86	0	22	8	44	2
Brown	24	4	66	3	18.5	2	60	4
Milton	2	0	13	0				
Cook	20	11	38	0	8	1	22	0
Mortimore	28	7	82	0				
Allen	8	4	6	2	6	0	20	0
Bernard	13	1	67	1	8	1	23	2

GLOUCESTERSHIRE

D.M. Young	b Knight	14	c Ralph b Bailey	0
*C.A. Milton	c Ralph b Knight	99	run out	23
R.B. Nicholls	c Taylor b Hurd	64	c Milner b Knight	41
J.B. Mortimore	c Taylor b Hurd	30	c Williams b Ralph	12
D. Carpenter	c & b Greensmith	1	b Greensmith	13
A.S. Brown	b Knight	35	c Taylor b Bailey	91
J.R. Bernard	c Insole b Bailey	9	b Knight	1
D.R. Smith	c Williams b Knight	1	c Taylor b Greensmith	6
D.A. Allen	c Bailey b Greensmith	37	lbw b Knight	5
+B.J. Meyer	c Taylor b Greensmith	21	not out	13
C. Cook	not out	0	c Milner b Knight	0
Extras	b 3, lb 12, nb 3	18	b 4, w 1, nb 1	6
		329		211

1-19, 2-133, 3-199, 4-211, 5-238, 6-263, 7-267, 8-276, 9-326, 10-329
1-0, 2-61, 3-73, 4-82, 5-104, 6-110, 7-111, 8-131, 9-209, 10-211

Bailey	29	5	74	1	14	1	46	2
Knight	25	4	69	4	17.4	2	64	4
Ralph	23	6	56	0	7	1	30	1
Greensmith	30.2	4	80	3	8	1	65	2
Hurd	18	6	32	2				

Umpires: A.E. Fagg and T.W. Spencer

Bill Alley

THEY COULD NOT BE BEATEN

Somerset v Yorkshire
August 1959
with Ken Biddulph

Ken Biddulph played for Somerset from 1955 to 1961. He was a fast-medium bowler, and he played in the Somerset side of 1958 that reached third place in the championship, the county's highest ever position. From 1962 to 1972, he played for Durham. He remembers a game at Bath against a resurgent Yorkshire side.

The sun shines on the Bath Recreation Ground. A week earlier, there have been floods in the West Country, but summer has re-asserted itself. It is August 1959. Yorkshire have just gone top in the championship table. It is their chance to end Surrey's seven-year reign, and they have not lost to Somerset since 1903, not since the days of Lord Hawke and Lionel Palairet.

"Yorkshire were a hard team to play," Ken remembers. "The atmosphere was always a bit different. They had this self-belief. When you went in to bat, they used to look at you as if to say, 'How dare you come out here!' They could not be beaten."

It is August 1959. Harold Macmillan is preparing for his 'Never had it so good' election, the Queen is expecting her third child and Cliff Richard is top of the hit parade with 'Living Doll'.

On the first morning, Somerset are batting, and the teenage Roy Virgin opens with ex-Lancastrian Geoff Lomax. "Geoff was so laid back," Ken says. "I think they invented the phrase for him. It's a wonder he didn't fall asleep while he was batting." In winter Ken walks past Geoff's house on his way to the sports shop where he works, and he spots Geoff, reading his newspaper in the armchair. He passes on his way home for lunch, and Geoff is still there, though he has moved to the other armchair. "By the end of lunch he was laid out on the sofa, fast asleep."

For this game at Bath there is no Fred Trueman, for England are about to complete a five-nil rout of India, but twenty-year-old Barry Stead makes his championship debut, a week after catching the headlines with seven Indian wickets at Bradford. His opening overs are lively, but the pitch offers nothing but a little bounce. At lunch Somerset are 75 for no wicket from forty overs.

Forty overs in the morning, 123 in the day. As soon as the action is complete, the bowler is on his way back to his mark. "We got on with the game. These days people make an awful lot of fuss about nothing." There are no fielding helmets, no changes of gloves, no drinks breaks. "We had to go on our knees to get a drink," Ken recalls. "Most of the time they couldn't afford it." There is even a day at

Taunton when the county secretary appears at the pavilion gate to tell him off for wasting thirty shillings on a second new ball.

Yorkshire and Somerset, what contrasting counties! Only the Yorkshire-born play for Yorkshire. None of Somerset's established players are county-born. 'Those were the days when the rest of the counties would take the mickey out of Somerset,' Bill Alley writes. They are called the Foreign Legion. Peter Wight and Abbas Ali Baig, Yawar Saeed, Bill Alley and Colin McCool, they all arrive at Somerset in the fifties from different corners of the Commonwealth. Ken has grown up in Essex, Geoff Lomax in Lancashire and Harold Stephenson in County Durham.

Maurice Tremlett, himself born in Stockport, is the Somerset captain. 'It was that happy era,' Bill Alley writes, 'when Maurice managed to mould a group of outsiders together, to have faith in one another and pride in their adopted county.' And there is something of the spirit of the old Somerset in the way they play their cricket. "Everywhere we went, we drew the biggest crowds," Peter Wight recalls. "We were always happy-go-lucky."

After lunch, Brian Close drops Roy Virgin: *'Close missed, juggled, had a last desperate bite at the cherry, then the ball came to earth.'* Roy Virgin goes on to 68, his maiden fifty. In time he will score over 20,000 runs, but from such moments are careers built or broken. Graham Tripp has spent eight summers on the Somerset books, and he has never turned his immense talent into first team runs. But Roy Virgin will, and he has built a solid start by the time Don Wilson beats him in the air.

Enter Colin McCool, the Australian who is enjoying his cricketing twilight in the West Country. The quiet one in the corner, smoking his pipe. He has modelled his batting on his idol Don Bradman, and in his Test-playing days they shared rooms. Somerset are staying at the Francis Hotel in Queen's Square, and now he shares with Ken Biddulph. "I was sharing a room with a bloke who shared a room with Don Bradman," Ken likes to boast. Throughout the following summer Colin will be on his typewriter. "Two o'clock in the morning I'd wake up. Clink-a-clink-clink. 'Colin, what are you doing?' 'Get back to sleep, I'm writing a book.'" 'Cricket Is A Game', he will call it. It will sell for eighteen shillings. 'England 1959 was paradise,' he types. 'Day in, day out, up and down the length and breadth of the country, I found that I had a sight of the ball and the pace of the pitch from the very first delivery I received.'

'McCool began his attack at once,' the Times records, *'firing off four boundaries in his first volley.'* McCool, Tremlett, Alley, Stephenson. Is it any wonder that Somerset are nicknamed the biff-bang boys? Runs start to flow, but wickets fall. At one stage Don Wilson has figures of five for 32 as Somerset stand at 237 for five. Bill Alley and Chris Greetham join forces. *'It was here that the crowd saw the real jewel of the day's batting.'*

Bill Alley, the noisy Australian. How old is he? The books say forty, but has he counted the war years? "He played every shot in the game when he came to us in 1957, but he kept getting out," Ken recalls. "Gradually he cut them out till in 1961 he only had three left: the dab wide of gully, the hook - he loved to hook - and the hoik over mid-wicket. The dab, the hook and the hoik, he got 3000 runs in 1961 with those three shots." 3000 runs in a season, he is still the last man to achieve the feat. *'The score fairly raced along with a great profusion of boundaries'*. A century partnership in 58 minutes. 342 for five at close of play. *'There were many sunburned and smiling countenances in Bath this evening,'* Ron Roberts observes in the Daily Telegraph.

Bill Alley, the great talker at the wicket. Fred Trueman cannot get the better of him. "He used to make Fred laugh. Fred would run up. That lovely long, flowing run of his, he'd get to the crease, then he'd burst out laughing. Bill was talking the whole time." It is not so with Peter Wight, Somerset's most gifted batsman, their Guyanese stroke-player. On a raging turner at The Oval in 1956, he scores 62 and 128, not out both times, against Laker and Lock, and his team mates in two innings manage 142 between them. "A beautifully delicate player," Ken calls him, but Fred Trueman has a psychological hold over him that is never broken. "That's four wickets for me this season," he says whenever he spies Peter Wight in May, and from '58 to '61 Peter falls seven times in single figures to Fred. Revenge of sorts comes in '62 at Taunton. Fred is dropped for arriving late at the ground, and Peter compiles an elegant 215.

Fred and Peter are both missed by the Bath crowd in August 1959. Fred is performing at The Oval, but Peter is suffering from the after-effects of being hit by Mickey Norman of Northants while fielding at short leg. "It was that Kenny Biddulph," Peter curses. "Half-volley on the leg stump. Terrible ball." He has never forgotten. "I put my hand on my forehead, and there was just the one spot of blood, that and the name of the maker of the ball, in gold. Stuart Surridge." Bill Alley and Brian Langford carry him off, but they are laughing so much they keep dropping him. He is fifth in the national averages with over 1600 runs, and his season never recovers.

It is August 1959. There are strikes at Morris Motors and De Havilland Aircrafts, and the House of Fraser is fighting Debenhams for control of Harrods. The Science Museum is building an extension for its aeroplanes, and Charles Laughton opens as King Lear at Stratford-on-Avon.

The second day brings more sunshine, and the spectators fill the Recreation Ground, sitting in the valley of this city of hills, the high Georgian buildings providing such a splendid backdrop to the cricketers. "There was always a good crowd at Bath," Ken remembers. At Taunton, 'the local people don't seem to appreciate cricket,' Bill Alley writes. 'I would back moving the headquarters to Bath.' When he finishes playing, Peter Wight will settle in Bath and open his cricket school. "Taunton seems to be a sleepy town," he says. "I like Bath. It's more go-ahead."

With matches at Weston-super-Mare, Bristol and Glastonbury, Somerset play nine of their fourteen championship home games away from their Taunton headquarters. It all adds to the miles on the road. They have just come back from

Swansea. There is no Severn Bridge so they travel by the ferry at Weston-super-Mare. "We were all taking these pills to stop sea sickness," Ken remembers. "Quells they were called. Geoff Lomax had been in the Navy. 'You don't need Quells,' he said. 'We're only going across a river.' And he was the only one who was sick." At least they no longer travel by rail. "Can you imagine going by train from Taunton?" Ken asks. "We spent about four hundred hours each summer at Bristol Temple Meads, waiting for connections. I remember arriving at Old Trafford after three in the morning. Of course we'd always lose the toss and be in the field."

It is August 1959. The M1 stretches as far as Rugby. A plan to extend it to Doncaster is under consideration.

Bill Alley has a Morris 1000 van, painted yellow and black. It is known as The Wasp. "At the end of a game, we'd all pack our bags and leave them beside Bill's van. And off we'd go. We'd drive as fast as we could. Then, when we got to the hotel, there was Bill. 'Where have you been then, lads? There's a good dinner.' He's had dinner, he's had a pint, but we never saw him on the road, he never passed us." Peter Wight remembers differently. "Geoff Lomax used to go with him to read the map, and he'd fall asleep. Bill got lost on quite a few occasions. But, if you like, leave it as Ken says. It's a good story."

It is hard to imagine how anybody can fall asleep with Bill as a travelling companion. In a fog outside Birmingham, he has Ken shinning up a road sign to read the directions. At Nottingham he is caught speeding and, by the end of his sob story, the policeman is offering to escort him to the hotel. "He'd find something to talk about every five minutes on the road," Ken recalls. "Everything he ever did was a story." Bill works one winter in a cider-making factory, and "his story of how they made cider was incredible. He made it seem so exciting." Gloucestershire's George Lambert works there too and, when he joins in, it seems the dullest place. And if there is nothing happening on the road and he is not in the mood to tell the story of his life, there is always the day's play to go over. "Langford can't spin it ... Peter's frightened of the quicks ... Maurice can't judge a declaration." "And that would be just the first mile out of Taunton."

On the second day, the Times reports, *'Yorkshire's fortunes rocked to and fro violently'*. Ken Taylor goes early, thinking he has nicked a straight one through the slips for four till Colin McCool, *'resplendent in a floppy sun hat',* calls his attention to a dislodged bail. Bryan Stott follows soon after, and the scoreboard reads 9 for two. The Times takes up the story: *'In a humdrum match the call would probably have been for a sober approach to the troubles; but when Close arrived, his immense skill, which was evident from the beginning, and some Somerset bowling far short of the standard required, enabled Yorkshire to prosper.'*

122 for two at lunch. Close takes eighteen off a Whitehead over and seventeen off one from Atkinson. Doug Padgett, *'not unnaturally subordinated by such a performance',* provides support. At four o'clock, the 200 partnership is being clapped all round the crowded ground. "If you played against Closey," Ken

154

recalls, "you knew you were going to have a tough game. A great opponent." Like most left-handers, everything at his legs is whipped away. "If you bowl at me legs, lad," he chides, "it's got to go." But Brian Close does not just play a good game, he talks one, too. "If you listened to him," Ken tells, "he was never wrong. You tended to get into the habit of believing everything he said."

The new ball is taken. Another thirty shillings for the secretary to find. Padgett falls to Bill Alley for 83, Close to Ken for 128. In the words of the Times, *'the innings petered out with scarcely another spark'*. 275 all out, a deficit of 67. Bill Alley finishes with four for 19 in 13 overs, but it is Ken who is saluted at the end of the day, three for 66 but it is enough to see the tall, thin man presented with his county cap. "It was something worth having in those days. I worked a few years for it." Tradition requires him to buy champagne for the two teams, and he gets it on credit from Bill Moor the caterer. "It took me about a month to pay for it."

"The players all played because they enjoyed it," Ken reflects. "The question of money didn't arise that much. Nowadays the money's taken over."

Somerset end the day on 66 for no wicket, Roy Virgin and Geoff Lomax again looking steady. *'The situation at the close,'* the Times declares, *'was such that Yorkshire can hardly expect even a crumb from this match'*. Warwickshire are in control at Edgbaston, and Yorkshire's championship lead is looking like a three-day affair.

It is August 1959. Under the Times report, Shell is advertising Phosdrin, an organo-phosphorus insecticide with 'dramatic killing power'. At Bath's Theatre Royal they are playing 'The Happiest Days of Your Life'.

On the third day the sunshine gives way to cloud and rain. Even on a damp day Yorkshire attract a crowd and, as Ken reflects, "we would be very conscious that they paid to watch us play." Rain arrives during the morning, *'but by then,'* the Times records, *'Yorkshire had got their teeth into Somerset and were not letting go.'* The openers are soon parted, a magnificent throw by Ken Taylor running out Roy Virgin. The overnight 66 for no wicket is soon 127 for six as Brian Close and Don Wilson set to work on the turning wicket.

Brian Close, the great competitor. An eighteen-year-old in 1949, he is the youngest cricketer to perform the double. He bowls medium-pace, he bowls off-spinners. Is there any truth in the story that, as England captain, he volunteered in a selection committee to keep wicket? "Get off, you lot, you're no good," he says to his fellow bowlers. "Give me the ball, I'll get some wickets." "He liked to put a few fielders round the bat," Ken recalls. "Probably more than he ought to have." Today he takes six wickets to go with his first innings century.

Only Bill Alley lasts long after the openers. "You had to watch Bill, even if only to see his jaws going." He talks to everybody, and one year Yorkshire decide to ignore him. "I don't think Fred could have been playing." "What's the matter with you lot?" Bill asks. "What have I done?" It puts him right off his game, but "it didn't last for long. You couldn't ignore Bill for more than a few minutes."

Here at Bath he makes 45, but Somerset are all out by lunch. There is no need for one of those declarations that Bill likes to curse. "Stupid declaration, that, they'll get them with an hour to spare." If opponents declare, the lament is different: "Ridiculous declaration, we'll all get ourselves out". "He could destroy his own team sometimes. If you were next in to bat and Bill was beside you, he'd frighten you to death with the things he could see the bowler doing."

Brian Close has Ken caught behind for a duck. Has Bill frightened Ken to death? Or is Ken unnerved by the 'How dare you come out here!' looks of the Yorkshire fielders. Whichever way, he is unable to repeat his little triumph at Swansea four days ago. An innings of 11 and first innings points secured. The crowd claps as he reaches the foot of the eighty-four steps up to the dressing room. "Halfway up, the members started to stand up. It was wonderful. I raised my bat, then I heard the loudspeaker announcement. It was McConnon's hundredth wicket of the season. I shoved my bat back under my arm, got my head down quick and thought, 'What am I doing here?'" Next summer at Southend Ken will make a career best 41, and the last wicket partnership of 75 will save an innings defeat. But there will be no celebrations from his team mates. They have all changed and packed their bags in the Wasp, and now they have to take the field for Essex to score four runs. Colin McCool throws his whites over his everyday clothes. "We could be halfway back to Taunton by now," Bill Alley curses.

Look up Ken in any book about Somerset cricket, though, and it will tell of his finest half hour - when he and Brian Langford hold on for a draw against the 1961 Australians at Taunton. Ron Gaunt hurls the ball down at a ferocious pace. "I got bouncers, wides, no balls, yorkers, everything from the fellow." At the other end Ken Mackay is bowling, "a tiddly little medium pacer". Brian Langford meets Ken in the middle. "I think I'd better take Mackay," he says. "He swings it about a bit."

The tourist match is the highlight of the county's season, and never is Ken sadder than when he is made twelfth man against the 1957 West Indians. No chance to bowl at Weekes, Walcott and Sobers. Still, look on the bright side. He avoids having to face a fiery spell of bowling from Wes Hall and Roy Gilchrist. Peter Wight is unfit to play, and a young Kenny Palmer battles it out for a brave 23. Back in the pavilion Kenny starts to examine the colours of his bruises, but there is no colour left in his face when he goes to pull out his box and discovers that he has batted without it.

Once against Yorkshire Ken has a whole over to face against Fred Trueman, with Bill Alley marooned at the non-striker's end. How can he possibly survive? "Is that right what they're saying about you, Fred?" Bill asks. "What's that, Bill?" "They reckon you've lost it. You can't bowl the outer anymore. It's all round the counties." What are you talking about?" Fred explodes. "Can't bowl the outer? I'll show you." He takes the new ball, and he bowls six perfect out-swingers to Ken. "If only we had somebody who could make the ball swing like that now," Ken sighs. He shoulders arms to all six, and only at the end of the over does Fred rumble Bill's game.

In London, thunderstorms cause flooding that shuts Liverpool Street Station for two and a half hours, but, though *'rain during the luncheon interval had a sombre air of finality about it'*, only five minutes are lost. There are two sessions for Yorkshire to score 255. "We didn't run for cover at the first drop of rain," Ken recalls, "like they do now."

Bath is not Taunton. At headquarters the bowlers get their help on the first morning. Here at Bath the help comes on the last day in the form of a turning wicket. It is Brian Langford's favourite ground. Breaking into the Somerset team as a seventeen-year-old in 1953, he takes 26 wickets in the three games of the Bath Festival and briefly heads the national averages. Three years later, National Service done, he returns to take 28 wickets in three games. Throughout his long career he will take wickets at Bath. An average of 16.97 there, 26.22 elsewhere.

Ken Taylor, who has failed in his two Tests at the start of the summer, hits an attacking 70, and he and Brian Close look in control during a third wicket partnership of 78. In the field it falls to captain Maurice Tremlett to tease out the batsmen. With the experience of Colin McCool at his side, he gets the best out of his bowlers. "He read the game well, he knew where to set the field, he knew all the players around the counties," Ken remembers. "He was the best captain I played under." Peter Wight agrees, and so does Bill Alley: 'Maurice was the best captain I played under," he writes. "He was completely unflappable and, if we were having a rough day, he would say: 'Well, lads, we can't push this brick wall over. But keep on trying.'"

It is still the age of amateurs and professionals, and in the first ten seasons after the war Somerset have eight amateur captains. "Nice blokes," Ken says, "but they weren't all great readers of the game." For four successive summers from 1952, Somerset finish last. "I made my debut in '55," Ken recalls. "Against Worcestershire. It was our first win at Taunton for a season and a half. We won before lunch on the third day, and it started to rain. Johnny Lawrence was standing in as captain, and we drove around the town in his Land Rover. Every time we came up to a bunch of people, Johnny would lean out of the window and shout 'Who won the game?'. And we'd all sing in chorus, 'ZUMMERZET'." This victorious Somerset side sports an Australian, a Pakistani and a West Indian, a Lancastrian, a Durhamite and Ken from Essex, but 'ZUMMERZET' they happily sing.

In 1956, they turn to Maurice Tremlett, a professional, and by 1958 they are up to third place, a position the county is still to better. Ten years earlier he has played three Tests as a bowler, but some unhelpful coaching leads to a loss of line, the crowd turns cruel and he never bowls again. "I don't suppose I saw him bowl a dozen overs in the whole time I was there," Ken says with sorrow. "But I learnt a lot from him. He was a great skipper of bowlers."

"I talked Maurice into bowling one game," Peter remembers. "I went short fine leg, and I dropped this catch. It didn't please me, and it didn't please him. He didn't bowl again."

157

At 146 for three Yorkshire need 109 in 90 minutes. The ball is wet, but *'the pitch has shown enough to suggest it might be Langford's line of country'*. Brian Langford, "a lovely off-spinner" is Ken's judgement, "lot of variation. He had a lovely loop. If he was around today, he would walk into the England team." Peter Wight is not so sure. "The laws, the pitches, everything has changed. The wickets don't turn. You can't buy your wickets like you used to years ago. Batting is a lot easier now."

Brian Langford bowls at Taunton, Jim Laker bowls at The Oval. How would their deeds look if they swapped grounds? "To me he was better when conditions were against him," Ken says. "That's probably because he had so much bowling at Taunton, which didn't help him at all. On a real turner Brian lacked that special accuracy. You got Laker on a turner and you'd got no chance." Unless your name is Peter Wight.

It is six years since this square at Bath has been relaid, and it is still unpredictable. "It changed from one year to another," Ken remembers. At least there has never been a repeat of that first ever game on the new square. Bertie Buse, Bath born and bred, serves Somerset loyally from 1929 to 1953, and he selects the Lancashire fixture for his benefit match. Starting at eleven thirty on Saturday morning, it is all over by six o'clock, Lancashire's off-spinner Roy Tattersall taking thirteen wickets for 69 in an innings victory. It is Brian Langford's debut match, the square is peppered with acorns and gravel, and desperate measures are taken before the next match on Wednesday. Liquid marl and cow manure are spread across the wicket, with sprinklings of cut grass for camouflage. The two remaining games of the Festival last longer, but Brian takes 25 wickets in them. What a different world from the standardised pitches of the 1990s. "Batting these days is made so easy," Ken reflects. "It's like a bank holiday every day for batsmen. Brian Lara comes over here, playing on covered wickets at Edgbaston, he must think it's a private birthday party."

Brian likes Bath, *'he began spinning to his heart's content'*, and wickets fall with regularity. "Brian was a superb bowler, but he was a little excitable. He wasn't a great thinker of the game. He needed Maurice's experience." Taylor and Close are caught behind, later Wilson is stumped, three more victims for the Langford-Stephenson partnership. 'Steve', Colin McCool writes, clink-a-clink-clink on the typewriter, 'has as good a pair of wicket-keeping hands as I have seen in the business. If I had to choose between him and Godfrey Evans, I would go for him every time.' Two weeks earlier at Bristol he stands up to Ken's fast-medium in-swing, and he performs a wonderful leg-side stumping. Colin is at slip. "Why don't you let one go?" he suggests. "That'd show them how difficult it is." "Brilliant keeper," Ken says. "I never saw him have a bad day."

Ronnie Burnet is a moderate player, but in 1958 Yorkshire promote him from the second eleven to be their amateur captain. "For God's sake get your left foot down the pitch," Brian Close tells him before he goes out to bat. "Hit Langford anywhere between mid-on and fine leg." Brian demonstrates the sweep shot in the pavilion. 'The informed riposte', he calls it. "Well, Ronnie got his leg down the pitch all right," Brian tells, "but somewhere outside the line of the leg stump! The whole lot went over." "You told me to do that," he accuses Brian, and he will spend the rest of his life regretting that he took the advice. It is 165 for six. 196 for seven when Don Wilson is stumped.

There is time still for Yorkshire to win the game. Jack Birkenshaw is just eighteen years old, and he plays 'with remarkable maturity'. He and Jimmy Binks lift the score to 221 for seven, just 34 to win, when he backs up too far and is *run out by Whitehead's direct hit*. "Run out," Ken pauses. "I don't remember that." Bill Alley bowls the debutant Barry Stead, but Yorkshire are not yet beaten. Somerset's tail-enders may accept their fate with good-humoured resignation, but nobody in this Yorkshire side believes that they should be batting at ten or eleven, certainly not Bob Platt. *'Bob Platt's place in the Yorkshire batting order is not settled,'* the Daily Mirror writes, *'except that he shuttles between numbers ten and eleven.'* All his life this will rankle with Bob. "More unkind, distorted and downright inaccurate statements have been made about my batting than about almost anything else in cricket." Why, last month he turned the match at Chesterfield with a thrilling 57 not out, and still he is going in last. Here is another chance to show them that he should be at eight or nine. He and Jimmy Binks add vital runs, the winning target is down to 17, and there is still the extra half hour to be claimed. There is a championship at stake, and they are not to be beaten.

Brian Langford continues to flight the ball in a teasing loop, Bob Platt pushes too firmly and Geoff Lomax pouches the catch at short leg. The game is won for Somerset, and the cheers of the crowd echo off the high Georgian houses. Lionel Palairet and his 1903 side can be forgotten now. This Bath crowd can cheer Maurice and Bill, Geoff and Harold, Brian and Ken, as they leave the field victorious. *'Yorkshire Beaten After 56 Years'* is the headline.

Yorkshire's championship challenge has suffered a setback, and Ronnie Burnet knows where he places the blame. "As a business stroke, the sweep was virtually unknown," he will write in 1994. "I am convinced that, if we had batted in an orthodox manner, we would have won." It will be another eight years before Somerset beat Yorkshire again. And that will be at Bath, too, Brian Langford still at home with five for 14 and three for 78. By the 1970s, Yorkshire are easier to beat - but by then the Somerset captain is Brian Close. "He taught them how to really play cricket," is Ken's verdict. "Before that, I think they were playing at it a bit."

Yorkshire are off to Bristol, where Gloucestershire will bowl them out for 35. Somerset are to stay in Bath, where the whole Surrey team will come into the dressing room in the morning to congratulate Ken on his county cap. "I had a lot of friends at Surrey, people who helped me when I was a kid. Alec Bedser was wonderful. Locky and Laker even bowled at me at Alf Gover's. They all came in and said 'Well done'. That probably meant more to me than getting my county cap." On another spinners' pitch, Jim Laker will take seven second innings wickets and Brian Langford will have no second innings to bowl in.

It is August 1959. Within a month, Maurice Tremlett will be sacked as captain. "Committees used to work in funny ways in those days," Ken says. "I think they still do, don't they?" Within three months, Harold Macmillan will have won his 'Never had it so good' election. Ken and Peter Wight play a charity match at Haywards Heath, and Ken finds himself sitting next to the Prime Minister at tea. "I was dying to know what it was like to be the PM, but he just wanted to talk cricket. He wanted to know what it was like to be a first-class cricketer." His own efforts are preserved on a 1955 scorecard. Macmillan, hit wicket b Hearne, 2. The Hearne in question is Richard, television's Mister Pastry.

It is August 1959, and this Friday evening Yorkshire are off to Bristol, Somerset staying in Bath. There is to be no journey for The Wasp, and some of the Yorkshire team stay for drinks. A wonderful opportunity for Brian Close to talk through the game, to explain to the Somerset lads how his batsmen could have swept Brian Langford with ease, how the victory was there for the taking. Yorkshire have been beaten after 56 years, and Ken has a county cap to add to the glow of these post-match drinks. "But after half an hour of listening to Closey, we thought we were the ones who'd lost. They were unbeatable. Yorkshire had lost the match, but he didn't believe it. They could not be beaten."

SOMERSET v YORKSHIRE

Bath. 19, 20 & 21 August 1959

SOMERSET WON BY 16 RUNS

SOMERSET

Batsman	1st innings		2nd innings	
J.G. Lomax	c Burnet b Wilson	92	c Bolus b Close	49
R. Virgin	st Binks b Wilson	68	run out	37
C.L. McCool	c & b Wilson	32	c Bolus b Close	17
G. Atkinson	b Wilson	0	c Padgett b Wilson	12
*M.F. Tremlett	c Binks b Wilson	30	c Burnet b Wilson	1
W.E. Alley	not out	56	c Bolus b Close	45
C. Greetham	not out	49	c Platt b Wilson	0
+H.W. Stephenson			c & b Close	13
B. Langford			not out	5
K.D. Biddulph			c Binks b Close	0
A. Whitehead			b Close	0
Extras	b 9, lb 6	15	b 8	8
	(5 wkts, dec)	**342**		**187**

1-118, 2-158, 3-162, 4-230, 5-237
1-74, 2-98, 3-103, 4-104, 5-127, 6-127, 7-156, 8-185, 9-187, 10-187

Bowler	O	M	R	W	O	M	R	W
Platt	20	4	57	0	6	2	8	0
Stead	13	1	35	0	2	0	4	0
Close	32	13	72	0	33.2	8	87	6
Taylor	11	1	39	0				
Birkenshaw	25	5	67	0	7	2	16	0
Wilson	22	8	57	5	28	9	64	3

YORKSHIRE

Batsman	1st innings		2nd innings	
W.B. Stott	c McCool b Alley	8	c Langford b Biddulph	19
K. Taylor	b Biddulph	1	c Stephenson b Langford	70
D.E.V. Padgett	b Alley	83	c & b Langford	12
D.B. Close	c McCool b Biddulph	128	c Stephenson b Langford	34
J.B. Bolus	lbw b Alley	4	c Alley b Whitehead	11
D. Wilson	b Alley	6	st Stephenson b Langford	19
*J.R. Burnet	c Greetham b Langford	20	b Langford	3
J. Birkenshaw	not out	12	run out	31
+J.G. Binks	c & b Biddulph	0	not out	28
R.K. Platt	c Alley b Langford	1	c Lomax b Langford`	1
B. Stead	c & b Langford	8	b Alley	0
Extras	lb 4	4	lb 10	10
		275		**238**

1-7,2-9,3-214, 4-222, 5-226, 6-243, 7-260, 8-260, 9-261, 10-275
1-26, 2-55, 3-133, 4-152, 5-156, 6-165, 7-196, 8-221, 9-221, 10-238

Bowler	O	M	R	W	O	M	R	W
Biddulph	20	2	66	3	10	1	49	1
Alley	13	4	19	4	18	4	57	1
Langford	34	11	58	3	16.4	0	85	6
Whitehead	20	5	69	0	5	1	20	1
Atkinson	4	1	25	0				
Lomax	6	2	23	0	2	0	17	0
Virgin	1	0	11	0				

Umpires: C.S. Elliott and J.S. Buller

Fred Trueman

THE END OF AN ERA

Sussex v Yorkshire
August & September 1959
with Jim Parks, Bryan Stott & Ken Taylor

Jim Parks played for Sussex from 1949 to 1972 and for Somerset from 1973 to 1976. He started his career as a forcing right-hand batsman, winning his first Test cap in 1954, but in 1958 he took up wicket-keeping, in which role he played a further 45 times for England. His father played for Sussex and England before the war, and his son kept wicket for Hampshire from 1980 to 1992. Jim is now Sussex's Marketing Manager.

Bryan Stott played for Yorkshire from 1952 to 1963. An attacking left-handed opening bat, he scored 1000 runs in a season five times and played in four championship-winning teams. He left cricket to join his father's building firm.

Ken Taylor played for Yorkshire from 1953 to 1968. A right-hand bat and occasional medium-pace bowler, he played in seven championship-winning teams. He played three Test matches for England and football in the old Division One with Huddersfield Town. A graduate of the Slade, he became an art teacher when he retired from professional sport.

They all remember a match at Hove at the end of the 1959 season.

Cricket at Hove. What better a place to bring to a close a long, hot summer! It is the last stop in Yorkshire's Southern tour. Lord's, Bath, Bristol, Worcester, Hove. Seventeen days on the road at the end of a tiring season. There are 35 matches on their fixture card, 105 days of cricket. "The heatwave was unrelenting," Yorkshire's skipper Ronnie Burnet writes. "With a combination of continual blazing sunshine and grounds as hard as concrete, several of us were looking a bit weary."

Cricket at Hove. The holiday crowd watches Robin Marlar, Old Harrovian and Sussex skipper, toss the coin, and once more Ronnie Burnet calls wrong. Robin, sporting a colourful cravat, opts to bat. It has been a long, hot summer and only six times have Yorkshire enjoyed first knock. They are top of the championship table, but they are having to do it the hard way.

It is the end of August 1959. It is eight years now, back in the days of King George VI and the Festival of Britain, since a county other than Surrey has hoisted the championship pennant. Lying in second place, with a game in hand, Surrey are still favourites to extend this winning sequence, but Yorkshire are determined to shake off their weariness for one last victory. Never before in their history have they gone so long without a title, and their yearning for success adds an edge to this game at Hove. "There were lots of Yorkshiremen in the crowd,"

Bryan recalls. "Some were travelling with us on the Southern tour. Others were living down there. It was amazing."

Alan Oakman and Les Lenham open for Sussex while Freddie Trueman takes the new ball with Brian Close. *'Trueman started the Sussex troubles,'* Tony Goodridge writes in the Manchester Guardian, *'by having Lenham caught off the handle of his bat from a bouncer.'* "Hove was a magnificent track," Jim remembers. "It was always green on the first morning but, if you'd only lost two or three wickets by the afternoon, you could cash in on it. On the second day it was absolutely magnificent. Then on the third it would turn a little bit, not really that much. It was perfect for a good game of cricket. We had marvellous games here."

It is August 1959. The average household spends one pound eight shillings a week on food.

Ken Taylor replaces Brian Close and sends down his gentle seamers. 'Phantom seamers,' Jim calls them. "I was just a bits and pieces bowler," Ken says. "I was put on when it didn't happen for the strike bowlers." Today, to add to their difficulties, Bob Platt is twelfth man, resting sore shins. *'For the benefit of the modern mechanically minded,'* Tony Goodridge explains, *'shin soreness is roughly the human equivalent of metal fatigue.'* Does Ken find some early greenness in the wicket? Or does the ball wobble as he bowls uphill into the offshore wind? Whichever way, there is *'some undistinguished stroke-making'* as Oakman, Suttle, Dexter and Parks all find themselves dismissed by Ken, a spell of four for 13. Hubert Doggart is lbw Close, and it is 67 for six.

Cricket at Hove. It is Brighton in Alan Ross's poem.

'Trains will decant
People with baskets, litter and opinions, the seaside's staple
Ingredients.'

Opinions. Why haven't England chosen Jim Parks for the West Indies? He's scored 2000 runs, and he's top of the wicket-keeping list. Okay, he only took up keeping last summer. Okay, maybe Keith Andrew is technically better. But what an asset he would be with the bat! Were you down at Worthing last week for his hundred against Derbyshire? What about his century at Old Trafford? Fastest of the season, wasn't it?

Jim has spent his boyhood on this ground, watching his father. He was here as a six-year-old the day Hugh Bartlett caned a 57-minute century against the 1938 Australians. Hugh won the Lawrence Trophy for the fastest hundred that summer, and now Jim will win it for his innings at Old Trafford. "I went in just as they took the new ball," he recalls. He curses Ted Dexter as they cross. "What a time to get out," but Ken Higgs bowls too short and in two overs Jim hits him for 34. "And Brian Statham the other end. Well, you didn't slog Brian too far, but I managed to get a few through. In fact, I broke my bat trying to hit Brian over the top. So we wasted a couple of minutes on that." His century takes 61 minutes. "It was one of those things that happen. It was incredible. Every time I hit the ball it went for four."

"The light was so wonderful at Old Trafford," Jim recalls. "And the crowd really knew their cricket." It is not so wonderful for Ken Taylor when he first plays there, a youngster going out to bat in front of a Whit Monday crowd. "It's a long way from the changing room down to the middle. You have a lot of time to think. There was a gate onto the field with a man to open it. 'Don't be long now, son,' he said as I went past him. Tattersall was bowling. A great off-spinner. He had three men close in on the leg side for the catch. So I told myself not to play anything which set off on the leg stick or outside. Well, he sent down this ball on the leg stick, so I brandished arms. It was his floater. Off and middle went over first ball. Twenty-three and a half thousand people there. I could have died on the spot. I dragged myself off the pitch and, as I passed the gateman, he touched his cap and said 'Thanks very much, son'."

Cricket at Hove. Don Smith and Tiger Pataudi at the wicket. *'Trueman was recalled at 1.15 to dismiss the final pair of ranking batsmen,'* the Daily Telegraph reporter writes. *'Almost his final fling before lunch, a bouncer, flew off Pataudi's bat and lobbed wicket-keeper and slips.'* Survival is achieved, and lunch is taken at 76 for six.

And who writes this report in Monday's Daily Telegraph? Why, none other than Robin Marlar. He is Sussex's amateur captain, but the game supports him financially in other ways. The Duke of Norfolk is President of the county, and Robin is his librarian at Arundel Castle, though there are not many books catalogued in the course of a cricketing summer. "This may be the twilight of the amateur," E.W. Swanton declares on the same page of the Daily Telegraph. For Robin, there will be this one last week of captaincy, then he will be off to the election hustings. The Conservative candidate for the Derbyshire mining town of Bolsover. "Why he did it, I don't know," Jim says. "He was always an adventurous sort of person," Hubert Doggart recalls.

Don Smith and Tiger Pataudi return to the fray after lunch. The seasoned pro and the schoolboy amateur. They still talk of the day here in 1957 when Don plundered the Gloucestershire off-spinners. The prepared strip is waterlogged, and they agree to play on the edge of the square, just forty yards from the pavilion. Don is a forcing left-hander, and he hits the ball like a tracer bullet again and again into the crowd. Young Derek Hawkins bowls two overs for 33, then, as Bomber Wells is brought back, the members start to leave their seats. "You've never seen such an exodus," Bomber laughs. "Then this old chap runs on the field with a little umbrella." He approaches the umpire and points to Bomber. "That man there will get someone killed. You've got to take him off." Bomber hears rumours that Don's contract is not to be renewed at the end of that season, but his assault on Bomber sets off a run spree that by the Lord's Test sees him in the England team.

Tiger Pataudi is just eighteen years old, a schoolboy at Winchester College where Hubert Doggart is now a master. Sussex has always been a county to welcome amateur guests in their summer holidays. Hubert and Tiger, Ted Dexter when he was at Cambridge, the Reverend David Sheppard. As late as 1962, Jim will find himself playing in the second eleven to accommodate the Oxford University keeper. By this time Jim will have kept wicket six times for England, but "it was still the old days of the amateur committee, kindred spirits." It is not the best way to maintain morale among the professionals. "In the early fifties," Jim remembers, "the amateurs stayed in one hotel, the pros in another. And until the mid-fifties, they had a dressing room at the front so they could look out at the cricket, and we were at the back." Hubert Doggart remembers differently. "That's complete bunkum," he says. "We all stayed together for away matches. It was only in Eastbourne week that the amateurs stayed at the Grand Hotel and the pros went home. And the front dressing room was for the senior pros as well as the amateurs."

Tiger Pataudi. His father played for England and for India. He is a popular young man, and this is his third summer holiday in the Sussex team. He has grown up a lot since that debut at Worcester. "He got roughed up by Jack Flavell," Jim remembers. Flav bounces him out in the first innings and, when he joins Jim at the wicket in the second, they know what to expect. "Get on the back foot," Jim tells him and, when the inevitable bouncer comes down, Tiger is quick to duck. "But he left his bat in the air. The ball hit it and went down to third man for four." His first runs in senior cricket. Here at Hove, two years later, he compiles a maiden fifty. *'Smith and Pataudi knew exactly how to deal with all inadequacies of length or direction and in the next hundred minutes they added 90 runs before Pataudi who had just passed an excellent 50 lost his off stump to a ball from Trueman that came back very fast.'* 157 for seven.

Cricket at Brighton.
'ladies clap from check rugs, talk to retired colonels;
On tomato-red verandas the scoring rate is discussed.'

Cricket at Brighton. Or is it cricket at Hove? Brighton is raffish Regency, Hove is Edwardian respectability. Brighton is hills and hotels, the extravagant Pavilion and the two pleasure piers, Hove is well-laid out streets and family housing. Brighton is the Sussex of Ranjitsinhji and Duleepsinhji, Lord Edward Dexter and Tiger Pataudi. Hove is the Parks family, the Langridge brothers, George Cox father and son. Sometimes, as in that golden summer of 1953, David Sheppard's single year of captaincy when they come so close to the championship, it all seems to fuse together. Sometimes, alas, it does not. In his career Jim will serve under more than a dozen captains, but he will rate none higher than the Reverend David. "He got the best out of everybody. And he was a tremendous player as well."

It is late August 1959. 'Men are going bright and gay,' the Brighton and Hove Gazette declares. 'Colour has taken a long time to arrive in the conservative world of men's clothing, but it is here at last and here, so the experts say, to stay.'

Ian Thomson hits Illingworth for six, and Sussex reach 210 all out. *'Sussex at least had a score of respectability,'* Tony Goodridge writes, *'with which to test*

Yorkshire's batting.' At the Oval, Middlesex's lower order batting is making life harder for Surrey.

Opinions. Why are Surrey struggling this year? Well, Peter May's been out since July. Had a major operation, hasn't he? They won six of the seven games he played, and they've only won six more all season. And Tony Lock has had to change his bowling action, hasn't he? He hasn't done so well.

Throwing and dragging are now the great controversies of world cricket. Through the seven years of Surrey's success, England have been the best team in the world, but Australia have beaten them 4-0 in the winter, and in every state there are bowlers with suspect actions. The clean-up in England begins with Tony Lock. "I remember down at Hastings," Jim recalls. "Little Arthur McIntyre was keeping wicket, and Locky let his quick one go. Down the leg side to a left-hander. It was four byes before little Mac could move. He suddenly looked up at Locky. 'What do you think I am?' he said. 'An Aunt Sally.'" But Tony Lock is a great bowler, he has changed his action, and he will become a great bowler again. "It was marvellous to see Locky with a straight arm." In 1958, he takes 170 wickets at 12.08. In 1959, 111 at 21.38.

Opinions. Yorkshire did right last summer to sack Wardle and the others, didn't they? Okay, Wardle was the best slow left-arm bowler in the country, but they weren't a happy team. All those star players, and they finished eleventh, didn't they? Now, with this team of youngsters, they're top of the table. "Certainly there was a better spirit," Ken remembers. "Johnny had the temperament that, if he thought something, he had to say it. A lot of people in that side were niggling and niggling, and he was the spokesman. He didn't do anything worse than one or two others, but he was the scapegoat."

The previous summer Ronnie Burnet, a chemical engineer by profession, jumps up from captaincy of the seconds to first team skipper. He has six Test players in his side, and he has never played a game of first-class cricket in his life. But, at the end of that first disastrous summer, the committee takes his side and in 1959 he brings through some of the young players he has captained in the second eleven. Phil Sharpe and Brian Bolus, Bob Platt and Don Wilson. He is forty years old, and nobody else is more than twenty-eight. "He created such a great atmosphere in the team," Ken recalls. Ronnie is not a bowler and he scores few runs, "but he got this extra ten per cent out of everybody else so it was worth it." Everybody knows that he will retire at the end of the summer, and this game at Hove will determine whether his young team can bring glory to his brief moment in Yorkshire's illustrious history.

It is August 1959. 'Carry On Nurse' is showing at the local Odeon, and the town's first family planning clinic opens.

Robin Marlar leads Sussex onto the field. "Mad Marlar," Bomber Wells says mischievously. "They used to say how the Sussex team only followed him onto the field out of curiosity." "He did some odd things as captain," Jim admits, "but he always had Sussex cricket at heart."

Ian Thomson runs down the slope with the new ball. For years he will carry this Sussex attack. Then, as he fades from the scene, a young John Snow will replace him. "Had Snowy been young with Ian Thomson," Jim hypothesises, "we could have won the championship." Ian Thomson, at the start of 1952 he comes down for a trial. He is a batsman, making runs in Essex club cricket, and he scores a century in a pre-season friendly with Hampshire. Then they give him a bowl. By the end of the summer, he is taking the new ball for the county. But in fourteen years he never comes close to another century.

Ted Dexter comes uphill. "Ted was very quick when he wanted to be. He had a magnificent physique, lovely action. But he liked to swing it around so he mostly bowled medium pace. I used to stand up to him. The only trouble was, if they nicked a four or something, he'd suddenly bowl a bouncer without any warning, and I'd be heading for cover."

Opinions. "If Dexter had been a professional," Somerset's Ken Biddulph says, "he'd have been a great bowler. He'd bowl four or five overs, then he'd lose interest and give the ball to somebody else."

'Dexter drove Bolus so far back that he knocked down his wicket.' "Brian used to play back a long way," Jim recalls. *'In the same over Padgett, having played one dreadful stroke at an outswinger that he could not reach anyway, nibbled at the next, a very much better one, and was caught at the wicket.'* Yorkshire are 6 for two. Ken Taylor has turned an ankle in the field and is batting down the order but, when Close and Bryan Stott are out, it is 78 for four when he comes to the crease. 81 for five when he is lbw Thomson 3. *'Yorkshire, the leaders, are in something of a mess. By the day's end they had mustered a rather frail-looking 89 for five wickets.'*

It is the second Saturday of the football season. Wolverhampton Wanderers are defending champions, but in May next year they will lose their title to Burnley. Brighton and Hove Albion are in the old Division Two, along with great clubs like Aston Villa, Liverpool and Huddersfield Town. When Brighton visit Huddersfield, will little Kenny Suttle come up against Ken Taylor? Most of the Sussex professionals play a good class of football around the county. "In those days," Jim remembers, "when we came back for the start of the cricket season, we were a lot fitter."

Ken is studying Fine Art at the Slade, and his football training is two evenings a week with his brother Jeff at Fulham. "Nowadays there's so much more money in football," he reflects. "The clubs can demand more of the players. They're much fitter than we were, and the skills are much better. Our game was slower." And cricket skills, have they improved, too? "No, they're not as good now. The fielding has improved tremendously, but that's the only aspect that has. We were brought up on uncovered wickets. Technique was so much more important than it is today. Nowadays I think we come unstuck when the ball does anything."

168

On Monday morning another large holiday crowd settles onto the benches and into the deck chairs. There is no pre-session circuit training by the Sussex team, just a few stretching exercises in the changing rooms, a few balls by Ian Thomson before play starts. "They do it an hour before the start now," Jim says. "Then they go back in and stiffen up. I don't think it does them any good whatsoever. We did it at the right time, and we did it off our own bat. We didn't have somebody saying, 'Go on, get out there, you've got to do this, that and the other'. I'm convinced we were far more conscientious in what we did."

Jim has broken his left thumb at Eastbourne, and he is playing four days later. For this match at Hove, Sam Cowan the masseur has fitted him up with an iron thumb-stall. "It was very painful every time I got one on the end, but it wore off after a while." Ian Thomson has sore shins, but he plays through them. "These days you'd have a stress fracture, and you wouldn't play for a month. You have these physiotherapists who have to justify their existence. We just had Sam Cowan, and all he had were his hands and an infra-red lamp." He quotes with approval what his friend Fred Titmus always says to him. "They keep on saying they're fitter than we were. They may be, but they're not tougher."

It is the last day of August 1959. From the fairgrounds and the transistor radios, the latest pop songs tell of teenage love.

'We'd laugh and we'd sing and do the little things that made my heart glow,
But she was too young to fall in love and I was too young to know.'

Eight of this Yorkshire side have played for the county as teenagers. "At that time," Ken explains, they were prepared to push younger players through. Now there's plenty in the Academy who are 20, 21, that haven't had a second team game. I don't know how they stick at it."

Jack Birkenshaw is just eighteen years old, and he goes out to bat with Ray Illingworth on Monday morning. He will never score a fifty in his three seasons with Yorkshire but, according to Tony Goodridge, *'he looked so unruffled and composed as if he had been playing this type of innings all his life.'* A partnership of 112 with Ray Illingworth tilts the contest crucially. *'Once again it was on the solid, competent and intelligent Illingworth that Yorkshire had to rely, and right admirably did he get down to the work in hand.'* Ray Illingworth, he is such a shrewd cricketer and he makes so much of his talent. Brian Close, by contrast, he always leaves you wondering how much more he might have achieved with a less quixotic personality. "Closey had so much ability," Jim reflects. "He should have played a hundred Tests."

Jack Birkenshaw is content to let the runs come slowly but *'as soon as he had bigger ideas,'* the Times reports, *'he was leg before, sweeping at Marlar'.* It is only Robin's 57th wicket of the season, a long way short of his tally in those glory years in the early fifties when he came down from Cambridge University. 34 wickets in three games at the end of 1952. "Jim Langridge used to stand at mid off and literally tell Robin how to bowl. He bowled magnificently. He spun it, he flighted it, he had control." He takes 136 wickets in David Sheppard's year of triumph, he only just misses out on Len Hutton's tour of the West Indies, but captaincy brings other cares and his loop grows flatter with each passing summer. "Dexter and I used to bait him about flighting the ball," Hubert Doggart recalls. His name has long stopped cropping up when Test selectors meet.

Hubert Doggart captained Sussex the year after David Sheppard, and now he pops back during his school holidays. He is still a fine player, and he brings a genuinely amateur spirit. "He swallowed a wasp once at Bournemouth," Jim recalls. "It hit the headlines. We told him it was because he always had his mouth open."

At half past two Ray Illingworth brings up his fourth century of the summer and, when he finally falls to a legside catch by Jim Parks, ouch, that left thumb again, Yorkshire have a healthy lead of 49. *'All season,'* the Times records, *'Yorkshire have complained of a tail that is impossibly long. Sometimes it has started at No. 6, with due respect to Wilson, who quite recently was going in last for his club side.'* While Ray is scoring at the other end, Don Wilson is happy to play second fiddle. *'For the best part of an hour he played virtually the same stroke to every ball. A telescopic forward prod.'* Now, with Fred as his partner, he competes for the limelight, lofting the ball with confidence into the deep. A straight six off Marlar brings up the 300 and his first ever fifty. With the lead standing at 97, he is last man out, caught one-handed by Alan Oakman at slip. Alan does not drop many. In the second of his two Tests, he snaps up five of Jim Laker's record nineteen wicket haul.

At the Oval, Surrey, still without Peter May, are all out 79 runs behind Middlesex. But this Hove wicket is giving no help to the bowlers, and there is plenty of work yet for Yorkshire to do.

Cricket at Brighton. *'Trains will decant*
People with baskets, litter and opinions, the seaside's staple
Ingredients.'

Opinions. Who's the best fast bowler in county cricket? Brian Statham is top of the averages; he takes some beating. Frank Tyson is quick. Not as quick as he was five years ago, though. Les Jackson, why do they never pick him for England? "The greatest fast medium bowler ever," Bomber Wells declares. "Better than Trueman or Statham. I could take a chair, sit down by the sight screen and watch him bowl all day." No, Fred has to be the best. "He swung it more than any genuinely fast bowler," Jim remembers. "I rate him as the greatest because he was at you all the time. Fred never bowled wide of the off stump. He made you play. That's where his greatness was."

1959 is a long, hot summer. Fred is a fast bowler with a long run, and he will bowl 1072 overs before summer is out. On this batsman's wicket at Hove he cannot make the vital breakthrough. But Brian Close can. He gets an in-swinger to jump and hit Alan Oakman on the arm, and the ball falls back onto the stumps. Then Don Wilson lures Kenny Suttle out of his crease and has Les Lenham caught in the covers. Sussex are just two runs ahead with three wickets down.

170

It is 1959. "Hove was a magnificent track," Jim remembers, "but it got very poor in the late sixties. Then Bert Lock became Inspector of Pitches and advocated Surrey loam everywhere. That made a featherbed of all the wickets. It's getting better again, but it'll be a long time before we get the Surrey loam completely out of the system."

'Dexter and Parks took the war into the other camp,' E.W. Swanton writes, *'and we saw some fine driving by both to end the long day. Trueman was withstood, and Parks set hundreds of children making parrot noises by hitting Illingworth successively for six and four.'* Tony Goodridge waxes more poetic. *'As the slanting rays of the sun gave way to a foreboding autumnal chill, Dexter and Parks went briskly about the getting of runs. There is still all to play for today.'*

"We played fairly and squarely and straight," Ken remembers. "There was no team that I didn't look forward to playing against. The manners, the way the game was played, it was a really super way of playing cricket. I don't see how today you can spend eight hours playing cricket against a team who cheat and shout and scream and then expect to have a nice friendly drink in the bar afterwards."

Here they all sit in the bar at Hove. "It was lovely playing against Yorkshire when Fred and Closey were young," Bomber Wells recalls. "At the end of the day, you'd split up into parties. Fred would be up one end of the bar, Closey up the other. When you got fed up with listening to Fred, you could go and listen to Closey." Neither of them is short of an opinion.

"There were some fabulous chaps playing cricket then," Bryan Stott recalls. "Real good pals around all the counties."

It is the last day of August, and television viewers watch President Eisenhower in relaxed armchair conversation with Prime Minister Harold Macmillan. The country is two months away from its General Election, and Robin Marlar will soon be off to Bolsover to tell the mining community that they have never had it so good. Derbyshire's Les Jackson is one who receives his election address.

In Brighton's coffee bars Elvis Presley sings from the juke boxes.

> *'When you're gone, yes I dream a little,*
> *Dream as years go by.*
> *Now and then there's a fool such as I.'*

In Hove magistrates are insisting on licenses for juke boxes. According to the Gazette, *'teenagers sit gloomily around in an eerie silence'.*

Tuesday brings further sunshine and, as E.W. Swanton writes, *'there was every possible ingredient of a perfect day's cricket except one: time.'* An eleven o'clock start and a four thirty finish. Should Sussex press on and set a tempting declaration? Or should they dig in and force Yorkshire to bowl them out? Opinions differ in the crowd, and opinions differ in the Sussex side.

There is certainly a spirit of adventure in the way that Jim Parks and Ted Dexter set about the bowling first thing. *'Trueman, downhill and downwind, fired the first salvoes with authentic fire and speed'*, but he is safely despatched. Jim and Ted are on their home patch after all. It is not like facing Fred at Bradford. "The old gate at Bradford would clang behind you," Jim remembers. "It was like a bull-ring. You'd drop down. And Fred invariably would be running down the hill at you." Ted is caught at extra cover, but Jim is at the peak of his game.

Jim Parks. "I do not think there has been a more fluent stroke-maker in England since Denis Compton," David Sheppard will write in 1964. "When he goes to make a drive every part of the body seems to flow into the stroke: every stroke in the game is at his command." *'One could not escape the thought,'* E.W. Swanton writes. *'How greatly might his batting have been appreciated in the West Indies.'* Little does he know that Jim will take up a coaching post in Trinidad and be called up for the final Test, scoring a match-saving century. Today he plays his shots in the hope of an early declaration. *'Parks,'* Robin Marlar writes later in the Brighton Gazette, *'launched himself into one of those bursts of hitting which are at once delightful and infuriating. He tried to hit Wilson for a series of sixes and in the end fell, as he was almost bound to do, to a catch at deep extra.'* He has made 85, and lunch comes at 280 for seven, 183 runs on. Tiger Pataudi and Ian Thomson are the not out batsmen, and Tiger is again equal to Fred's new ball burst.

"Tiger didn't always play straight," Hubert Doggart recalls, "but he cut and hooked beautifully. He had a wonderful eye." So wonderful that, within two years, he will become only the tenth batsman ever to hit a century in each innings against Yorkshire, despatching Trueman, Illingworth, Close and Wilson to every corner of the Parks in Oxford. Later that summer a car crash will see a splinter of glass destroy the lens of his right eye. How much greatness he might have achieved is underlined six months later at New Delhi when he employs his new one-eyed stance to hit a two-and-a-half-hour century against England. At Hove in 1959 he is still a schoolboy, and the ups and downs of his cricketing career are all ahead of him.

Opinions. They should get rid of the amateurs now, have professional captains. It's got to come. "The old amateur captains did rely on the senior players," Jim reflects. "The senior pro would be a very responsible position. I think the captain now is on his own a lot of the time." And the genuine amateur did have an independence. "Being an amateur," Ken says, "Ronnie Burnet could dictate to a certain extent to the committee. If he didn't agree, he could resign, and they wouldn't have wanted that."

When will the declaration come? "I remember," Jim says, "several of us saying, 'Come on now, Robin, we've got to declare.' But he wouldn't. No way. I don't think he wanted to give Yorkshire anything. That was his attitude." Hubert Doggart remembers differently. "He went to a committee meeting. He wasn't there."

The Yorkshire players also remember the declaration debate. "Robin Marlar didn't like the North," Ken recalls. "He didn't like the Yorkies in particular." Ronnie Burnet writes of their response to his batting on: "Robin Marlar made it absolutely clear that under no circumstances was he going to declare since the championship was at stake. He had the whole Yorkshire team seething." "Well, that's true," Bryan Stott says. "We were all willing him to declare, to make a game of it. Mind you, if we'd been in his position, we wouldn't have declared."

Yorkshire have their own problems. Fred is knackered, and Brian Close gives him hell at lunch. "Wash your hands of Fred," he tells Ronnie as they walk back out, and it is left to the slow bowlers to winkle out the tail, with the batsmen under instructions to stay in. "The wicket was so good," Bryan says. "It wasn't turning. If the Sussex lads had really wanted to keep it going, they could have stayed all day." But do they? *'Pataudi continued to play well and freely until he seemed to think his part had been played,'* E.W. Swanton writes. *'Thomson followed him.'* "A couple of them gave it away," Jim recalls. It only leaves the captain himself between Yorkshire and a run chase.

Robin Marlar the batsman. They still tell the tale of the evening at the Oval, when Doug Insole sends him out as night-watchman. In one version of the story he is already in evening clothes, and Doug is enjoying some mischief at his expense. He attempts to refuse the duty and he returns to the pavilion, stumped second ball for 6. "As I was saying," he says. "I'm not a night-watchman." Here at Hove he is caught first ball by Jack Birkenshaw. And Jack is fielding on the square leg boundary. It is 2.37, and Yorkshire have to score 215 in 103 minutes. Surrey are struggling at The Oval, and it looks increasingly that victory here will settle the championship race.

It is September 1959. British Nylon launches BRI-LON. 'Super-soft sheets and cosy night-dresses. Washing in the morning and dried by bed-time, that's the BRI-LON touch.'

Cyril Turner, the Yorkshire scorer, has gone home ill from the previous game, and the young Philip Sharpe is deputising for him. He joins the team in the feverish atmosphere of the Yorkshire dressing room. Ronnie Burnet announces a batting order - Taylor, Stott, Close, Padgett - and that provokes debate. Dougie Padgett at four? Not every member of the side thinks he is the man for such a frantic run chase, but Ronnie stands his ground. His style is good humour and discipline. And Philip Sharpe is sent off to calculate Sussex's over rate in the first innings. "It was the first time we'd decided to look at runs per over," Bryan recalls. "We insisted that they put the overs up each time. We reckoned we needed eight or nine per over from the start."

Eight or nine per over, and the ever accurate Ian Thomson to come downhill, downwind, with the new ball. "He used to swing it in," Jim explains, "bowl a cutter. He was very, very accurate. I can remember Denis Compton trying to get after him down here when Tommy was quite young, and Denis couldn't. If you stopped Denis going for runs, you'd achieved something."

The Yorkshire scorebook is safely stored in the Chief Executive's office, but the neat, bold writing of Philip Sharpe is still quite legible, though the black ink is starting to fade with the passage of almost forty years. Thomson, first over: dot, four, four, five, one, one. Second over: six, one, six, dot, four, dot. Two overs, nought for 32. "I hit Thomson over his head for six," Bryan recalls. "I can remember his eyes. They popped a bit." Ken is lbw Dexter, but Brian Close hits the ball high over the scoreboard, causing an unwanted delay, before he too falls to Ted Dexter. It is 40 for two in the fourth over.

"We were always prepared to go in and throw our wickets away," Ken says. "You only need one or two selfish players, and your chance of winning the championship is over." And nobody has ever accused Brian Close of that sort of selfishness. In time he will captain this side, and Ken can still hear him sending out Philip Sharpe and himself for quick runs before a declaration. "We want 100 in forty minutes," Brian instructs. "Don't get out, and don't make it look easy." What a contrast to playing for counties like Kent and Glamorgan! "They were never challenging for the championship," Ken reflects. "Their batsmen could play every innings however they wanted. '100 in forty, don't get out and don't make it look easy.' They had none of that. The game would be much better if these statistics were not made as important as they are."

Bryan Stott is left-handed. He always flashes outside the off stump, and he runs so well between the wickets. Dougie Padgett is right-handed, and he is the more correct batsman. "He was the perfect man at four," Bryan says. "I was chancing my arm. Batting like that, it's pure luck rather than good management that decides whether you succeed. But Dougie's was a real cricket innings. He batted beautifully." The 100 is up by half past three, 150 by ten to four.

Opinions. I'd stop bowling so straight. I'd put the fielders on one side of the wicket and bowl to that side. *'Sitting in the press box,'* Tony Goodridge writes, *'one felt that one would have arranged the field differently.'* No, Robin Marlar argues in the Brighton Gazette, *'with a right- and left-hander batting, it would have meant an immense field change with every ball and would, I think, have been hardly sporting.'*

"Cricket's become a defensive game now," Jim says. "We had spinners; we were attacking all the time. Because of one-day cricket, we've brought in the medium pace seamer who bowls just short of a length. Our medium pacers swung it and seamed it. They bowled a fuller length and let the ball do the work."

Robin Marlar takes to fielding on the boundary. "We got on top of him too fast," Bryan explains. "It was the running that did it. He couldn't set a field to stop the singles." Bryan is on 77 when he hits the ball high to leg and Tiger Pataudi takes a wonderful running catch. "But he stepped over," Bryan recalls. "He immediately said it was no catch." But Robin Marlar runs all the way across to talk to Tiger. Thirty-eight years have passed, but the memory still sends Bryan into paroxysms of laughter. "He tried to convince him he'd caught it." It is a six, but, when Bryan lofts the ball once more towards Tiger, the catch is held inside the boundary. He has made 96, and it is 181 for three.

Whatever is in his mind that afternoon, Robin Marlar is the model of generosity in the Brighton Gazette. *'The strokes that Padgett and Stott played were perfectly executed, their running was miraculous in its understanding, and there was no sign of crudeness or bludgeoning in their stroke play.'* He will have one more game here as Sussex captain, Kenny Suttle will deliberately give away his wicket so that he can walk out to bat on the final day, and the crowd will cheer him all the way to the wicket. "He certainly wasn't the greatest captain," Jim says, "but he always had Sussex cricket at heart." 22% of the Bolsover constituency will prefer him to his Labour opponent - though not, they say, Les Jackson. And he will not be the last Sussex captain to wear the blue rosette. At the next election, when Labour's white heat of technology will triumph, Ted Dexter will stand in Cardiff South-East. "Against James Callaghan," Jim says. "Another masterly move."

Fred is promoted for a quick biff, and Jim stumps him. "I do remember that one. He hit over the top, and he dragged a little. I was quite pleased with that one." The 200 is up in 24 overs. Dougie Padgett is caught at deep mid-wicket for 79, but there are still seven minutes to spare when Brian Bolus glances the winning four. Surrey wickets are falling like nine pins at The Oval, and the champagne is soon flowing. "Tommy, 87 off ten," Jim reads in Wisden. "That was incredible. He was one that never got slogged."

The celebrations last long into the night, and Ronnie Burnet leads them in his Jaguar to his favourite pub, The Bell in St Neots. "He'd fill two petrol tanks so he wouldn't have to stop," Ken remembers. "He'd do 139, and it wasn't even motorway in those days." He stays for a steak and a bottle of Burgundy, and he does not make it to Scarborough till the morning. "The one thing that still gets to my heart and soul," Bryan tells, "was the reception back in Yorkshire." It is two or two thirty when they arrive in Scarborough. "We were all in different cars so we arrived in penny numbers. But everybody was up waiting in the hotels. It will stay with me for ever."

The next morning they play M.C.C. at the Scarborough Festival, and there is no need for the captains to toss. "You have to field," Doug Insole tells Ronnie, and the opposition and crowd form a tunnel from pavilion to wicket for the players to walk down. "I'm almost in tears now thinking about it," Bryan says. "And I remember thinking to myself, 'By Gosh, this is something I'm never going to forget.'" Ken Taylor's twisted ankle keeps him out of the game and, when it is Yorkshire's turn to bat, his place alongside Bryan is taken by Dickie Bird, his last game for the county. "He was temperamentally unsuited to be a player," Ken recalls. "If a wicket fell and it was his turn to bat, you knew where to look for him. He was on the loo." "Come on, Dickie, take deep breaths," Bryan tells him all the way to the wicket, and they put on 146 together.

Connie Francis has hit the Top Ten with her version of 'Who's Sorry Now?', but in the world of county cricket the song is 'Who's Surrey Now?'.

'The era of Surrey's domination has ended,' the Times correspondent writes. *'With May to guide their fortunes it might have been another story. But the change of champions will do our cricket good and it is often said that when Yorkshire thrive then England prosper with them. The truth of which we shall duly*

see.' And Yorkshire do prosper. This young side will win seven titles in ten years. But England? Have they ever regained the supremacy they enjoyed during Surrey's reign?

Ronnie Burnet will give way to Vic Wilson, Yorkshire's first professional captain, and in three years' time there will be no amateurs and professionals, no gentlemen and players, just cricketers. Affluence will bring a greater classlessness, and people will find other things to do than to spend their days watching cricket at grounds like Hove. Trains will no longer decant people with baskets, litter and opinions. Instead, there will be holidays on Spanish beaches and a great axing of branch lines. The world will move on, and cricket will have to move with it.

"I consider myself lucky to have played in the fifties," Jim says. "It was a fun game then. I think getting the money's the fun these days." There is certainly no easy money for cricketers in the fifties. "I remember," Ken says, "Ray Illingworth and his family coming back to Headingley from a Test match. The Test had finished early, and they ate some of the sandwiches left over from our tea. Do you know, they gave him a bill. Can you believe it?"

"You didn't always think so then," Bryan reflects, "but it was the most wonderful time."

SUSSEX v YORKSHIRE

Hove. 29 & 31 August, 1 September 1959

YORKSHIRE WON BY 5 WICKETS

SUSSEX

A.S.M. Oakman	st Binks b Taylor	33	b Close		7
L.J. Lenham	c Taylor b Trueman	4	c Stott b Wilson		66
K.G. Suttle	c Illingworth b Taylor	5	st Binks b Wilson		22
E.R. Dexter	c & b Taylor	14	c Birkenshaw b Wilson		33
+J.M. Parks	c Bolus b Taylor	6	c Birkenshaw b Wilson		85
D.V. Smith	c Close b Illingworth	49	c Bolus b Taylor		31
G.H.G. Doggart	lbw b Close	5	c Birkenshaw b Illingworth		10
Nawab of Pataudi	b Trueman	52	c Close b Illingworth		37
N.I. Thomson	lbw b Illingworth	21	b Illingworth		12
A.E. James	b Illingworth	4	not out		0
*R.G. Marlar	not out	13	c Birkenshaw b Illingworth		0
Extras	lb 4	4	b 4, lb 4		8
		210			**311**

1-28, 2-40, 3-51, 4-62, 5-63, 6-67, 7-157, 8-192, 9-193, 10-210
1-14, 2-80, 3-99, 4-174, 5-195, 6-247, 7-266, 8-306, 9-311, 10-311

Trueman	19	5	40	2	24	5	60	0
Close	17	3	54	1	19	6	51	1
Taylor	22	9	40	4	8	5	5	1
Illingworth	14.2	3	51	3	28.3	8	66	4
Wilson	5	1	21	0	24	7	78	4
Birkenshaw					7	0	43	0

YORKSHIRE

W.B. Stott	c & b Suttle	34	c Pataudi b Marlar		96
J.B. Bolus	hit wkt b Dexter	1	not out		6
D.E.V. Padgett	c Parks b Dexter	0	c Dexter b Thomson		79
D.B. Close	b Dexter	14	c Parks b Dexter		12
R. Illingworth	c Parks b James	122	not out		5
K. Taylor	lbw b Thomson	3	lbw b Dexter		1
J. Birkenshaw	lbw b Marlar	38			
D. Wilson	c Oakman b Marlar	55			
*J.R. Burnet	c Marlar b Dexter	1	st Parks b Marlar		11
F.S. Trueman	c Pataudi b James	7			
+J.G. Binks	not out	1			
Extras	b 24, lb 6, nb 1	31	b 1, lb 4, nb 3		8
		307	(5 wkts)		**218**

1-6, 2-6, 3-38, 4-78, 5-81, 6-193, 7-259, 8-264, 9-305, 10-307
1-18, 2-40, 3-181, 4-199, 5-206

Thomson	31	7	65	1	10	0	87	1
Dexter	29	7	63	4	10.3	0	69	2
Smith	4	1	14	0				
James	24	4	67	2	2	0	15	0
Marlar	15.4	7	29	2	6	0	39	2
Suttle	6	1	20	1				
Oakman	6	1	18	0				
Doggart	1	1	0	0				

Umpires: R.S. Lay and F.S. Lee

THE STUMPS ARE DRAWN

Arthur Milton looks back. "We used to learn just as much in the bar afterwards as we did on the field."

'The past is a foreign country: they do things differently there.'

Crowds fill the grounds, even for routine county games. In 1950 there is an average of 8,000 spectators at the three days of each championship match. There are few television sets to provide an easier, more comfortable entertainment. "If you weren't there," Don Shepherd reflects, "you didn't know. You could talk to your mates, that's all. There were no playbacks."

The players travel to the people. There are only two million cars in 1950 so the cricket goes out to towns like Kidderminster and Burton-on-Trent, Stroud and Huddersfield. "We used to go down to a place called Ashby-de-la-Zouch," Bernie Constable remembers. "What a bloody place that was! Just a village. The cricket ground was at the back of the pub, and that was it. You went in to change in the dressing room, and you were tripping over your own bags." "It was like climbing over an obstacle course," Maurice Hallam recalls. "Vic Munden was allocated the job of bringing some six inch nails to make sure we'd got enough pegs."

The championship is contested at a wide variety of venues, and the uncovered wickets add to the unpredictability of it all. Batsmen play fully forward and back, bowlers strive for lateral movement, and captains analyse the changing conditions. There is no question of waiting in the pavilion till the pitch eases. "The umpires would have you out there," Terry Spencer says. "Now everything has got to be perfect."

By the 1960s the world will be a faster place, and people will want more instant entertainment than three-day matches provide. "Limited over cricket?" Bomber Wells says. "Neville Cardus said to me, it's like trying to play Beethoven on a banjo." "You get the excitement of knowing that someone's going to win," Dickie Dodds says, "but I don't see the crowd excited by an art form, their spirits revived or re-created." There is artistry here in the fifties as Doug Wright runs through the repertoire of his medium-pace wrist-spin and Jim Laker teases the batsmen with his masterly control of flight. But, with covered wickets, heavy bats and three one-day competitions, do their modern equivalents have the opportunity to reach such levels of skill? "Nowadays," Malcolm Heath says, "it seems to me that the most important aspect is to get the overs in. It never seems to be about bowling the other side out."

39 wickets tumble in a day at Burton-on-Trent. Nobody there that day has ever forgotten it. But what shudder would the prospect of such a match send down the spine of today's Marketing Manager as he sells his corporate hospitality schemes?

Standardised facilities, standardised pitches. Today we are ill at ease with inconvenience and unpredictability. "We were put to the ultimate test almost every day," Tom Cartwright reflects. "An uncovered wicket could change four times in a day to suit four different bowlers." Suit the bowlers, yes, but what of the poor batsmen? In the fifties they struggle for a season's average of 30 or 35, whereas today they can play their shots with freedom. "One of the reasons our batsmen have problems with technique," Harold Rhodes says, "is that they play on too many wickets where the ball does nothing. When they get on a wicket that does a bit, they haven't got the technique. Once you've learnt to play on all sorts of wickets, you'll always be able to play on a covered wicket." "Peter May was the best post-war English batsman by a parish," John Pretlove believes, and Peter plays half his games on the Oval's bowling paradise. "I think we've got to give something back to the bowler, give him some help," Jim Parks says. "Then your batsmen will become better players."

The players of the fifties have learnt to play in city streets. "My early cricket was played against the lamp post," Sonny Avery says of his East End childhood, "or up in the park with a stick with a coat over it." They have learnt to play in schools with playing fields. How many of those playing fields are gone now? And in summer there is just this one sport for them to play. "It's one of the problems with cricket now," Arthur Milton says. "The talent that might be playing cricket is probably playing golf or tennis." In modern Britain, golf clubs have ten times as many members as cricket clubs. "We shall have to accept a lower standard," Dennis Brookes reflects.

For young boys after the war, childhood is an outdoor world. There are no video recorders and computer games, no car journeys to and from school. "Physically they're not as strong as they used to be," Ken Taylor says, a schoolmaster since his retirement from cricket. "I can see that at school. They haven't got that built-in stamina anymore. Thirty years ago they did have it."

"We had niggling injuries but we didn't say anything," Terry Spencer says. "If you didn't play, you didn't get paid. So we would bowl it off, grin and bear it, which you had to do in those days." There will no physical fitness routine to watch when you take your seat before play at a 1950s game, but the players are cricket fit. Not perhaps for thrilling dives on the boundary. "Maurice Tremlett used to tell me off if I did anything like that," Ken Biddulph recalls. "Forget the two runs, I want you fit to bowl." There are ninety-odd days on the fixture card. Opportunity for Johnny Wardle to bowl 1,857 overs in 1952, for Mike Smith to play 67 innings in 1959. "You can't play too much cricket," Bernie Constable says. "When you're only playing four months a year, that's not hard work. I think people make out they're working harder than what they really are."

"One day I was keeping at Lord's," Jim Parks remembers. "Les Lenham threw in. Well, Les was the worst thrower going. When Les got the ball, there'd be a cry of 'Back up', and everybody backed up all over the place. Anyway, he threw this one in, and my finger went right back. Totally dislocated. I whipped my gauntlet off and ran into the dressing room. 'Oh right,' Sam Cowan, the masseur, said. 'Turn away.' Crack. Back in. Plaster on. Straight onto the field again. Nowadays you'd be down the hospital for an x-ray." Geoff Edrich has been reduced to six-and-a-half stone in a Japanese prisoner-of-war camp. He is willing to bat on with a broken thumb. No elaborate physiotherapy equipment to justify, no injury insurance scheme to worry about. "They keep on saying they're fitter than we were," Fred Titmus says. "They may be, but they're not tougher."

There is food rationing in the early fifties, national service for all young men, a world still rebuilding from a long and hard war. There is little money for professional cricketers, certainly no sponsored car or free equipment. The journeys from ground to ground are long and arduous, and the hotels are often spartan. "The professionals were serfs," Richard Bernard says. "They were paid a pittance, then they had a benefit."

Yet around the counties there is a sense of community among the cricketers and a code of what is fair on the field of play. "The war was still so close," Tom Cartwright says. "People could see the consequences of doing wrong." Derbyshire's Cliff Gladwin is as hard a man as any on the circuit, but he uses his hardness to maintain standards as the young David Green discovers when he fails to walk in a benefit match. "We don't play cricket like that," Cliff growls at him. "The manners and the way the game was played," Ken Taylor reflects. "It was a really super way of playing cricket."

"I never saw players cheat," Bomber Wells says. "I caught Dick Spooner once, and I had this queer sensation that the ball had bounced. Dick started walking, and I said 'No, Dick, it landed'. Cooky was bowling. "You daft bugger," he says to me. The next ball Dick comes waltzing down the pitch, misses the ball by about five yards, and gets stumped. It wouldn't happen today, would it?"

Cricket is not yet a game for the television screen and the advertising sponsors. It is a game played by the people and for the people. It is a game with roots deep in the country's sporting culture, and its players nurture the skills that have been passed down to them. What else is there to do in a Stroud hotel lounge or a Kidderminster club bar but to talk cricket? How Sydney Barnes bowled a leg-cutter, how Wally Hammond took a slip catch, how Frank Woolley played the pull. Does anybody tell the players of today how Jim Laker gripped the ball? Bomber Wells tells of one current off-spinner. "He didn't even know who Jim Laker was."

"We used to enjoy our cricket in those days," Brian Close says. "Now they just walk around as if tomorrow will do. There's no urgency in it. 'Oh well, we've so many overs to bowl so we'll take our time.'" At Brentwood in 1952, Essex and Lancashire manage 370 overs in three days, and there are three changes of innings during playing time. The match regulations for such a game in the 1990s will allocate four days and stipulate a minimum of 386 overs, "and more often than not," Brian complains, "they have to do overtime to get that in."

"Each generation has its own pressures," Dickie Dodds says. "These matches are of the spirit in which we played our cricket. Because that spirit went, they tried to legislate to make people play the way the game should be played." "Cricket has changed its format almost totally," Tom Cartwright says. "When you take away some of the facets, which we have done, it shrinks in its artistic form, certainly in the disciplines required."

"I don't think the game's changed all that much," Bernie Constable says. "We always think they're not as good as we were, let's face it." "The game is still the same, isn't it?" Terry Spencer says. "But it's more intense. Nobody played any harder than we did, but we seemed to enjoy it a bit more back in them days."

"English cricket was at its best in the fifties," Dennis Brookes says. The skills, the spectators, the fair play, the sense of community. "I still maintain that it was a golden age," says Malcolm Heath.

'There are few personalities in the game today.' ... *'Technical developments have all been defensive, especially in bowling tactics and field placing.'* ... *'The truth is that the majority of players do not adopt a dynamic attitude towards the game.'* ... *'Our first-class cricketers seldom are allowed to play for fun.'* All these four statements can be found in the Wisden of 1952.

Arthur Booth bowled slow left-arm for Yorkshire on either side of the second war, and he often said that it was a better game when he started than when he finished. "Mind you," he would add, "my father said the same." His father's playing days began in the Golden Age before the first war. "And his father before him said the same as well. My word, it must have been a hell of a game when it started."

Perhaps the past is a foreign country that the old, who once inhabited it, will always see through rose-tinted spectacles. Or are their memories our last contact with a lost world of well-honed craft skills and shared good sportsmanship? Could it be that, in the drive for profit and prosperity, we have started to forget why we created such a wonderful game? "The more money you get into a game," Martin Horton says. "The more cut-throat it gets."

"The trouble is," Brian Close says, "the game doesn't come first these days. The money comes first."

"It's all become very materialistic," Tom Cartwright says. "The other things were easier to achieve. Getting out into the country, doing the garden, going to cricket. Today people seem to be pursuing things that are beyond their reach."

"Money is not an adequate motive," says Dickie Dodds. "You've got to love cricket."

*

The stumps are drawn. The last orders are drunk. It is time to go home.

"Wonderful days in the sun," Arthur Milton recalls. "The days were never long enough."

"I'm glad I played when I did," Tom Cartwright reflects. "It was a magic time. I'm just sorry I'm not still playing."

COUNTY CHAMPIONSHIP TABLES 1952-1959

Where the total of results does not add up to the total matches played, there have been games in which no first innings decision was reached.

1952

		P	W	L	D	Pts
1	Surrey	28	20	3	5	256
2	Yorkshire	28	17	2	8	224
3	Lancashire	28	12	3	11	188
4	Derbyshire	28	11	8	9	164
5	Middlesex	28	11	12	4	136
6	Leicestershire	28	9	9	9	132
7	Glamorgan	28	8	7	13	130
8	Northants	28	7	8	12	128
9	Gloucestershire	28	7	10	11	124
10	Essex	28	8	4	13	120
10	Warwickshire	28	8	10	8	120
12	Hampshire	28	7	11	9	112
13	Sussex	28	7	12	6	96
14	Worcestershire	28	6	11	10	90
15	Kent	28	5	15	8	84
16	Nottinghamshire	28	2	12	13	72
17	Somerset	28	2	12	13	44

Lancashire, Essex, Warwickshire and Sussex each tied a match

1953

		P	W	L	D	Pts
1	Surrey	28	13	4	10	184
2	Sussex	28	11	3	13	168
3	Lancashire	28	10	4	10	156
3	Leicestershire	28	10	7	11	156
5	Middlesex	28	10	5	11	150
6	Derbyshire	28	9	7	9	136
6	Gloucestershire	28	9	7	10	136
8	Nottinghamshire	28	9	10	8	128
9	Warwickshire	28	6	7	14	124
10	Glamorgan	28	8	4	14	120
11	Northants	28	6	3	15	114
12	Essex	28	6	7	13	100
12	Yorkshire	28	6	6	13	100
14	Hampshire	28	6	11	11	96
15	Worcestershire	28	5	12	10	72
16	Kent	28	4	14	8	64
17	Somerset	28	2	19	6	36

Middlesex and Northants each tied a match

1954

		P	W	L	D	Pts
1	Surrey	28	15	3	8	208
2	Yorkshire	28	13	3	8	186
3	Derbyshire	28	11	6	9	168
4	Glamorgan	28	11	5	10	148
5	Nottinghamshire	28	10	6	8	144
6	Warwickshire	28	10	5	10	140
7	Middlesex	28	10	5	10	136
7	Northants	28	9	9	9	136
9	Sussex	28	8	7	12	120
10	Lancashire	28	6	3	12	108
11	Kent	28	5	7	15	100
11	Worcestershire	28	5	12	9	100
13	Gloucestershire	28	5	11	10	96
14	Hampshire	28	4	10	13	80
15	Essex	28	3	11	12	64
16	Leicestershire	28	3	9	11	62
17	Somerset	28	2	18	8	40

Yorkshire and Leicestershire each tied a match

1955

		P	W	L	D	Pts
1	Surrey	28	23	5	0	284
2	Yorkshire	28	21	5	2	268
3	Hampshire	28	16	5	6	210
4	Sussex	28	13	8	6	196
5	Middlesex	28	14	12	2	192
6	Leicestershire	28	11	10	7	154
7	Northants	28	9	10	9	148
8	Derbyshire	28	9	10	9	146
9	Lancashire	28	10	9	8	140
9	Warwickshire	28	10	9	9	140
11	Nottinghamshire	28	10	11	7	132
12	Gloucestershire	28	9	13	6	128
13	Kent	28	8	13	7	104
14	Essex	28	6	15	7	100
15	Worcestershire	28	5	17	6	84
16	Glamorgan	28	5	14	8	80
17	Somerset	28	4	17	7	64

Hampshire and Sussex each tied a match

182

1956

		P	W	L	D	Pts
1	Surrey	28	15	5	6	200
2	Lancashire	28	12	2	12	180
3	Gloucestershire	28	14	7	5	176
4	Northants	28	8	5	15	148
5	Middlesex	28	11	9	7	144
6	Hampshire	28	9	6	10	140
7	Yorkshire	28	8	7	10	136
8	Nottinghamshire	28	7	4	15	128
9	Sussex	28	7	10	9	112
9	Worcestershire	28	8	4	14	112
11	Essex	28	6	10	9	110
12	Derbyshire	28	7	6	11	102
13	Glamorgan	28	6	9	9	100
14	Warwickshire	28	5	11	9	80
15	Somerset	28	4	15	8	76
16	Kent	28	4	12	10	60
17	Leicestershire	28	3	12	9	56

1957

		P	W	L	D	Pts
1	Surrey	28	21	3	3	312
2	Northants	28	15	2	10	218
3	Yorkshire	28	13	4	11	190
4	Derbyshire	28	10	8	9	162
5	Essex	28	11	6	10	158
6	Lancashire	28	10	8	8	156
7	Middlesex	28	10	12	3	148
8	Somerset	28	9	14	5	138
9	Glamorgan	28	10	9	8	136
9	Sussex	28	8	9	9	136
11	Warwickshire	28	9	7	11	134
12	Gloucestershire	28	8	13	6	132
13	Hampshire	28	7	12	8	116
14	Kent	28	6	13	9	90
15	Nottinghamshire	28	5	13	9	88
16	Worcestershire	28	4	9	14	72
17	Leicestershire	28	2	16	9	40

1958

		P	W	L	D	Pts
1	Surrey	28	14	5	8	212
2	Hampshire	28	12	6	10	186
3	Somerset	28	12	9	7	174
4	Northants	28	11	6	6	160
5	Derbyshire	28	9	9	8	151
6	Essex	28	9	7	7	146
7	Lancashire	28	9	7	8	142
8	Kent	28	9	10	7	139
9	Worcestershire	28	9	7	8	134
10	Middlesex	28	7	4	16	130
11	Yorkshire	28	7	5	10	126
12	Leicestershire	28	7	13	6	104
13	Sussex	28	6	7	11	102
14	Gloucestershire	28	5	9	11	89
15	Glamorgan	28	5	11	11	82
16	Warwickshire	28	3	7	14	68
17	Nottinghamshire	28	3	15	8	50

1959

		P	W	L	D	Pts
1	Yorkshire	28	14	7	7	204
2	Gloucestershire	28	12	11	4	186
3	Surrey	28	12	5	11	186
4	Warwickshire	28	13	10	5	184
5	Lancashire	28	12	7	9	184
6	Glamorgan	28	12	8	7	178
7	Derbyshire	28	12	6	10	174
8	Hampshire	28	11	10	7	168
9	Essex	28	11	7	9	168
10	Middlesex	28	10	9	9	157
11	Northants	28	8	10	10	146
12	Somerset	28	8	13	7	130
13	Kent	28	8	12	8	128
14	Worcestershire	28	6	8	13	106
15	Sussex	28	6	11	10	102
16	Leicestershire	28	5	16	7	72
17	Nottinghamshire	28	4	14	9	62

Gloucestershire and Essex each tied a match

ACKNOWLEDGEMENTS

I would like to express my thanks to all those cricketers who were so welcoming and talked to me so freely during my writing of this book. Their hospitality told me so much about their love of the game.

I met in person: Sonny Avery, Richard Bernard, Ken Biddulph, Dennis Brookes, Tom Cartwright, Bernard Constable, Dickie Dodds, David Green, Malcolm Heath, Martin Horton, Arthur Milton, Jim Parks, John Pretlove, Harold Rhodes, Don Shepherd, David Smith, Terry Spencer, Ken Taylor, Derek Ufton, Bomber Wells, Peter Wight and Merv Winfield.

I spoke on the telephone to: Brian Close, Hubert Doggart, Geoff Edrich, Colin Griffiths, Maurice Hallam, Doug Insole, Brian Reynolds, Ken Smales, Bryan Stott, Alan Townsend and Charles Williams.

I exchanged letters with Peter Pickering.

I hope that I have done justice to the many memories they shared with me.

Additionally I would like to thank the following for their help:

John Featherstone at Headingley, Jeff Hancock and William Hasledene at the Oval, David King at Stroud, Alec Lodge at Huddersfield and Malcolm Webb at Brentwood.

I have made regular use of the following cricket reference books:

Wisden Cricketers' Almanack

Bailey, Thorn & Wynne-Thomas, *Who's Who of Cricketers*
        (Newnes Books, 1984)

Robert Brooke, *A History of the County Cricket Championship*
        (Guinness, 1991)

Bill Frindall, *England Test Cricketers*
        (Willow Books, 1989)

Jim Ledbetter & Peter Wynne-Thomas, *First-Class Cricket, 1934-39*
        (Limlow Books, 6 volumes, 1991-6)

I have read and occasionally quoted from the following autobiographies:

Bill Alley, *My Incredible Innings* (Pelham Books, 1969)

Trevor Bailey, *Wickets, Catches and the Odd Run* (Willow Books, 1986)

Alec Bedser, *Twin Ambitions* (Stanley Paul, 1986)

Brian Close, *I Don't Bruise Easily* (Macdonald & Jane's, 1978)

Colin Cowdrey, *M.C.C. The Autobiography of a Cricketer*
        (Hodder & Stoughton, 1976)

Tom Dollery, *Professional Captain* (Stanley Paul, 1952)

Dickie Dodds, *Hit Hard And Enjoy It* (The Cricketer, 1976)

Tom Graveney, *The Heart Of Cricket* (Arthur Barker, 1983)

Eric Hollies, *I'll Spin You A Tale* (Museum Press, 1955)

Ray Illingworth, *Yorkshire And Back* (Queen Anne Press, 1989)

Colin Ingleby-Mackenzie, *Many A Slip* (Oldbourne Books, 1962)
Doug Insole, *Cricket From The Middle* (William Heinemann, 1960)
Jim Laker, *Spinning Round The World* (Frederick Muller, 1957)
Colin McCool, *Cricket Is A Game* (Stanley Paul, 1961)
Peter May, *A Game Enjoyed* (Stanley Paul, 1985)
Jim Parks, *Runs In The Sun* (Stanley Paul, 1961)
H.A. Pawson, *Runs And Catches* (Faber, 1980)
Harold Rhodes, *The Harold Rhodes Affair* (Breedon Books, 1987)
David Sheppard, *Parson's Pitch* (Hodder & Stoughton, 1964)
Frank Tyson, *A Typhoon Called Tyson* (William Heinemann, 1961)
Bomber Wells, *Well, Well, Wells* (Cabdene, 1981)
Don Wilson, *Mad Jack* (Kingswood Press, 1992)

from the following county histories:
Jack Bannister, *The History of Warwickshire CCC* (Christopher Helm, 1990)
Brian Bearshaw, *From The Stretford End* (Partridge Press, 1990)
Matthew Engel & Andrew Radd, *The History of Northamptonshire CCC*
    (Christopher Helm, 1993)
David Foot, *Sunshine, Sixes and Cider* (David & Charles, 1986)
Andrew Hignell, *The History of Glamorgan CCC* (Christopher Helm, 1988)
David Lemmon, *The History of Worcestershire CCC*
    (Christopher Helm, 1989)
Don Mosey, *We Don't Play It For Fun* (Methuen, 1989)
Grahame Parker, *Gloucestershire Road* (Pelham Books, 1983)
Anthony Woodhouse, *The History of Yorkshire CCC*
    (Christopher Helm, 1989)

from the following biographies:
Andrew Hignell, *Wilf Wooller, The Skipper* (Limlow Books, 1995)
Alan Hill, *Johnny Wardle, Cricket Conjuror* (David & Charles, 1988)
Don Mosey, *Laker* (Queen Anne Press, 1989)
Patrick Murphy, *'Tiger' Smith* (Readers Union, 1981)
Christopher Sandford, *Godfrey Evans* (Simon & Schuster, 1990)

from the following other books about cricket:
Trevor Bailey, *Championship Cricket* (Sportsman's Book Club, 1962)
Trevor Bailey, *Cricket* (Eyre & Spottiswoode, 1956)
Trevor Bailey & Fred Trueman, *From Larwood to Lillee*
    (Queen Anne Press, 1983)
Jack Bannister, *The Innings Of My Life* (Headline, 1993)
Mike Brearley, *The Art Of Captaincy* (Hodder & Stoughton, 1985)
Michael Marshall, *Gentlemen and Players* (Grafton Books, 1987)
Patrick Murphy, *The Centurions* (J.M. Dent & Sons, 1983)
Patrick Murphy, *The Spinner's Turn* (J.M. Dent & Sons, 1982)

Leslie Thomas, *County Champions* (Heinemann, 1982)
Donald Trelford, *Len Hutton Remembered* (H.F.& G. Witherby, 1992)
Fred Trueman & Don Mosey, *Champion Times: Yorkshire CCC 1959-68* (Dalesman Publishing, 1994)
Frank Tyson, *The Test Within* (Hutchinson, 1987)
Nick Yapp, *A History Of The Foster's Oval* (Pelham Books, 1990)

and from the following non-cricket book:
Lettice Cooper, *Yorkshire, West Riding* (Robert Hale, 1950)

I have quoted from the following national newspapers:
Daily Herald, Daily Mirror, Daily Telegraph, Manchester Guardian, Observer, Times and Sunday Times.

from the following local newspapers:
Bath Chronicle, Birmingham Post, Brentwood Gazette, Brighton and Hove Gazette, Bristol Evening Post, Burton Daily Mail, Huddersfield Weekly Examiner, Kent Messenger, Kidderminster Shuttle, Leicester Mercury, London Evening Standard, Manchester Evening News, Northampton Chronicle and Echo, Nottingham Evening Post, Stroud Journal, Walthamstow Gazette and Western Daily Press.

and from the following cricket magazines:
The Cricketer, Wisden Cricket Monthly.

A shorter version of the chapter, *They Could Not Be Beaten*, appeared first in *Cricket Lore* magazine, and I would like to thank Richard Hill, the editor, for his help. *Cricket Lore* contains articles about cricket's past and its future and can be obtained from Richard at 22 Grazebrook Road, London N16 0HS.

For permission to reprint copyright material I would like to acknowledge:
Faber & Faber Ltd for 'Burnt Norton' by T.S.Eliot, and
The Harvill Press for 'Cricket At Brighton' by Alan Ross.

Finally I would like to thank all those who have offered me encouragement, advice and critical feedback during the writing of this book, particularly:
Andrew Chalke, David Foot, Peter Griffiths, Andrew Hignell, Humphrey Keenlyside, Richard Parry, Barry Phillips, Geoff Wallis and, most of all, Sue and Martha Kendall, who have also had to live with me through all the ups and downs.

I hope that you enjoy reading it as much as I have enjoyed writing it.

Stephen Chalke

Bath, 1997

INDEX

Aitchison, Jimmy 105
Allcock, Bert 106
Allen, David 140-1,143,146
Allen, Gubby 23,30,140
Alley, Bill 115,**150**,152-7,160
Alston, Rex 109
Ames, Les 35,118
Andrew, Keith 68,164
Appleyard, Bob 80,83-4,94,102-3,108
Arlott, John 17,54,109,112
Arnold, Peter 69
Ashdown, Bill 35,37
Atkinson, Graham 154
Avery, Sonny 15,18,37,39,41,179
Baig, Abbas Ali 152
Bailey, Trevor 14,33-6,38-43,77,
138,140-1,143-7
Banerjee, S.S. 47
Barker, Gordon 140
Barnard, Mike 132
Barnes, Sydney 50-1,56,180
Barrick, Desmond 62,71
Bartlett, Hugh 164
Bedser, Alec 47-51,56-7,65,112,
117,119,121,159
Bedser, Eric 48,52,56,119-20
Benaud, Richie 70
Bernard, Richard 88,139-48,180
Berry, Bob 65,70-2,106-9
Biddulph, Ken 11-3,16-8,108,119-20,
130-1,134,151-60,168,179
Binks, Jimmy 103,108,159
Bird, Dickie 79,175
Birkenshaw, Jackie 79,159,169,173
Bloodworth, Bernie 144
Bolus, Brian 168,175
Booth, Arthur 181
Booth, Roy 107
Boshier, Brian 76-7,81,84-5
Botham, Ian 36,43,142
Bowes, Bill 75,80-1,113
Boycott, Geoffrey 84
Bradman, Donald 24,38,41,54,89,117,144,152
Brailsford, Jim 127,129,133
Bridle, David 144
Broadbent, Bob 102,104,108-9
Broderick, Vince 65,68
Brookes, Dennis 15-6,28,61-72,179,181
Broughton, Peter 102
Brown, Bill 23
Brown, Freddie 28,61-5,67-9,71-2
Brown, Sid 22.25,28-30
Brown, Tony 141-4,146,148
Burden, Mervyn 128-9
Burnet, Ronnie 76,158-9,163,167,172-3,175-6
Buse, Bertie 158

Butler, Harold 9
Cannings, Vic 126,134
Cardus, Neville 39,147,178
Carpenter, David 146
Carr, Donald 126,129-31,133-5
Cartwright, Tom 9-10,16-7,22,46-58,178-81
Charlton, Michael 109
Clark, Tom 53,104,116,120
Clarke, Bob 63,65-8,71-2
Clift, Phil 22,26-7
Close, Brian 13,76,80-2,103,106,108,134,
152,154-60,164,168-74,180-1
Coldwell, Len 106,109
Compton, Denis **20**,21-5,29-30,77,80,
119,141,172-3
Compton, Les 27,30
Constable, Bernie 15,52-3,57,81-2,116,
119-120,178-9,181
Cook, Sam 90-1,93-4,96-8,139-42,147-8,180
Cowan, Mick 103,132
Cowan, Sam 169,179
Cowdrey, Colin 82,113-22
Cox, George 166
Crabtree, Harry 78
Crapp, Jack 92-3,142
Crawford, Tom 113
D'Oliveira, Basil 109
Dalton, Harold 36
Davidson, Alan 70
Davies, Dai 23
Davies, Emrys 22-3,25,27,30
Davies, Haydn 22,25,30
Davis, Eddie 65,67-9
Dawkes, George 102,107,109
Denness, Mike 118
Dewes, John 27
Dews, George 103,107,109
Dexter, Ted 53,164,166,168,170-2,174-5
Dixon, Alan 115,122
Dodds, Dickie 14-8,33-43,93,145,178,180-1
Doggart, Hubert 164-6,170,172
Dollery, Keith 49,51,58
Dollery, Tom 47-56,58
Dooland, Bruce 89,91-4,96-7,115
Duleepsinhji, K.S. 166
Eagar, Desmond 125
Edrich, Bill 21-2,24-5,29-30,66,72,107
Edrich, Geoff 35,38-9,63,66-8,72,179-80
Emmett, George 89-95,97,142
Etheridge, Bobby 146
Evans, Godfrey 68-9,113,117,120-1,158
Fagg, Arthur 113,122
Firth, Jack 79,82,84
Flavell, Jack 104,106,109,166
Fletcher, David 52-3,116,120
Foot, David 18

Freeman, Tich	116-8
Gardner, Freddie	48,50,55-6
Garland-Wells, Monty	50
Gaunt, Ron	156
Gaustad, John	15
Gibb, Paul	34-5,38-41,43
Gibbons, H.H.	106
Gifford, Norman	109
Gilchrist, Roy	156
Giles, Ronnie	91,96
Gimblett, Harold	63,128
Gladwin, Cliff	57,127,130-1,180
Goddard, Tom	140,147
Goodridge, Tony	101,164,166-7,169,171,174
Goodyear, Walter	127
Gover, Alf	159
Grace, E.M.	139
Grace, W.G.	21,28,56,139,143,146
Graveney, Ken	142
Graveney, Tom	50,80,89,109,140,142-3
Gray, Jimmy	130,132,135
Gray, Lawrie	49
Greasley, Derek	69
Green, David	14,125-36,180
Green, Jack	14,127-9,133
Greensmith, Bill	36,38,145-6
Greetham, Chris	152
Grieves, Ken	36,63,67
Griffith, Billy	61
Griffiths, Colin	37-8,40-1,43
Grove, Charlie	47,51-2,55,57
Halfyard, David	115,117-22
Hall Payne, Mrs	33,37-8,42
Hall, Wes	156
Hallam, Maurice	75-85,178
Hamer, Arnold	129
Hammond, Wally	143-4,180
Hansell, Bill	35,37
Hardstaff, Joe	9,34
Harris, Charlie	39
Harris, Lord	114
Hawke, Lord	76,151
Hawkins, Derek	165
Headley, Ron	104,109
Heath, Malcolm	14,16,18,125-36,178,181
Hedges, Bernard	26
Hendren, Patsy	37
Hilton, Malcolm	34,37-42,65,69-71
Hirst, George	76,84-5
Hitchcock, Ray	49,51,56
Hobbs, Jack	113
Hollies, Eric	46-9,51-4,57,93
Holmes, Percy	140
Holt, Arthur	125
Horsfall, Dick	34,37,40-2
Horton, Henry	131-2,135-6
Horton, Margaret	13,102,104,107
Horton, Martin	13,53,101-10,139,181
Howard, Geoffrey	17,63
Howard, Nigel	37,42,62-4,67,70-1
Howorth, Dick	106-7
Hurd, Alan	143-4,147
Hutton, Len	47,67,72,**74**,75-7,80-2,170
Ibadulla, Billy	49
Ikin, Jack	34,63,67
Illingworth, Ray	79,103,107,166, 169-70,172,176
Ingleby-Mackenzie, Colin	95,105,**124**, 125-9,132-4,136
Insole, Doug	14,33-5,39-40,42-3,51, 139-42,144-6,148,173,175
Iqbal, Asif	118,122
Jackson, Les	122,127,129-36,170
Jackson, Vic	77-8,81
Jenkins, Olive	104
Jenkins, Roly	13,**100**,101,104-9,143-4
Jepson, Arthur	9
Johnson, Laurie	129
Johnston, Brian	112
Jones, Willie	24,26-7
Kardar, Hafeez	49
Keating, Frank	17
Kelly, John	129,136
Kenyon, Don	101-4,106-9
King, David	88,98
Knight, Barry	139,142-3,146-8
Knightley-Smith, William	92-3,97
Knott, Alan	118
Laker, Jim	41,**45**,48-9,51,54-7,81-2,95,102, 105,109,112-4,117,119,121,127, 140,153,158-9,170,178,180
Lamb, Allan	63
Lambert, George	154
Langford, Brian	153-4,157-60
Langridge, Jim	166,169
Langridge, John	166
Lara, Brian	43,158
Larwood, Harold	23
Lavis, George	27
Lawrence, Johnny	157
Leach, Clive	49
Leary, Stuart	116
Lee, Charlie	127-8
Lee-Cox, Major-General	96
Lenham, Les	164,170,179
Lester, Gerry	78-80
Lester, Ted	77-8,81,83
Leyland, Maurice	80
Lightfoot, Albert	63,65,67,70
Livingston, Jock	62,72,82,89
Loader, Peter	48,82,85,112,114, 117,119,121,142
Lock, Bert	47-8,171
Lock, Tony	48,50-1,55,57,95,97,102,105,109, **111**,112,114-5,117-22,127,153,159,167
Lomax, Geoff	34,36-7,39-40,151-2,154-5,159

188

Lowson, Frank 75,77,81,107-8
Luckhurst, Brian 118,122
McConnon, Jim 26,28-9,156
McCool, Colin 28,115,152,154,156-8
McDonald, Colin 66
McGrath, Glenn 63
McHugh, Frank 91,94-7
McIntyre, Arthur 51,56,120,167
Mackay, Ken 156
McKenzie, Graham 70
McMahon, John 115
Mailey, Arthur 95
Major, John 17
Marlar, Robin 163,165,167,169-75
Marner, Peter 71
Marriott, Father 116-7
Marshall, Roy 12,130-1,134-5
May, Peter 12,48,50-1,77,93,112, 116-20,167,170,175,179
Melford, Michael 130,132,135,141
Meyer, Barrie 142-3,146-8
Miller, Keith 146-7
Milne, A.A. 21
Milner, Joe 141,144,148
Milton, Arthur 13-4,16,19,**87**,88,90-5,97, 139-48,178-9,181
Moor, Bill 155
Morgan, Derek 91,129,133-5
Mortimore, John 91,93-4,96,140-2
Mosey, Don 102
Moss, Alan 23-4,27
Muncer, Len 26-9
Munden, Vic 77,83-4,178
Nicholls, Ron 90-2,142-3,145-6
Noble, Denis 23
Norman, Mickey 153
Nutter, Albert 62
Oakman, Alan 164,170
Oldfield, Buddy 62
Outschoorn, Laddie 101-2,104,106,108-9
Padgett, Doug 103,106,108,154-5,168,173-5
Page, Colin 117,121
Palairet, Lionel 151,159
Palmer, Charles 75,77,81-3
Palmer, Kenny 156
Parker, Jack 54
Parkhouse, Gilbert 24,27,29
Parkinson, Michael 17
Parks, J.H. 163-4,166
Parks, Jim 121,163-76,179
Pataudi, Nawab of 165-6,172-3
Pawson, Tony 114
Perks, Reg 72,106-7
Pettiford, Jack 114-7,120-1
Pickering, Peter 16,61-72
Pitman, Ray 132
Place, Winston 36
Platt, Bob 159,164,167
Pocock, Pat 122

Poole, Cyril 91,96
Pope, George 50
Preston, Ken 34,36,41,144
Pretlove, John 16,112-22,179
Pritchard, Tom 49
Prodger, John 112,114,117
Pugh, Tom 142
Ralph, Roy 144,146
Ranjitsinhji,K.S. 166
Reynolds, Brian 62,65,67-72
Rhodes, Dusty 125,136
Rhodes, Harold 14,125-36,179
Rhodes, Wilfred 76,83-5
Richardson, Dick 53,103,107-8
Richardson, Peter 101,103,108,120
Ridgway, Fred 40
Roberts, Ron 153
Robertson, Jack 22,25,28
Robins, R.W.V. 105,140
Rochford, Peter 92,97
Ross, Alan 164
Routledge, Reg 26,29
Rowbotham, Denys 63-4,66-7,71,128,131-2, 140-1,144,146
Rowe, Eddie 97
Saeed, Yawar 152
Sainsbury, Peter 134
Sarwate, C.T. 47
Savill, Les 140,144,147
Shackleton, Derek 122,127-34,136
Sharp, Harry 25
Sharpe, Philip 105,180,186-7
Shaw, Hazel 12,18
Shepherd, Don 14,21-30,178
Shepherd, John 118
Sheppard, David 75,107,166,169-70,172
Simpson, Reg 89-90,95-7
Sims, Jim 23,27,30
Singh, Swaranjit 49
Smales, Ken 88-98
Smith, David 94,142-4,146
Smith, Don 165-6
Smith, Edwin 134
Smith, Mike 97,179
Smith, Ray 34-6,38-42
Smith, Tiger 51,53,56
Smithson, Gerry 79-80
Snow, John 168
Sobers, Gary 96,156
Spencer, Terry 16,75-85,178-9,181
Spooner, Dick 49-50,52,54,56,130,180
Standen, Jim 104
Statham, Brian **32**,34,36-7,39-40,65,67-72, 78,84,164,170
Stead, Barry 151,159
Stephenson, Harold 152,158
Stewart, Micky 113,116,120
Stocks, Freddie 89,95
Stott, Bryan 14,17,154,163-76

Strudwick, Herbert 51
Subba Row, Raman 72
Surridge, Stuart 46,48,50-1,53-4,56-7,118,153
Sutcliffe, Herbert 140
Suttle, Ken 164,168,170,175
Swanton, E.W. 17,47-8,165,171-3
Tattersall, Roy 34,39-41,65,68-9,84,158,165
Tayfield, Hugh 54
Taylor, Brian 14,140,144
Taylor, Derek 51
Taylor, Derief 49
Taylor, Don 49-50,56
Taylor, Ken 14,16-7,106-7,154-5,
157-8,163-76,179-80
Taylor, Will 129
Thomson, Ian 166,168-9,173-5
Tinniswood, Peter 36
Titmus, Fred 27,169,180
Tompkin, Maurice 79-80
Townsend, Alan 49,51-3,56,58
Tremlett, Maurice 152,154,157-8,160,179
Tribe, George 63-6,69-72,115,127
Tripp, Graham 152
Trueman, Fred 12,50,61,63,76-8,80,82-4,
101,103,117,130-2,134-5,151,
153,155-6, **162**,164-6,170-3,175
Turnbull, Maurice 27
Turner, Cyril 173
Tyson, Frank 12,23,**60**,63,65-70,82,
95,97,127,135,170
Ufton, Derek 114,119-22
Underwood, Derek 118
Van Geloven, Jackie 79
Verity, Hedley 83-4

Vigar, Frank 38-9,41
Virgin, Roy 151-2,155
Walcott, Clyde 156
Walker, Alan 89,93,96
Walsh, Courtney 145
Walsh, Jack 77-8,84,115
Wardle, Johnny 76,80,83-5,97,102-3,105-6,
108-9,117,119,146,167,179
Warr, John 135
Washbrook, Cyril 26,34,71
Watkins, Allan 22,24-7,29,33
Watson, Willie 78-9,81,106-7
Webb, Malcolm 35
Weekes, Everton 156
Weeks, Ray 53,56
Wells, Bomber 16-8,51,83-4,88-98,140,
147,165,167,170-1,178,180
Wharton, Alan 34-5,40-2,63
Whitehead, Alan 154,159
Wight, Peter 16-7,152-4,156-8,160
Williams, Charles 141,144-8
Wilson, Andy 79
Wilson, Bob 113
Wilson, Don 152,155,159,167,170,172
Wilson, Vic 77-8,81,107-8,176
Winfield, Merv 88-98
Wooller, Wilf 22-4,26-30
Woolley, Frank 35,113-4,116,118,180
Wright, Doug 116-8,120,178
Wyatt, Bob 105-7
Yardley, Norman 40,76,80-1,83-4
Yarnold, Hugo 107
Young, Jack 24,27,30
Young, Martin 142,145,148

(illustrations in bold type)

Also available from Fairfield Books

AT THE HEART OF ENGLISH CRICKET
The life and memories of Geoffrey Howard
by Stephen Chalke
with illustrations by Susanna Kendall
and a foreword by Scyld Berry

The 92-year-old administrator looks back with insight and humour on his long involvement with cricket – including full accounts of the three M.C.C. tours which he managed: six months in newly independent in India in 1950/51, Ashes victory in Australia in 1954/55 and a diplomatic storm in Pakistan in 1955/56.

One of the most valuable documents in English cricket history. **Scyld Berry**

Cricket's most delightful book for a long time. **Frank Keating**, The Guardian

A cracking read, studded with invaluable historical insight.
David Llewellyn, The Independent

Rich in anecdotes of human and cricketing interest.
Christopher Martin-Jenkins, The Times

I have been totally engrossed. Normally I would never have considered buying a book about a cricket administrator, but knowing Stephen Chalke's inimitable style I was tempted and what an inspired decision I made. **A reader in Leeds**

I have seldom read a cricket book with so many first-hand insights into the game.
A reader in Bury St Edmunds

FRAGMENTS OF IDOLATRY
FROM 'CRUSOE' TO KID BERG
by David Foot

Character studies of twelve sportsmen and writers whom the award-winning author has admired in his life: Raymond Robertson-Glasgow, Carwyn James, Patsy Hendren, Alan Gibson, Tom Cartwright, Reg Sinfield, Jack 'Kid' Berg, Maurice Tremlett, Walter Robins, Alec Stock, Alf Dipper, Horace Hazell.

Sports writing on another plane. **Ian Wooldridge**, Daily Mail

Irresistible. He is the most felicitous of cricket's current authors.
Robin Marlar, The Cricketer

David Foot's first collection of portraits Beyond Bat and Ball *is the best book about cricketers I have ever read. His new collection is a splendid successor.*
Stephen Fay, Wisden Cricket Monthly

CAUGHT IN THE MEMORY
COUNTY CRICKET IN THE 1960s
by Stephen Chalke
with illustrations by Ken Taylor

Twelve more county matches recreated, these ones remembered by David Allen, Keith Andrew, Roy Booth, Alan Castell, Alan Dixon, Robin Hobbs, Mick Norman, Alan Oakman, Peter Robinson, Peter Walker, Don Wilson and others.

A second innings as salty, charming and free flowing as the first.

Colin Chinery, Eastern Daily Press

I thought Mr Chalke could never repeat his success. He has. Triumphantly. 'Caught in the Memory' is a delight. Read the book. Read the book, I beg you. I commend it wholeheartedly - and not least for the splendid illustrations by Mr Ken Taylor. He won't remember, but once he trod on my toe in the tea interval at Bramall Lane. He could grind my whole body into the ground without trace if he compels Mr Chalke to produce another volume.

Peter Tinniswood, Wisden Cricketers' Almanack

ONE MORE RUN
by Stephen Chalke
with Bryan 'Bomber' Wells
with illustrations by Ken Taylor and Susanna Kendall

The uplifting and joyful reminiscences of Gloucestershire off-spinner 'Bomber' Wells, one of cricket's greatest characters, all set in the context of Sam Cook's benefit match against Yorkshire at Cheltenham in 1957.

A blissful remembrance of a time when cricket and the world were different. Bomber Wells – there was a summer's day in his face and laughter in his soul.

Michael Parkinson, Daily Telegraph

The monumental, unforgettable book all writers hope they have in them.

Robert Brooke, The Cricket Statistician

All these books are available post free from Fairfield Books, 17 George's Road, Fairfield Park, Bath BA1 6EY. Telephone 01225-335813

At The Heart of English Cricket	**£16.00**	Hardback, b&w illustrations, 224pp
Fragments of Idolatry	**£15.00**	Hardback, b&w illustrations, 176pp
Caught in the Memory	**£16.95**	Hardback, colour illustrations, 224pp
One More Run	**£8.00**	Paperback, b&w illustrations, 128pp